KNOWING THE NAME OF GOD

A TRINITARIAN TAPESTRY OF GRACE, FAITH & COMMUNITY

RODERICK T. LEUPP

InterVarsity Press
Downers Grove, Illinois

InterVarsity Press® is the book-publishing division of InterVarsity Christian Fellowship®, a student movement active on campus at hundreds of universities, colleges and schools of nursing in the United States of America, and a member movement of the International Fellowship of Evangelical Students. For information about local and regional activities, write Public Relations Dept., InterVarsity Christian Fellowship, 6400 Schroeder Rd., P.O. Box 7895, Madison, WI 53707-7895.

Cover photograph: David Muench

ISBN 0-8308-1874-X

Printed in the United States of America ⊖

Library of Congress Cataloging-in-Publication Data

Leupp, Roderick T., 1953-
    Knowing the name of God: a trinitarian tapestry of grace, faith
and community/Roderick T. Leupp.
        p.   cm.
    Includes bibliographical references and index.
    ISBN 0-8308-1874-X (pbk.: alk. paper)
    1. God—Name.   2. Trinity.   I. Title.
BT180.N2L45   1996
231'.044—dc20   96-9123
                                                                          CIP

21	20	19	18	17	16	15	14	13	12	11	10	9	8	7	6	5	4	3	2	1
14	13	11	10	09	08	07	06	05	04	03	02	01	00	99	98	97	96			

Dedicated to my father
Thomas Andrew Leupp (1922-1991)
a Christian gentleman
a triune presence in my life
bestowing life, crafting character, kindling enthusiasm

Introduction

The birth of my brother enlivened all of us. Just before he arrived my family was breathing death. Sorrow had blighted the family landscape with the death of our maternal grandmother four months earlier. Then cancer claimed my mother's only sister a few days prior to my brother's birth. Eight months later our maternal grandfather would pass away. Since I was not yet seven, death was still a stranger to me. And having three older sisters, I was delighted to get a brother at long last.

We exercised family democracy in choosing my brother's name. Mother convened a family council that resulted in our choosing the name Braden Timothy Aldridge Leupp. Four names seemed elaborate at the time, but Aldridge was our recently deceased grandmother's maiden name. It fit my brother well, and Tim seemed to fit him even better, so that is what we still call him.

At the time of his first real job, as he established his professional identity, Tim all of a sudden became Braden. It was his choice. His wife has never known him as anyone else, and their children, when they are born, may have the dilemma of choosing between his "new" name and his "traditional" name, which is still the name of choice for the entire Leupp family. His children will likely feel most comfortable with a simple "Dad."

What is in a name? Some of the most obvious things are personal identity, honor, reputation, power, creativity and continuity through time. Among the few genuine cultural universals found in all times and places, the promise and weight wrapped up in a person's name is surely near the top of the list. Names are much too important to be relegated to booklets filled with them sold near supermarket check-outs. We are reminded that "in the earlier stages of culture, by 'name' is normally meant not the mere name, but the person, the power, the nature of the one named."[1] What was true then is just as true today. A contemporary African theologian writing about the Igbo tribe reports that for them names "convey the deepest feeling of those who name, and they sometimes describe the characteristics of the named."[2] Nicknames bestowed on Filipinos are even more colorful than the renowned jeepneys that carry passengers around the archipelago. Female nicknames are limited only by the imagination originating them. Girlie, Cherry Pie, Sunshine and Tweetie are by no means uncommon. Men generally stick to the more utilitarian Boy, although Bong Bong can name the son of former president Marcos or the lowliest street vendor.

If names are universally esteemed as windows into personal identity and essence, in biblical religion names bear special watching. When my brother self-consciously opted for his first name, Braden, as his professional name, he did not thereby cancel the two dozen years of our knowing him as Tim. He was Braden to some, Tim to others, but one and the same man. But in biblical religion the changing of a name typically, perhaps even always, means a new identity. A changed name means a transformed character.[3] Many whom God used to implement the history of salvation are best known to us by their new, God-granted names. Sarai and Abram become Sarah and Abraham, while "Jacob, the usurper, becomes Israel, the friend and servant of God."[4] In the New Testament the vacillating Simon becomes the rock-solid Peter; Saul the persecutor becomes history's greatest Christian missionary, Paul.

In giving new names to biblical figures, God gave with them new and deeper responsibilities. For the newly named the vernacular of the marketplace somehow became elevated into the language of Canaan, and one's horizon of obligation was now circumscribed by God's providence. What God required of the newly named, God would enable in them. For Abraham this meant becoming the "ancestor of a multitude of nations" (Gen 17:4-5), a task out of proportion with Abram's abilities.

The fixing of names, the power of naming, arises from God. God is, in the words of H. Richard Niebuhr, "the source and center of all being and value,"[5] and therefore when God gives a name, God also gives identity, meaning and a definite place in his sovereign will. What is God's by nature, his power to name, God grants to Adam by grace, and Adam names every living creature brought to him by God (Gen 2:19).

Perhaps God's entrusting Adam with this naming task is, from the human perspective, the first recorded act of theological reflection. Adam was called and commissioned by God to name the animals, and whatever name Adam gave to each was its name. Theology, which is disciplined thinking about God, must always be carried out within the expansive parameters of grace provided by God. So Adam did in naming the animals. Only presumption could have dictated Adam's seeking out this task for himself. Only grace enabled him to perform it acceptably in God's sight.

What is in a name so far as God is concerned? Here we do well to err on the side of caution, of reverence, of the fear of the Lord that is the beginning of wisdom. Some philosophers, practicing what we can safely call reductionism, have claimed that *God* is only a haphazard collection of three randomly arranged letters, the reversal of which, in spelling out "man's best friend," is closer to the truth. But theistic religion has always claimed otherwise, that the divine name, so far from inviting canine comparisons, is frankly unutterable. Moses, wondering what he can say to those Israelites curious about the divine name, receives only the tantalizing "I AM WHO I AM" (Ex 3:14). Perhaps more knowing on this point than Christians, Jews sometimes refuse even to complete the divine name in written form, fearful of trespass and presumption. "G D" is as much of the divine name as any righteous Jew can commit to writing. A chance visit to a rabbinic training school in upper Manhattan reminded me of this, as posted notices would not compromise the divine mystery by spelling the divine name fully.

God is not a member of the Republican party any more than God belongs to any other coalition, club or caucus. Any name we affix to God blunts God's freedom and aligns God with a particular cause. Groucho Marx remarked that he would not want to belong to any club that would have him as a member. God is not a snob like Groucho was; God wants nothing more than to belong to every club and every family, redeeming everyone and re-creating all things in his own image. But for this to happen, it must be on God's terms of universal grace freely offered, not on human terms of God held captive to this or that slender strand of advocacy. Never far below the surface is our desire to turn God into our private idol to suit our special needs. Those who would be bold enough to name God must bear the responsibility for their actions, for "the possibility of misnaming and lying is always present in names. Names seem not to reveal the true God, but rather to reveal what we think the characteristic of any true god should be."[6] Everyone who would presume to name God must self-consciously practice the "hermeneutics of suspicion," suspicious of motives, intent and outcome.

Christians are as prone to the misappropriation and abuse of God's name as anyone else. Paul's admonition to the Romans (12:2) not to be squeezed into the world's mold reminds Christians not to squeeze God into the mold of their own desires and ends. For even Christians, and maybe especially Christians, enthusiastically recruit God for every moral crusade, political stand and theological battle. Yet at least Christians, by virtue of owning the name of Jesus Christ and remaining open to the Holy Spirit's leading, do not begin to ponder the divine name as though it were the foundational principle of a philosophy or the launching insight of a worldview. Christians cannot run from God's concreteness and actuality into a comforting haze of abstractions. Nicholas Lash perceptively notes that "Christianity is not a 'worldview,' or a system of beliefs. It is a people with a memory and, for all the world, a hope."[7]

The great I AM is not a name that humankind could have anticipated or invented, for this God is the living God whose Spirit swept
over the face of the waters in the beginning (Gen 1:2). He is the Father
whose eternal Word became incarnate in the fullness of time (Gal 4:4),
the Father's Son who said, "Before Abraham was, I am" (Jn 8:58).
Father, Word and Spirit. From everlasting to everlasting God's name
is triune. God does not have three names; God has one name "above
all names," uttered in three distinct yet inseparable ways, God's
thrice-blessed name.

This book is about the name of God. It is not about every biblically
sound and theologically appropriate name of God (for that would be
a theological project without end), but rather about the name Christians have from the beginning worshiped, in whom they have been
baptized, to whom they have prayed—this is the name we seek to
illumine. This name is the Triune God. God's triunity is not only the
summit of the task of theology, it is absolutely foundational for the
very living of the Christian life in devotion, in witness, in consecration.
If God is triune, then it is as triune that the privilege of knowing God
is accorded to us, an offer graciously extended to us in Jesus Christ.

God as triune is therefore God's self-expression given to us, God's
self-interpretation offered in sacrificial love for our salvation. God's
triunity is not the ultimate end in theological cleverness, but is the
fullness of God condescending to engage the deepest needs and
longings of humanity. Obviously, then, "the significance of the doctrine of the Trinity is not philosophical but redemptive."[8] Certainly
one can sharpen one's intellect on the Trinity. But to do this and no
more is surely to have missed "the better part" (Lk 10:42). That better
part is the sentence with which John Wesley ended his long life: "Best
of all, God is with us." In the Father's depths, the Son's incarnation
and the Holy Spirit's indwelling, God is with us. Depth, incarnation
and indwelling are not three isolated moments in a divine life that is
otherwise seamless, and not temporary manifestations of some
deeper underlying reality. The uniqueness of each triune Person is
constituted by his relations to the other two. The Father is depth

because of his unfathomable love for the Son, the Son is the visualization and representation of the Father's mystery, and the Holy Spirit is the One through whom the Father speaks his Word eternally.

Every human name is given in the hope that its recipient will indeed become worthy of it, will in fact develop into a fit bearer of it. What is possible in humans is actual in God so that only God's triune name is an absolutely appropriate engagement of what could be with what truly is. The reason for this is simple: God's triune name is self-bestowed. God's name is triune. God is the Triune God. Because the name is God's own, he alone is capable of a full investigation of its eternal richness. Only God can truly examine God, "for the Spirit searches everything, even the depths of God" (1 Cor 2:10). God does reward those "who seek him" (Heb 11:6), but the search must be carried forth in the spirit of *The Imitation of Christ*: "Of what use is it to discourse learnedly on the Trinity, if you lack humility and therefore displease the Trinity?"[9] Openness before the mystery of God is the hallmark of a humble spirit, coupled with certain confidence that the end of human wisdom is the beginning of God's clarity:

Blind unbelief is sure to err,
And scan His work in vain;
God is His own interpreter,
And He will make it plain.[10]

1

GOD'S NAME REVEALED

*E*VERYONE SEARCHES FOR GOD. God searches for everyone. These two statements contain the same words, but they are far from identical. To say "God is love" (1 Jn 4:8, 16) is not the same as to say "Love is God." Love is not God. God is God, and love is one of the ways that God has of being God. God is also God as truth, mercy, compassion, righteousness, holiness and innumerable other traits.

Every way that God has of being God, the totality of God's self-awareness and expression, is summed up in the Trinity. The Trinity is the fullness of God, the length and breadth and depth of all that God is. Searches for God apart from God's triune identity are futile. At best they are only investigations of innate religious curiosity. They can in time turn toward God, but only under the realization that God has first turned toward humankind in Jesus Christ. God's only begotten Son is the climax of God's search for humanity, and naming him "only begotten" already witnesses to the pervasiveness of the triune premise: begotten of God the Father and anointed by God the Holy Spirit.

The God Who Would Be Known

No one could have discovered the Trinity. No one could have named

God triune. Some names are affixed by popular declaration. A city gaining a new professional sports franchise may conduct a contest to name the team. At the birth of an exotic animal a zoo may have a contest to name the animal, thus taming the mystery. But God is a case unto himself, a case of divine disclosure. God has named himself as triune, because that is who God is.

When the angel spoke to Joseph, not all of the triune persons were named, but the name of Jesus means nothing apart from the Trinity. Mary, the angel said, "will bear a son, and you are to name him Jesus, for he will save his people from their sins" (Mt 1:21). Jesus cannot be named, and his mission cannot be launched, unless it is a name triunely bestowed and a mission triunely undergirded. Salvation is itself an event of all of God, for it is reconciliation with the Father, through the Son, nurtured and sustained by the Holy Spirit.

Yet for most people and, sadly, for most Christians also, the Trinity is the great unknown. The Trinity, to use a familiar equation, is viewed as a riddle wrapped up inside a puzzle and buried in an enigma. A riddle, for how can any entity be at the same time multiple (three) yet singular (one)? A puzzle, for the Trinity is so clearly contrary to any rational thought as not to warrant a second thought from sensible people. An enigma, for even if the Trinity could be understood, of what practical value, even what religious value, would it have for ordinary people?

The Christian tradition describes the Trinity in another word—pure, deep, undefiled mystery. Pure mystery, because the mystery derives from God and in fact is God. Deep mystery, because this mystery shines in its own light and is its own depth. Undefiled mystery, because nothing can be added to or subtracted from it. The idea of mystery is itself multifaceted. At a minimum, mystery "is the idea of something hidden which has been revealed, something unapproachable which invites entry, something unknowable which offers true under-standing."[1] Mystery, then, implies revelation, invitation and offering. It is precisely here that we wish to focus our thoughts on the Trinity, on the generosity and graciousness of God. The Trinity is not an intellec-tual problem to be pondered and finally solved. Problems can be

explained away when further explanations come to light, but a true
mystery can only be deepened, never solved. The reality of revelation,
the unveiling of that which had been hidden, is not the end of mystery,
but its very beginning.

The Trinity's fundamental mystery is not how one can be three and
yet remain one, but simply that God desires that his creatures should
fully share in God's triune life. Human life is completed and fulfilled
only as it becomes triune life. God's mystery invites our participation;
and our joining in the mystery intensifies it for us, for God's life
"remains an even deeper mystery to those who do share in it and . . .
becomes ever more mysterious as the sharing deepens."[2] It is in that
sense that Paul can call the union of man and woman as husband and
wife a mystery (Eph 5:31-32).[3] As the years of union unfold, the
mystery lingers and lengthens.

The Trinity is the Christian doctrine and understanding of God. It
would be needlessly shortsighted and dogmatic to say that the Trinity
is the *only* acceptable way for Christians to think about and experience
God. While all Christian thought about God must ultimately be rooted
and grounded in the Bible, the Bible has many ways of speaking about
God. I will briefly mention some of these other ways later. But as the
very name demands, a Christian is not interested in just any approach
to God. A Christian is captivated, ultimately and finally, only by God's
approach to us in Jesus Christ. Jesus is the Christ only as begotten of
the Father in or by the Holy Spirit.[4] Any responsible thinking about
Jesus is bound to lead one emphatically into the presence of the Triune
God. Otherwise Jesus remains only human.

Christians are therefore not simply monotheists. Jews and Muslims
are monotheists, and anyone who believes in any sort of god that
excludes all other gods could conceivably be named a monotheist.
Some have even theorized that the ancient Egyptians "invented"
monotheism when they worshiped the sun as the only god in the
universe. Christians need to begin to think of themselves as trinitarians. It would not do a great deal of harm if *monotheist* were to be
dropped from the Christian vocabulary. Certainly this traditional
designation must always be clarified and qualified by the word *trini-*

tarian. The only monotheism Christians can in good conscience affirm is a trinitarian monotheism.

Any badge of orthodoxy shines only as brightly as the knowledge of God it reflects. Trinitarian or monotheist, it matters not, if the heart is still alienated from God. John Wesley frequently complained that a religion of the purest orthodoxy, what he called "a religion of opinions," is false religion. Neither does true religion consist for Wesley in "forms of barely outward worship," the religion of righteous formality, nor in "a religion of works, of seeking the favour of God by doing good to men."[5] Orthodoxy, formality, works—none of these was true religion for Wesley, and all of them could do more harm than good, because people would imagine themselves to be saved thereby.

The essence of true religion is not for Wesley validated by an elaborate theology, regimented by propriety of worship, or approved by good works. It is simple. It can be tested by two words. Wesley believed that "true religion is right tempers toward God and man. It is, in two words, gratitude and benevolence: gratitude to our Creator and supreme Benefactor, and benevolence to our fellow creatures. In other words, it is the loving God with all our heart, and our neighbour as ourselves."[6] Religion has therefore to do with God and humankind, thanksgiving to God followed by generosity to one's neighbor. True religion is keeping the great commandment, utter devotion to God, and its corollary of service to humanity (Mt 22:36-39; Mk 12:28-31; Lk 10:27). The God toward whom our worship is to be directed is for Wesley none other than the Triune God. True religion has to do with the true God, and this can only be the Trinity. In Wesley's view, authentic religion "properly and directly consists in the knowledge and love of God, as manifested in the Son of his love, through the eternal Spirit. And this naturally leads to every heavenly temper, and to every good word and work."[7] Knowledge and love of God must be added to gratitude and benevolence to constitute true religion.

"The knowledge and love of God" is unsurpassed as the goal toward which all Christians, indeed all of humanity, must point. Religious creatures that we are, we *will* worship something. "To what you give your heart and in what you trust, that is actually your God,"[8] said Martin

Luther. The accent of this study is that the very nature of the Triune God is self-giving love. God in Christ Jesus has already given his heart to humanity. The Holy Spirit offers the gift of Jesus and confirms Christ's presence within whenever a soul opens up to Christ's full and free benefits.

Not every vision of the divine is a vision of self-giving, even self-emptying, love. In fact, this is what makes the Triune God the Christian God. In other perspectives, God may have better things to do than to be concerned with the fates of pathetic mortals. Aristotle's god, although unquestionably noble, can by definition have contact only with what is equal to it. No one is equal to Aristotle's god, so it is left to contemplate only its own perfection throughout eternity. It is futile to love this god, because this god can never return human love. Here is a god that is curved in upon its own self [9] and consequently is best thought of as "it" because it is subpersonal.

"Curved in upon itself" is exactly how Martin Luther described original sin. Humanity is very far gone from original righteousness, because "all we like sheep have gone astray; we have all turned to our own way" (Is 53:6). Does this make Aristotle's god out to be a sinner? Not exactly, because the category of sin cannot ultimately be applied to a god of naked perfection, as is Aristotle's. But anyone who tries to imitate this god's self-sufficiency will only reinforce his or her own lostness and become more and more isolated from fellowship with the one true God, who encounters us in the history of Israel and the history of Jesus Christ. [10]

The Triune God, so far from being "curved in upon itself," is radically available. *Radical* means "at the root." Early church fathers, for example Tertullian (c. 160-c. 225), occasionally described the Trinity as "root, branch and shoot." The Father's root branched out in the Son's incarnation, and the shoots of the Holy Spirit sought to intertwine and therefore transform the human organism and indeed the whole created realm. The metaphor may be botanical, but the reality is divine: God's drawing and encouraging humanity toward true life. Charles Wesley captured God's intention when he preached that real religion is "a participation of the divine nature, the life of God in the soul of man."[11] From a human vantage point, such participation is not possible. Most people do not even know they are lost. Those who do are prone to search in the oddest places for some meaning upon which to anchor their lives. The Christian message honors the human search for a solid center but says two decisive things: (1) in creating us for himself, God is the primal author and motivator of the search, and (2) because God originated the search, its only satisfying goal must be God himself, the Triune God. Grace is the invitation and constant companion to this goal, grace that is not irresistible but efficacious.

The Christian life is not possible apart from grace. Indeed, no life at all would be possible if God's grace suddenly vanished altogether. The grace of God, described by John Wesley as "free in all, and free for all,"[12] undergirds all that is. Freely bestowed upon all, increasing in all who respond to its initial advances, God's grace is God's call to join freely and fully in the divine life. Grace is participatory and condescending, not exclusive and highhanded. The logic of grace is the pull toward inclusion, toward taking part.

This logic of participation can be seen in democracy, which depends on citizen awareness and involvement in voting, voicing opinions and keeping up on issues. Volunteer organizations and service groups could not exist without participation.

The terms of participation are often the terms of power. The dominant force determines who will take part, and those perceived to be lower in quality or ability—as often seen when grammar school children choose sports teams—are excluded. Exclusion is no respecter of persons. All have known exclusion in life, regardless of how rich or powerful. Some years ago I bought a third-row concert ticket and quickly lost it. When I returned to the box office and explained the problem, the ticket seller graciously gave me a note with my seat number on it, which would admit me if no one found the ticket. Although it was found by someone else who then claimed the seat I had paid for, I was fortunate still to hear the music, not in the third row, but at least on the main floor. Apart from the kindness shown to me by the ticket seller and the ticket taker, I would have recalled that concert only for what I did *not* hear.

The life that God offers us in Jesus Christ requires no ticket for admission, only our act of submission. The cross of Christ has already paid for everyone's admission into God's fellowship, and we must only submit and accept to receive entry into God's family. In the cross, God has already submitted to us; the very act of God's coming into flesh in Jesus Christ is the utmost humility. Under only his own inner compulsion, owing no one anything, God demonstrates his true character in sending Jesus Christ through the Holy Spirit, offering eternal life to those who will welcome God's Son. "This is eternal life, that they may know you, the only true God, and Jesus Christ whom you have sent" (Jn 17:3). Here are God's true colors, that God is "unalterably oriented toward us in love."[13]

Apart from God's grace, humans remain "unalterably oriented" not toward God but toward self. But in responding to grace, God turns the human heart toward the divine heart. Because God's entire being is enfleshed in Jesus Christ, nothing less than our entire being must be offered to God. In offering, we learn to love God, a knowledge that is not esoteric or privileged but practical, fundamental and transforming. "This experimental knowledge," Charles Wesley believed, "and this alone, is true Christianity."[14]

True Christianity is therefore an experiment—an experiment planned, constructed and overseen by God, not for God's own pleasure but for our knowledge of God, "the life of God in the soul of man." Although the experiment, meaning the plan of salvation, is God's, the response, and in that sense the completion of the experiment, is ours. Unlike the trial-and-error of high-school chemistry students, God's experiment is flawlessly designed and perfectly executed in the cross of Christ.

We can even say, intending no irreverence, that it is a "hands-on" experiment to which our God invites us. The apostle John begins his first letter fully convinced of how God can be known: "We declare to you what was from the beginning, what we have heard, what we have seen with our eyes, what we have looked at and touched with our hands, concerning the word of life" (1 Jn 1:1).

The availability and accessibility of God in Jesus Christ does not mean the end of God's mystery. Joy deep in human hearts comes only from God's own unsearchable—except by the Holy Spirit—depths. Every Christian's rightful relief of sins forgiven must compel the further thought: God is God. God remains God. As Karl Rahner has put it: "Revelation is not the bringing of what was once unknown into the region of what is known, perspicuous, and manageable: it is the dawn and the approach of mystery as such."[15] God invites us out of our mediocrity and laziness into his stern excellence. While we are certainly free to scorn the invitation, we must never forget its source, the sovereign freedom of God. "It is God who handles us, and not we who handle God!" confessed Martin Luther.[16]

The raw materials, we might say, for our experimental knowledge of God are, on one hand, God's eminent approachability and, on the other, God's utter mystery. The same God whom we meet in Jesus Christ, who is himself "God the only Son" (Jn 1:18), is also the One who "dwells in unapproachable light, whom no one has ever seen or can see" (1 Tim 6:16). The "hands on" God does not contradict Luther's "God who handles us." The God who enables every breath and step is also the God of infinite horizon, whose heights none can ever fully conquer.

If the results of a scientific experiment are written up in a lab report, no one confuses the report with the experiment itself. Family members gathering in front of the television to watch a video of a recent family vacation harbor no illusions that they are actually taking the trip over again. To use a crude analogy, theology is a little like the lab report and vacation video. It is not the thing itself, but it is certainly organically connected to what has gone before. Theology, from two Greek words meaning "thinking and speaking about God," should be a disciplined, reverent, and hope-filled discussion about God. Redemptive theology is cognizant of the riches of the Christian past and desirous of applying those riches joyously and expectantly to present tasks and future callings.

Christians are often tempted to dismiss theological reflection as not necessary and even dangerous to the integrity of confessional faith. Such fears are sadly misguided. Every practical application of Christian truth—preaching, missionizing, evangelizing, ministries of compassion and justice—has implicit and often clearly stated theological meaning. Theology as an intellectual exercise must never overwhelm devotional warmth, spiritual vitality, and evangelical persuasion. In truth, of course, reflection and devotion, so far from being enemies, deeply need each other. If theology, as Thomas Aquinas believed, is loving God with all of one's mind, and devotion is pursuing God with one's whole heart, then having "the eyes of your heart enlightened" (Eph 1:18) combines both. Enlightenment means both intellectual penetration and spiritual renewal.

The God who enlightens is the Triune God. While it is possible to separate the *doctrine* of the Triune God from the *experience* of the Triune God, such a separation does not exist within God. However nuanced and profound it may be, every theology finally fails in describing God with total adequacy, and no one, not even New Testament stalwarts of faith such as Paul, Mary or James, has *fully* experienced God. Aware of these limits, and not wanting to divide arbitrarily what for God is whole, we hope the reciprocal connection between piety and theology comes ever more clearly into focus.

Why the Trinity?

Were the apostle Paul to visit today's centers of culture and civilization, his judgment would be the same as he rendered to the men of Athens: "I see how extremely religious you are in every way" (Acts 17:22). We live today amid unprecedented religious options, and every religious practitioner carries an idea of God or the Absolute within. Good sense, so we are led to believe by influence-makers and the media, means that religion is a personal, even a very private, experience. It is so private that where different views of God or the Absolute are concerned, none is any better than any other. "True" religion in today's world is about sincerity (which no one can possibly criticize), about depth of commitment (although commitment to *what* is seldom at issue) and about "following your bliss."

Orthodoxy of any sort, especially Christian orthodoxy, is becoming increasingly out of fashion for shapers of public opinion. Those who cling to any orthodoxy are accused of blocking intellectual and social progress, and of trying to breathe light into a dying day. The very most that scoffers will admit is that a deep-rooted religious identity can sustain one in a psychological crisis. But those days are gone forever, skeptics say, when orthodox Christianity literally provided the value structure and intellectual cement of the Western world.

All observant Christians, and many secular sympathizers, will be disturbed by the radical relativism of our day. Inevitably, it will lead to nihilism, the abolition of all values whatsoever. Christian influence in such vital areas as medicine, education and culture has perhaps never been lower. Visible and empirical measures of Christian expression may be inching ever upward, but to what end? The Christian influence in the public forum, the Christian weight in the marketplace of ideas, seems battered, compromised and ineffectual.

There are no simple solutions to the current malaise. Every sector of the Christian world not only will define the problem differently but will offer various—we hope not contradictory—solutions. Theologians of many confessional locations have argued that until and unless "root metaphors," fundamental presuppositions and grounding insights change, behavior, whether small or great, never will. In short, without a proper understanding of God, no forward progress is possible. For our part, we must say, "Back to the sources!"

Our Source is God, the Triune God. So we believe, and so we preach. The great "cloud of witnesses" (Heb 12:1) of Christian antiquity testifies that God revealed himself to be three in one. All Christians, at least at some level, are aware of God's triunity. Christians confess Jesus to be Lord and Savior (Rom 10:9). This primal confession is immediately trinitarian because, as Paul continues, Jesus is Lord exactly because "God raised him from the dead," resurrected him through the Holy Spirit.

Yet confession alone may not be enough. The truth of Karl Rahner's accusation stings precisely because we recognize its intrinsic truthfulness: "Despite their orthodox confession of the Trinity, Christians are, in their practical life, almost mere monotheists."[17] Ordinary Christians (and that includes all of us!), too often fearing the Trinity as a theologi-

cal examination beyond their abilities and interests, have forfeited the
rich triune life that is rightly theirs. I hope to begin to close the
yawning gap between "orthodox confession" and "practical life" to
which Rahner rightly points. Since confession, if it be real, must fully
engage one's heart, mind, soul and strength, true confession in the
Triune God is bound to overflow in practical living. One may begin
at the confessional end of the continuum or at the practical end, but
a serious reckoning of either confession or practicality will soon
overcome this artificial dichotomy between thought and life. The
Trinity is an eminently practical doctrine, not for the sake of practicality alone, but because the Triune God is the living God who
invites all creation into the abundance of his life. Catherine
LaCugna weds theology to life in writing that "the extraordinary
import of the revelation of God in Christ, affirmed in the doctrine
of the Trinity, is that God's life does not belong to God alone: God's
life is shared with every creature. Living trinitarian faith entails
living as Jesus Christ did. . . . Living God's life means living
according to the power and presence of the Holy Spirit."[18]

My hopeful hunch is that Christians actually know more about the
Trinity than they think they know. If this is true, then the task is to
bring to conscious and practical awareness the deeply buried, almost
subconscious, understanding of the Triune God that Christians already evidence through such a simple yet profound act as reciting the
Apostles' Creed on Sunday morning.

Hand-lettered signs alongside many crowded streets in Manila, the
Philippines, warn of "deep excavation." Telephone lines, sewer sys-
tems, water pipes, subterranean electrical projects—all are marked by
wooden signs sounding the alarm in three ominous words: "Caution!
Deep Excavation!" When Christians pray, are baptized or read or hear
the Word of God proclaimed, they can allow the Holy Spirit to perform
a "deep excavation" on their hearts. The Spirit's ministry of presence
and witness opens us to God's triune fullness. God is there as Father,
Son and Holy Spirit even if unacknowledged or underappreciated.
Because the Trinity cannot be divided, God's fullness is present whenever God is. Where God is present at all, God is present clearly,

unmistakably, yet mysteriously, as triune. Rahner's intuition that
Christians are in reality practicing monotheists, and not trinitarians,
is a valid one; however, bringing to conscious awareness the theological foundations of time-honored devotional practices may help Christians not only to be more trinitarian, but also to realize that perhaps
they always have been. Can one really even pray to the "naked" God
of monotheism? Must not every prayer be through the Son and in the
Holy Spirit? Perhaps, after all, a practical Christian life is possible only
on triune terms.

That corn-flakes commercial that says, "Taste them again for the first
time" was much wiser than it knew. Christians have tasted the Triune
God whenever and wherever they have been worshiping, adoring,
pondering and investigating God. But in naming God triune, Christians
can experience God's riches, if not strictly speaking for the first time, then
with a freedom and integrity that will make it seem so. Like the pilgrims
traveling to the village of Emmaus in Luke 24, our eyes will be opened
to God's fullness, and we will recall how our hearts burned within us
when we walked with God but knew not the vast expanses of our
traveling Companion.

There is no substitute for experiencing God. The Triune God is the
inviting God, because the Trinity is really about the God who dares to
encounter us in Jesus Christ, redeeming us through blood and sanctifying us through the Spirit. As the early Christians experienced resurrection life, they were compelled to bear witness through preaching,
healing and ultimately through writing the Gospels, Epistles and
exhortations making up the New Testament. Their experiences were
not private. Real experience never can be private, self-enclosed and
solitary, but must be checked, cross-checked, validated and proven.
The rapid spread of Christianity proved the reality of Jesus Christ. If
only from human origin, the gospel would surely falter; but if from
God, there would be no stopping it (Acts 5:38-39).

As compelling as any one person's personal experience of God may
be, experience alone is not an adequate grounding for Christian theology.
Jaroslav Pelikan writes that Christian doctrine is "what the church of
Jesus Christ believes, teaches, and confesses on the basis of the word of

God."[19] Believing, teaching and confessing are all designed to reach their full bloom only within the Christian community. For the first Christians "the individual could confess Jesus only by taking over the confession of the congregation to its Lord, and also thereby confessing the work of the Spirit of Christ in this congregation."[20] The very act of confession itself was immediately communitarian. Indeed, "no one can say 'Jesus is Lord' except by the Holy Spirit" (1 Cor 12:3), and the Holy Spirit dwells within the church.

The church's doctrines, confessions and affirmations are necessarily rooted and founded in the Word of God, and the Word of God is Jesus Christ (Jn 1:1). The fullest witness we have to God's revelation in Jesus Christ is the Bible. The revelation is Jesus Christ, not the Bible, although we confess that "all scripture is inspired by God" (2 Tim 3:16).

The Bible speaks of God in many voices and accents. God occasionally appears almost as an abstraction, "I AM WHO I AM" (Ex 3:14), as if to remind us that God will finally transcend all of our concepts. But clarity is what interests the biblical writers the most—not clarity to rob mystery and majesty from God, but clarity to demonstrate, as Jesus did by speaking in parables, that God's greatness is not diminished by its appearing in humble symbols. God's greatness is that he can pour himself into biblical metaphors such as shepherd, light, rock, king, judge and fire.[21]

Suppose your house was recently ravaged by fire. Would that symbol for God appeal to you? Not likely. City dwellers may have only remote acquaintance with sheep; God as shepherd is strange to them. Others, however, may find altogether natural and helpful connections between their everyday experiences and biblical depictions of God. A trip to the seashore may convince one that God is light and rock if one sees a lighthouse beaming protection to fishing boats. The multiplicity of biblical symbols of God insures that everyone can discover meaning in at least one of them.

None of us would take literally the Lord God's walking in the Garden of Eden (Gen 3:8). Similarly, we know that God is not really fire, light and rock, although each of these conveys a wealth of meaning. When considering personal symbols, such as judge, king and shepherd, we instinctively sense we are getting much closer to the heart of divinity. Thinking of God as fire, light, rock or wind can be subpersonal and beneath God's dignity. Such thinking may be little better than pagan animism. But we need never apologize for using personal symbols, because all that we know about being authentic persons ultimately comes from God. We do not first create ourselves and then "invent" God. Self-created men and women finally have no need of God.

How is the understanding of God as triune related to these other biblical models? Is the Trinity a photograph of God and all of God's inner workings, whereas other models are merely paintings, and hence less accurate and revealing? Is the Trinity an alphabet of grace to be used to spell out clearly God's revelation to humanity? Are the other biblical portraits of God only so many hieroglyphics?

First and foremost, we humbly acknowledge that "only God has the capacity to fully comprehend God."[22] The early Christian bishop Eunomius (c. 325-c. 395), one of the leaders of the heretical Arian party, insisted that his knowledge of God was equal to, if not surpassing, God's own self-knowledge. Once truly in God's presence, enveloped in pure mystery, no one would ever make such a brash statement again. Any real knowledge of God convinces one that there is infinitely more to know about God than one already knows.

Our God is a giving God. God's revelation to us in Jesus Christ is pure gift and pure grace. Impressions of God as light, wind or fire are not wrong, but they are anticipatory and incomplete. Personal metaphors such as friend, shepherd and even mother cover more of the distance between God and us, but Jesus Christ is God's final revelation. All other revelations must be seen and judged through Jesus' finality.

Jesus Christ is the eternal Word of the Father who became incarnate in the fullness of time. The Holy Spirit, who in the beginning "swept over the face of the waters" (Gen 1:2) and spoke through the prophets, was the Spirit who enabled incarnation, who empowered Jesus' ministry, who in the present age cultivates God's life in human hearts. Self-giving love is the Trinity's signature, for this God is "not self-contained, egotistical and self-absorbed," but rather is "overflowing love, outreaching desire for union with all that God has made. The communion of divine life is God's communion *with us* in Christ and as Spirit."[23]

The Christian understanding of God takes its stand on the Trinity. Christian theology lives or dies with the Trinity. Christians are not "mere monotheists"; they are trinitarians. One of today's leading trinitarians, Jürgen Moltmann, has it exactly right: "Christian theology is hence, inescapably and of inner necessity, trinitarian theology; and only trinitarian theology is Christian theology."[24] What sets Christianity apart from all other religions, philosophies and worldviews is God's relentless search for community among those whom he created. The Word of the Father descended to human flesh so that we might ascend to God. God became incarnate, not for the sake of theology, but to save sinners from eternal death.

Theology therefore tries to focus, understand and interpret God's speech to humankind, but it is not the speech itself. Theology works to clarify God's message of salvation, to make certain the message is not obscured by careless language or odd customs. The theologian finally confesses that the Trinity is not human speech about God, but rather it is God's speech about his own nature unveiled in Jesus Christ and enlivened by the Holy Spirit. In the Trinity, and only there, we glimpse—even if through preliminary and imperfect lenses—"God's ways of being God."[25]

Biblical Foundations

For Augustine the Trinity was found on every page of the Bible. He did not mean that every page contained a detailed explanation of the doctrine, but rather that throughout Scripture God had graciously sprinkled countless clues of triune truth, which during the early Christian centuries would be drawn out and crafted into the doctrine of the Trinity. For Augustine the Bible is the book of God, the God who willingly gives himself in covenant with the ancient Israelites, a covenant finalized and perfected in Jesus Christ. There is continuity between the Old and New Testaments so that the seemingly "ruthless

God of Joshua" is the same God as "the loving God of Jesus."[26] The
Trinity's presence throughout the entire Bible, not as a detailed doctrine, but as a living reality, ensures this continuity.

The God of Abraham, Isaac and Ruth is the God and Father of Jesus
Christ. Ancient Christian commentators were impressed by this connectedness—so much so that they found many anticipations of the Triune
God in the Old Testament, for example, Genesis 1:1-2, 26; Numbers
6:23-26; Isaiah 6:2-3; 48:16; Haggai 2:1-7.27 God is supremely one in the
Old Testament, as in Israel's confession of faith: "Hear, O Israel: The LORD
is our God, the LORD alone" (Deut 6:4). While remaining one, God had
still to make himself known to his people, so God showed himself at
various times as Spirit, Word or Wisdom.[28]

Is the Triune God present in the Old Testament? We can allow that
"a primordial, implicit triune teaching appears in generalized form in
the Old Testament, as if a mystery were being prepared for subsequent
fuller disclosure."[29] This must be so, because the same God who called
Abraham later became incarnate in Jesus Christ. The salvation history
perspective that is today favored by most trinitarians urges us not to
neglect traces of the Triune God in the Old Testament. The doctrine of
the Trinity, after all, developed out of Jewish monotheism. The preex-
istence of Wisdom in Proverbs 8:22-31 was "the starting point both for
the Johannine concept of the Logos and for the doctrine of the Logos
in the early Christian Apologists."[30] These Old Testament hints and
anticipations are not to be lightly dismissed. This connection between
Old Testament promise and trinitarian fulfillment, writes Wolfhart
Pannenberg, "shows that the Christian view of the Son as a preexistent
hypostasis alongside the Father, and similar views concerning the
Spirit which developed in the course of the formation of the doctrine
of the Trinity, were not from the very outset opposed to Judaism and
its belief in one God."[31] Karl Rahner warns us against rejecting "too
simply, apodictically, and unreservedly the opinion of the ancients
that, even before Christ, there was already in some vague way a belief
in the Trinity."[32] God in the Old Testament is "the absolute mystery"
who yet communicates his nature through his Word and Spirit.
Rahner believes that "in a certain sense, theoretically no great distance

separates these three realities. His presence through the Word in the Spirit must be different from him, the lasting primordial mystery, yet it cannot stand before him and hide him as if it were something quite different."[33] Rahner is thus willing to contend for "an authentic secret prehistory of the revelation of the Trinity in the Old Testament."[34] It is surely "anachronistic"[35] to find in the Old Testament a full-blown trinitarianism. But considering the wide and deep sweep of salvation history, coupled with the considerable theological continuity between the two biblical testaments, the assessments of Pannenberg and Rahner are worth noting. Prooftexting the Trinity in the Old Testament, for example, "let us make humankind in our image, according to our likeness" (Gen 1:26),[36] does not advance the cause. But seeing hints and foreshadowings of the Triune God in the Old Testament does.

The folk wisdom about the forest and the trees is appropriate when thinking about the Trinity in the Bible. It is necessary to examine every twig of evidence for God's triune presence in the pages of Scripture. But in doing so, the bigger picture of the forest must be kept constantly in view. The center of the Bible's witness to God must be the revelation in Jesus Christ. The Triune God is to be found there, in "the fundamental recognition that Jesus Christ is Immanuel, God with us, a recognition which is itself enabled by awareness of participation in the Spirit in that same mystery."[37]

Since the center holds in Christ Jesus, sent from the Father and breathed into our hearts by the Holy Spirit, we can happily acknowledge biblical texts that, taken together, present a powerful witness to the Trinity. Many scriptural passages testify to God's oneness: Deuteronomy 6:4; Matthew 23:9; Mark 10:18; 12:29; Romans 3:30; 1 Corinthians 8:4, 6; Galatians 3:20; Ephesians 4:6; 1 Timothy 1:17; 2:5; James 2:19; 4:12.[38] God's forceful and total singularity was never out of mind for the first Christians. The Christian confession of Jesus Christ as God's perfect unveiling does not destroy God's unity, but confirms that God is a speaking and acting God.

God speaks and acts not only as Son, but also through Spirit. Numerous New Testament Scriptures could by considered dyadic, because they link the Holy Spirit and the Son in common cause and activity, or demonstrate the intimacy between Father and Son. Such passages include Romans 1:4; 6:4; 8:11; 1 Corinthians 6:14; 2 Corinthians 4:14; Galatians 1:1; Ephesians 1:20; 1 Timothy 1:2, 3:16; 1 Peter 1:21.[39] Virtually every dyadic passage is also triadic, because when any two of the three divine persons are present, the third is there also.

Many New Testament passages could be considered triadic in nature. Such passages are Acts 2:32-33; 1 Corinthians 6:11; 12:4-5; 2 Corinthians 1:21-22; Galatians 3:11-14; 4:6; Ephesians 4:4-6; 1 Thessalonians 5:18-19; 2 Thessalonians 2:13-14; Hebrews 9:14; 10:29; 1 Peter 1:2; 3:18.[40] Father, Son and Holy Spirit are to be found in all of these passages, yet they are more triadic than they are triune. The crucial difference between triadic and triune is simply this. Three of anything—beads on a string, for example—is a triad, yet these three need not be related to one another in any meaningful way. Washington, Jefferson and Lincoln may be widely esteemed as the three greatest U.S. presidents, but that does not make them a trinity. *Triunity* means just what the component parts of the word assert: there are three, and yet these three are one. Jesus' declaration that "the Father and I are one" (Jn 10:30) may not seem trinitarian since it mentions not three but only two, yet it is profoundly trinitarian because the Holy Spirit seals the union of Father and Son.

Therefore the Trinity is not simply about three parts or phases of God conceived and held in isolation from each other, but about how these three are dynamically related in the common goals of creation, redemption and consummation. Father, Son and Holy Spirit are indeed related to one another throughout the New Testament, so that with Augustine we can see the Trinity on every page. Later thinking about the Trinity did not improve God's internal relations, for they are eternally perfect. Later reflection, however, did sharpen our understanding of how the Triune God operates for personal and cosmic salvation. If the triadic God resembles three boxcars riding along the rails, connected to each other yet incapable of dwelling within each other, then the Triune God is more like a single locomotive whose three parts operate perfectly together to accomplish its tasks.

Isolating biblical texts that deal, respectively, with God's singularity, binity and finally trinity does serve a certain utilitarian purpose. If nothing else, the Christian will have abundant devotional materials. Ending there, though, is like unwrapping your child's swing set on Christmas morning and then not putting it together. Assuring and suggestive, if not always totally compelling, evidence can be found in the New Testament for God's triunity. The two clearest examples are Paul's benediction in 2 Corinthians 13:13, "The grace of the Lord Jesus Christ, the love of God, and the communion of the Holy Spirit be with all of you," and Jesus' baptismal command in Matthew 28:19, "Go therefore and make disciples of all nations, baptizing them in the name of the Father and of the Son and of the Holy Spirit."[41]

We are apt to get confused here. It does seem clear that "the doctrine of the Trinity cannot be derived from Scripture through proof texts."[42] We might even admit, following a conservative theologian, that "we are dealing with dogmatic foundations and not explicit biblical teaching."[43] For another this teaching "is a theological doctrine, not a scriptural proclamation."[44] The confusion comes if we do not see the deep and necessary connections between Scripture and doctrine. Not every Christian doctrine is fully and exhaustively explained in the Bible. Few, if any, Christian teachings, were "laid down once and for all in their complete form; they grew from simple beginnings . . . finally to emerge in mature form."[45]

The early preaching of Peter and Paul was not explicitly about the Trinity. "Jesus is Lord!" was on their lips, not "God is Triune!" Yet the apostolic preaching necessarily was implicitly trinitarian. Jesus is Lord only as coming from the Father and living in the Spirit's inspiration. The context of Peter and Paul's preaching was triune even if the explicit proclamation was the lordship of Jesus. Paul declared that "no one can say 'Jesus is Lord' except by the Holy Spirit" (1 Cor 12:3). The Trinity may be an elaboration of "the simple testimony of the New Testament,"[46] but nothing in the teaching in any way contradicts the New Testament's central message, the kingdom or reign of God. The reigning God is the Triune God, and therefore the Trinity, writes Emil Brunner, "defends the central faith of the Bible and of the Church."[47]

The apostle Paul testified that ministers of the new covenant are made competent by God, because this covenant is "not of letter but of spirit; for the letter kills, but the Spirit gives life" (2 Cor 3:6). God's triune fullness is God's new covenant with us. It is a covenant of presence and Spirit, not a covenant of letter and law. Approaching the Trinity legalistically can lead to loss of faith, because there simply are not enough New Testament passages that spell out the teaching fully and precisely.

We must, therefore, discover how God as triune is the sustaining power behind the central theme of the New Testament. This means that "every biblical reference to the mystery of redemption is ultimately important for a trinitarian theology of God,"[48] and not just those texts that explicitly spell out the three divine names. Ephesians 1:3-14 is deeply trinitarian,[49] not because it succeeds in solving the Trinity's mystery, but because it invites our direct participation in that mystery: "He has made known to us the mystery of his will, according to his good pleasure that he set forth in Christ, as a plan for the fullness of time, to gather up all things in him, things in heaven and things on earth" (1:9-10).

"The Lord has more light and truth yet to break forth out of his holy Word,"[50] testified the Puritan John Robinson. The psalmist affirmed, "In your light we see light" (36:9). Some church fathers compared the Trinity to three candles in one room. There are three candles but only one light. In the Bible, the Triune God does shine in three names, but for the sake of one goal—namely, our walking and sharing in God's eternal light.

God's Defining Name

Public opinion surveys reveal that almost everyone believes in some sort of "universal power" or "ultimate reality." Many of those thus believing would even be willing to call their object of belief "God." Such a belief in God is known as theism, and over the centuries a list of traits and qualities has slowly and surely established itself as accurately defining the God of theism. Thomas Aquinas can best speak for the theistic tradition. He believed that God was "simple, perfect, infinite, omnipotent, omnipresent, immutable, eternal, impassible, one."[51] In somewhat simpler language, theism views God as "timeless, changeless, passionless, unmoved, and unmovable."[52]

Thinking about the God of theism is really to ask, "What is the nature of the divine?"[53] This is certainly a necessary question. The greatest minds of history, those who love God supremely and those who despise God entirely, have given themselves over to pondering God's nature. Behind the dozen or so theistic characteristics listed above, there stand centuries of philosophical argumentation, literary exploration and cultural demonstration. Even limiting the discussion exclusively to ancient Christian witness provides innumerable viewpoints.

The riches of theism may be inexhaustible, yet it has seemed to many thoughtful persons that the God of theism bears only the slightest resemblance to the God of Abraham, Sarah and David, the God and Father of Jesus Christ. "What is the nature of the divine?" satisfies the intellectual need to know but not the heart's cry for reunion with God. Can God indeed be "timeless, changeless, passionless, unmoved, and unmovable" if we are to know God through God's only Son whom he sent?

"What is the nature of the divine?" is answered by the God of theism. Yet the theistic God who is so deeply ingrained in Christian history and tradition has in recent years come under increasingly heavy attack from many quarters. This God is often cast in the role of "an aloof monarch, removed from the contingencies of the world, unchangeable in every aspect of being, . . . an all-determining and irresistible power, aware of everything that will ever happen and never taking risks."[54] Regal, resplendent, philosophically compelling—God as monarch is all of this and more. Yet can this God care about his creatures? Can weak humans ever come to know this God more deeply than to salute as he marches past in the royal procession? Is not God more like "a caring parent with qualities of love and responsiveness, generosity and sensitivity, openness and vulnerability, a person (rather than a metaphysical principle) who experiences the world, responds to what happens, relates to us and interacts dynamically with humans"?[55]

The doctrine of the Trinity means that Christian thinking about God always begins with a person, Jesus Christ, never an abstraction into which the theistic God can easily devolve. Jesus Christ does not answer "*What* is the nature of the divine?" He is a "who," not a "what." "All the fullness of God" (Col 1:19) dwells in Jesus Christ. So he answers the question "*Who* is God?" The person of Jesus Christ must always correct and qualify the traits of the theistic God, however time-honored and culturally established they may be. If the priority of Jesus is kept center stage, then certain theistic qualities can indeed be helpful pointers to God's intentions for the world and humankind. That is because theism is then understood incarnationally, which makes all the difference. Not only Jesus is "the same yesterday and today and forever" (Heb 13:8), but also the full expanse of the Triune God. Precisely because of Jesus, however, the Triune God is unchanging in his passionate quest to be reconciled with his errant creatures. God's orientation toward humanity has never changed. It has always been filled with love, fellowship and communion. Exactly on account of God's incessant search for humanity did the Word become incarnate, to overcome sin that had alienated humanity from God.

God's overall purposes have not changed, and this fixity of purpose means that God is changeless and even immutable. God's immutability, for Clark Pinnock, means that "we can always rely on God to be faithful to his promises; he is not in any way fickle or capricious. Immutability ought to focus on the faithfulness of God as a relational, personal being."[56] God's purposes have not changed, but God's methods for accomplishing those purposes did change in the Incarnation. In his being "the same yesterday and today and forever," Jesus Christ testifies to God's fixed and immutable goal: to bring his people to know him, and ultimately to make them holy.

The hymn writer has said it better than I am capable of: "Thou changest not; Thy compassions, they fail not."[57] God does not change, and yet the mercies, the steadfast love, the compassions of the Lord are new every morning (Lam 3:22-23). God's compassions are God's passions extended and offered to us, for that is just what *compassion* means—"passion with or for."

A God who is "timeless, unmoved, and unmovable" is not apt to be a God of compassion and responsiveness. Even God's being changeless and passionless, two theistic traits that can be readily applied to God the Father, must be seen and revised through the Incarnation.

The God of theism is therefore not a total stranger to the God of Jesus Christ. It may be going too far, as I said earlier, to say that there is only a slight and passing resemblance between these two conceptions of God. Yet it is possible to trace historically the steps whereby the God of theism became disjoined from the God of Jesus Christ. The culmination of this process was in the thirteenth century, when Thomas Aquinas decided, on logical grounds, that the investigation of the One God must come before that of the Triune God.[58]

For Christians today the real challenge is not to maintain a strict stand of monotheism. Theism is too deeply ingrained in Western culture and institutions for it to evaporate suddenly. Christians will remain monotheists. But they should not remain monotheists at the great expense of forfeiting the Trinity, for the Triune God is the saving and keeping God, not the theistic God. To fight for the Trinity is to fight for God, and those who thus seek God will not be disappointed.

The theistic God is not disclosed in revelation. At the most, this God is most effective in the lecture hall instead of the pulpit, because the God of theism has no particular interest in our devotion, worship and loyalty. Too easily this God becomes merely "a closed circle of perfect being in heaven."[59]

The Triune God may be "perfect being in heaven" but is decidedly not "a closed circle." Revelation is God's radical openness to us, God's invitation to us to come and join and partake. Therefore, in Emil Brunner's words, "the Triune God is the God of revelation, not the God of the philosophers."[60] God as triune could only be revealed through God's generosity, never constructed through human ingenuity.

The uniqueness and finality of God's revelation in Jesus Christ is at the heart of Karl Barth's theology. He is one of the greatest trinitari-

ans in the history of Christian thought. For Barth revelation is "the
root of the doctrine of the Trinity."[61] Barth asserts that "revelation . . .
has no analogies, and is nowhere repeated. It stands alone and it
speaks for itself. It receives light from nowhere else; the source of its
light is in itself and in itself alone."[62]

Barth did not always make such strong statements. In his younger
years, at the beginning of the twentieth century, Barth was a theological and cultural liberal. Liberalism advised all people to look within
themselves, for having been created in God's image, surely they
would within their own persons encounter the divine purely and
truly. All of humankind was the best analogy of God. Barth's turn from
liberalism to the centrality of revelation started in an eleven-year
pastorate in a Swiss village. The religious longings of his parishioners
were simply not met by the liberal God. World War I destroyed this
God for Barth and for countless others. In the 1930s Barth saw some
of his theology professors from his student days defect to the Nazi
cause, ensuring that the liberal God was forever dead in his mind.

For Barth, God is the cause of revelation, the event of revelation and
the outcome of revelation. Using the language of grammar, Barth
declares that "God is He who in this event is subject, predicate and
object; the revealer, the act of revelation, the revealed; Father, Son and
Holy Spirit. God is the Lord active in this event."[63] Humanity is called
to hear the Word, but only the Father can speak the Word, in the Spirit's
power. The mistake of liberalism had been to presume that human
speech could imitate divine speech. In fact, for much of liberalism,
divine speech was nothing more than amplified human speech.
Against this stream, which finally ended in atheism, Barth declared
"that one can *not* speak of God simply by speaking of man in a loud
voice."[64]

Similarly, humanity can only receive the Word of God; God alone
can initiate revelation. From first to last, the drama of revelation is
God's and his alone. Barth writes that "God reveals Himself. He
reveals Himself through Himself. If we wish really to regard revelation from the side of its subject, God, then above all we must understand that this subject, God, the Revealer, is identical with His act in

revelation, identical with its effect."[65]

Recently a film actress lost a huge legal judgment because she backed out of a role she had earlier agreed to perform. She had not signed a contract, but she had given her word, which was ruled to be legally binding. Only of God can it be said that his word and act are always a perfect match. There is no duplicity or retreating from obligation in God. "God's word is identical with God himself,"[66] Barth assures us. Every person would like to make this statement about himself or herself, but only God can in truth make it. It is "the highest and last statement which can be made about the being of God," Barth believes—namely, that God alone "corresponds to himself."[67]

The source of this correspondence is God the Father, and the demonstration of it is Jesus Christ, who "does not merely reveal the truth. As the incarnate, earthly, and indeed crucified Christ he is the truth in person."[68] The Holy Spirit applies this correspondence in our hearts, restoring us through grace to God's initial intention for us. That is the meaning of sanctification—to be "restored to the favor and image of God."[69]

The Immanent and the Economic Trinity

The very idea of revelation is for many contemporary people foolishness. Science, so conventional wisdom has it, spells the end of mystery and hence the end of revelation. As science grows and is perfected, revelation shrivels and eventually expires. The scientific mindset supposedly argues about any given subject of inquiry that "the acquisition of further knowledge about the subject would reduce the mystery and reduce the necessity of revelation."[70]

This narrowing view is a disservice to both science and religion. As eminent a scientist as Albert Einstein pled, nearly sixty years ago, for a greater awareness of the mystery that pervades and sustains all things. Authentic science, Einstein implied, needs reverence every bit as much as curiosity. What science had no ability to investigate—the sheer awe of creation—could yet humble scientific, and all, inquiry.

Einstein placed himself before mystery and opened himself to mystery. Many thoughtful people would gladly follow him that far. The Christian, while rejoicing in the face of mystery, understands as no one else does the source of that mystery—God. The Christian understands, not totally but authentically, God's mystery, because that mystery has been made known in the person of Jesus Christ. The entire Christian approach to mystery is centered in Christ, not in the human desire to know ultimate things or in the human longing for convergence with the final truth. Christian truth begins in revelation, not in human intuition.

The modern mind stumbles on revelation, although it may grudgingly agree to the mystery of life. But that Jesus Christ is the One through whom God's mystery is presented to us is more than the modern mind can accept. Now, as then, to point to Jesus Christ and him crucified is "a stumbling block to Jews and foolishness to Gentiles" (1 Cor 1:23). This "scandal of particularity," that the God of all time and space should, when the time became full, pour himself into flesh, is simply unacceptable to the modern mind. Revelation may be provisionally accepted, proclaims modernity, if only it remains general and diffuse and requires no acknowledgment and commitment on my part.

The epistle to the Colossians understands that God's mystery is available only in one Person: "the mystery that has been hidden throughout the ages and generations but has now been revealed to his saints. To them God chose to make known how great among the Gentiles are the riches of the glory of this mystery, which is Christ in you, the hope of glory" (1:26-27). This mystery is available not through Jesus' solo effort divorced from Father and Holy Spirit, but through the Father's bestowing and the Holy Spirit's continued renewing, both in Jesus' heart and in our hearts.

God alone dwells in "unapproachable light" (1 Tim 6:16). Because we cannot approach God, God has approached us in Jesus Christ, the Light of the World. We have total and unfailing confidence that what Jesus reveals about God's character is accurate and truthful. Because we are mortal and not infinite, perfect knowledge of the divine is not possible. The creature cannot question the Creator's integrity, and neither is the creature capable of fully fathoming the Creator.

We are confident that the Son reveals the Father and that the Holy Spirit cultivates this revelation in human soil. Over time there may be a rich harvest, as grace is offered, extended and accepted. This harvest is nothing other than "Christ in you, the hope of glory" (Col 1:27). Mystery in the New Testament is always pointed toward Christ Jesus, flowing from the Father and stamped in our hearts by the Holy Spirit. It is not for the sake of mystery itself that God revealed himself. Mystery for its own sake is really mystification; it makes as much sense as steps that lead to nowhere or an unsolvable mathematical puzzle. The sort of mystery that God imparts to us is well summarized by Avery Dulles: "The mystery par excellence is not so much God in his essential nature, or the counsels of the divine mind, but rather God's plan of salvation as it comes to concrete realization in the person of Christ Jesus."[71] God's mystery is not mystery-in-itself but is rather mystery-for-us.

Much like the time-honored distinction between theory and practice, Christian theology has spoken about two approaches to the Triune God: the immanent Trinity of God's internal relations and the economic Trinity of God's relatedness to the world in creation and redemption. It is often the case when talking about the one God that the word *immanent*, meaning God's real presence in the world, is contrasted with *transcendent*, suggesting God's sovereign lordship over the whole created order. But immanent as applied to the Trinity does not mean God's connection to the world (for that is the economic Trinity), but rather God's internal relations, the inner dynamics of the Godhead, to use somewhat abstract language.

The immanent Trinity can also be called the essential or the ontological Trinity. For some theologians this is the "real God," the God whose knowledge all people ought to pursue for all they are worth. Theologian T. F. Torrance, for example, has written: "It is as our knowing God passes from what is called the 'economic Trinity' to the 'ontological Trinity' that we have [theology] in the supreme and proper sense, knowledge of God on the free ground of his own Being, knowledge of him in which our knowing is controlled and shaped by relations eternally immanent in God."[72]

Most recent thought about the Trinity has wished to begin with the economic Trinity revealed through God's desire to win back our allegiance lost through sin. Torrance also begins with the economic Trinity but suggests that God's authentic Being, God's true freedom, is best expressed through the ontological or immanent Trinity. This in turn seems to suggest that the immanent Trinity is somehow superior to the economic Trinity, that God's own internal thoughts (the immanent Trinity) are somehow more profound, revealing and illuminating than God's spoken Word of revelation that entered history in Jesus Christ.

Can there be different levels and realms within God? Is it possible that the immanent Trinity is somehow deeper and richer and fuller— more divine!—than the economic Trinity? Karl Rahner did not think so. His well-known assessment is that "the 'economic' Trinity is the 'immanent' Trinity and the 'immanent' Trinity is the 'economic' Trinity."[73] Catherine LaCugna perceptively asserts that "the central theme of trinitarian theology is the relationship between this economy and the eternal being of God."[74] If today we begin with God's economic manifestation in creation and salvation from sin, we do not thereby slight God's eternal Being. We honor and worship God's eternal Being and God's utter freedom, but we do so on the basis of that which God has revealed in Jesus Christ and made alive in us through the Holy Spirit. The whole idea of the immanent Trinity is to safeguard God's majesty, while at the same time acknowledging our humanness, remembering (as the Lord does) "that we are dust" (Ps 103:14). With Gregory of Nyssa, we exercise great caution, lest we claim to know more than we are capable of: "Following the instructions of Holy Scripture, we have been taught that [the nature of God] is beyond names or human speech. We say that every [divine] name, be it invented by human custom or handed on to us by the tradition of the Scriptures, represents our conception of the divine nature, but does not convey the meaning of that nature in itself."[75]

Today's stress on the economic Trinity does not diminish God's mystery, but intensifies it. Two Greek words meaning the management of the household are the basis for our English *economy*;[76] the economic Trinity, to continue the metaphor, invites us to close and familiar table fellowship with God. That is the true mystery—that God himself would want to know us and would desire our communion so keenly as to sacrifice willingly his only Son, Jesus Christ. God's making himself available to humankind is the all-surpassing mystery. Søren Kierkegaard confessed that "it is indeed less terrible to fall to the ground when the mountains tremble at the voice of the God, than to sit at table with him as an equal; and yet it is the God's concern precisely to have it so."[77] Kierkegaard, who elsewhere stressed the "absolute qualitative difference" between God and humans, is not diluting God's awe by claiming that God desires for us to sit at table with him as an equal. Human analogies fail us, but we are equal with God in the same way that a king makes himself equal to a peasant he has invited to a royal feast at the castle. Equality is altogether on the king's terms, as it is on God's terms. God has lowered himself in the Incarnation that we might be elevated in his likeness. "The great end of religion," John Wesley believed, "is to renew our hearts in the image of God."[78] To accomplish this end, God descends in Jesus Christ, that we by his grace may ascend to full participation in God's joys.

Mountain climbers often climb a mid-sized peak only by the light of the moon. A climb might begin around midnight so that climbers can reach the top and then begin their descent before the sun melts the snow and makes conditions treacherous. They climb by moonlight and by the rising sun's pink fingers. Picture, if you can, a mountain in total and complete darkness. There is no moon and no flashlights or climbing lanterns. Picture, too, a climbing team in total blindness. Progress up the mountain, if it can be made at all, is only by touch, bending over to touch the snow to be sure one is still heading up the mountain.

The immanent Trinity is vaguely like this mountain shrouded by impenetrable darkness. Even if we could climb it, we would know almost nothing about the mountain as we ascended it, for all of its secrets would be extremely well hidden. If we managed to reach the top, which would be highly unlikely, we would not know we had arrived and could therefore stumble to certain death.

No mountain can shine by its own light, but the immanent Trinity can. Yet apart from Jesus Christ, we have only anticipatory but not definitive knowledge of this inner light of God's own being, God's mystery. There are hints and foreshadowings, to be sure. The letter to the Hebrews says as much: "Long ago God spoke to our ancestors in many and various ways by the prophets" (1:1). God's veiled speech in the prophets was fulfilled by God's consummate utterance in Jesus Christ: "In these last days he has spoken to us by a Son, whom he appointed heir of all things, through whom he also created the worlds. He is the reflection of God's glory and the exact imprint of God's very being" (1:2-3).

"God's very Being" is another way of describing the immanent Trinity. But that we can describe it at all means that God has come near in Jesus Christ to make God's very Being known to us. The immanent and the economic Trinity can be distinguished from each other but cannot be separated, for they are not two but one. God's life is a life of perfect beauty, truth and goodness—a life worth sharing. The God of "infinite and independent Being" is the same God who, as John Wesley believed, "is in a peculiar manner the Father of those whom he regenerates by his Spirit, whom he adopts in his Son as co-heirs with him and crowns with an eternal inheritance."[79] Becoming "heirs of God and joint heirs with Christ" (Rom 8:17) does not deny God's mystery, but rather compels us to dive fearlessly into "God, the great ocean of love."[80]

Today's theological climate demands not that God be placed at human disposal, for to do that would reduce God to "a puny godling." But it is quite a different matter to claim that God *has placed himself* at human disposal, opening up the divine life to human participation. This new "openness of God"[81] suggests that the economic Trinity is the best methodological starting point for inquiring about God's purposes for his creation. This common move in recent trinitarian thought has been fluidly executed by Catherine LaCugna:

It used to be that a new doctrine of the Trinity meant a new way to explain "God's inner life," that is, the relationship of Father, Son and Holy Spirit to one another (what tradition refers to as the immanent Trinity). But now both Catholic and Protestant theologians who are working to revitalize the doctrine of the Trinity have shifted away from constructing theories about God's "inner life." Instead, by returning to the more concrete images and concepts of the Bible, liturgy and creeds, it has become clear that the original purpose of the doctrine was to explain the place of Christ in our salvation, the place of the Spirit in our sanctification or deification, and in so doing to say something about the mystery of God's eternal being. By concentrating more on the mystery of *God with us, God for us*, and less on the nature of God by Godself, it is becoming possible once again for the doctrine of the Trinity to stand at the center of faith—as our rhetoric has always claimed.[82]

If God cannot be known apart from his revealing himself to us, and if this happens supremely in the economy of salvation, then it would seem to be only a short logical jump from prioritizing the economic Trinity over the immanent Trinity to the total elimination of the latter. In fact, Thomas Weinandy has accused LaCugna of this conclusion, of relegating the immanent Trinity to unimportance. LaCugna's theology means, in his opinion, that "theories about what God is apart from God's self-communication in salvation history remain unverifiable and ultimately untheological,"[83] since the knowledge of God is only given in the economy of creation and redemption. Furthermore, Weinandy believes that LaCugna's thought leads to the virtual elimination of the immanent Trinity because she "so collapses the Trinity into the economy that the economy is no longer the realm in which the Trinity acts, but the only realm in which 'the Trinity' *is*."[84] LaCugna may not be guilty of all that Weinandy charges her with, but the reminder that *who God is* (the immanent Trinity) can never be absolutely identified with or totally reduced to *what God does* (the economic Trinity) is always timely and necessary. Weinandy rightly stresses that Christian theology can ill afford to lose "the noumenal God who actually exists in his wholly ontologically distinct otherness as God."[85] Hans Urs von Balthasar understands that to dissolve the immanent Trinity into the economic is to deny the finely tuned balance of the Triune God.

While, according to Christian faith, the economic Trinity assuredly appears as the interpretation of the immanent Trinity, it may not be identified with it, for the latter grounds and supports the former. Otherwise the immanent, eternal Trinity would threaten to dissolve into the economic; in other words, God would be swallowed up in the world process—a necessary stage, in this view, if he is fully to realize himself.[86]

New Names for God?

During his presidency, George Bush drew many smiles, and afterward many newspaper columns, when he declared in a presidential speech that he would not "mess" with social security. Commentators were amused that the president would use such a casual word for such a serious subject. Bush was thought to have dropped his pretense in using "mess" and to have really connected with the people.

Much as President Bush would not "mess" with something as urgent and vital as social security, affecting millions and millions of people, Christian theology must not "mess" with the classical names of God: Father, Son and Holy Spirit. There are at least two good reasons why this is so. Most tellingly, Father, Son and Holy Spirit are biblical speech. Jesus knew God as Father and knew that, in the bond of the Holy Spirit, perfect communion had prevailed among the three divine names from all eternity. Jesus' sonship did not begin at Bethlehem, for the Father's Word had no beginning; the Father was never without his Word. Jesus angered the Jews when he said to them, "Very truly, I tell you, before Abraham was, I am" (Jn 8:58). Flesh and blood cannot understand these realities, for only the Holy Spirit can illuminate one's spiritual senses.

Father, Son and Holy Spirit must also be retained for the sake of history and continuity. The time-honored means of entry into the Christian church has always been baptism in the thrice-blessed name. Christian worship, especially in the sacramental meal, has likewise always been offered up in praise to the Triune God. Communion has been celebrated to the glory of Father, Son and Holy Spirit almost daily

for nearly twenty centuries. "This repetition," states a leading histo-
rian of Christian thought, "for nearly three-fourths of a million days
in a row stands as a massive instance of the continuity of the church
across changes of culture and language, liturgy and theology."[87]

Father, Son and Holy Spirit therefore are deeply embedded in
Christian life, thought and practice. These names are undeniably a
part of what theologian Thomas Oden calls "classical centrist consen-
sual Christianity."[88] They are at the heart of the Christian proclamation—"what has been believed everywhere, always, and by all."[89] The
names are hence nonnegotiable and cannot simply be cast aside at will
because they are thought by some to be out of step with current
thought.

We must always remember, even so, that God's name is strong only
because God has spoken it, not because we have heard it. Human
hearing is inevitably distorted hearing. Human thoughts about God's
fatherhood are only an approximation of what that fatherhood really
means. God's fatherhood has been described as everything from
harsh, unbending and arbitrary to sentimental and indulgent.

Recognizing that God's fatherhood has many meanings does not
entail its being abandoned altogether but rather its need for clarifica-
tion. Some seemingly new names for God the Father are not really
new at all but are well attested in ancient Christian witness. Gregory
of Nyssa, for example, approached the Father as "the source of power,
the Son as the power of the Father, the Holy Spirit as the Spirit of
power."[90] The Trinity as Source, Word, Spirit[91] is a fresh yet dignified
way of naming God. The Father as Source is inexhaustible riches, a
treasure of grace made incarnate in the Word and applied by the Spirit.

The motherhood of God is a biblical yet frequently ignored way
of describing God's care for the world. Isaiah understood that
God's mercy was like a mother's touch: "As a mother comforts her
child, so I will comfort you; you shall be comforted in Jerusalem"
(66:13). Jesus applied maternal imagery to himself, calling himself
a hen desirous of gathering Jerusalem under her wings, but Jerusalem refused (Mt 23:37; Lk 13:34). The Holy Spirit could conceivably
be known as "she," because the Hebrew word for Spirit (ruaḥ) is

feminine and the Greek *pneuma* is neuter.[92]

I am not proposing a new Trinity of Mother, Daughter and Spirit. Such a flag dogmatically flown would only assert what all sides in the debate want most to deny—that God is gender specific. Insisting on a new Trinity of Mother, Daughter and Spirit would strongly suggest that God is not beyond gender after all but is in fact female. It would also not be biblical, because Jesus is not the daughter of God. God certainly could have become incarnate in a woman, because it is Jesus' humanity, not his being male, that really matters.

It is not necessary to sacrifice the traditional trinitarian language of Father, Son and Holy Spirit. Yet in speaking thus, we know that it is temporary speech, speech that attempts to convey ultimate reality but fails on account of our humanness. Any speech whatsoever about God is bound to have this temporary quality until "we will see face to face" (1 Cor 13:12). Because our speech about God is limited, we need not fear alternative ways of addressing God. We must only be certain that however we address God, respect, worship and love are what motivate us. Moreover, any speech about God must be finally rooted in the Bible and displayed at least intermittently throughout the history of Christianity. Notice that these two criteria—scriptural warrant and historical attestation—are the same two I initially invoked to protect the classic names of Father, Son and Holy Spirit.

Under these two criteria, we cannot allow the Trinity to be called "two bearded men and a bird."[93] This phrase can bring a smile to our lips, as its author no doubt intended that it should, but it is obviously not a serious proposal. Viewing God through the models of mother, lover and friend[94] is a serious proposal, and although its author did not put it forth as a new Trinity, God as mother and God as lover compel both our worship and our theological investigations. Christian tradition supports God as mother and lover, and has seen in Jesus not only the "friend of sinners" but also the highest possible expression of friendship: "No one has greater love than this, to lay down one's life for one's friends" (Jn 15:13). God's friendship does not, perhaps, as easily yield a triune interpretation as God's being mother and lover. Let us quickly and tentatively explore these two.

Late in fourteenth-century England, Julian of Norwich had a vision of Jesus that helped her see God's motherhood. Of her Savior, Julian declared: "Jesus is our true Mother in nature by our first creation, and he is our true Mother in grace by his taking our created nature."[95] God remained Father, but Jesus was Mother for Julian: "And so in our making, God almighty is our loving Father, and God all wisdom is our loving Mother, with the love and goodness of the Holy Spirit, which is all one God, one Lord."[96]

Augustine's vision of the Trinity understood the Father to be the divine lover. The Father's fathomless love fills the Son, the Father's beloved. The Holy Spirit is the love itself. God is thus "lover, beloved, love itself" for Augustine, or "he that loves, and that which is loved, and love" itself.[97] A recent writer is squarely on target in naming God "the radiating event of love."[98] Augustine confessed, "Thou seest the Trinity when Thou seest love."[99]

It turns out, then, that new names for God are really not new after all. They are well documented in Scripture and by Christian thought and action. Neglected themes such as God's motherhood and God as lover need not overwhelm and eliminate the received tradition of Father, Son and Holy Spirit. These neglected themes will not eliminate the traditional names but, positively, will supplement and illuminate all of Christian life and thought. Because the Holy Spirit is faithful, fresh formulas will emerge from the New Testament. A wonderfully fluid and expressive formula, knowing all about friendship, intimacy and service, is God as Abba (Mk 14:36; Rom 8:15; Gal 4:6), Servant (Mk 10:45) and Paraclete (Jn 14:16, 26; 15:26).[100]

A living faith has no fear of new ways of expressing ancient truths, provided that the continuity of truth and the vitality of tradition link new to old. The Triune God as the Abba, the Servant and the Paraclete does not transgress tradition, but rather elevates neglected strands of tradition that can forcefully address the present age. Other proposed trinitarian formulas, often advanced in hopes of overcoming the alleged gender bias of Father, Son and Holy Spirit, may not be deemed satisfactory once their theological merits are examined. To call God the Creator, Redeemer and Sustainer, as many have done, may obscure the full participation of all the triune Persons in creation, for it suggests that only God the Father creates, whereas the scriptural record attributes creation to God's Spirit (Gen 1:2) and Son (Jn 1:3; Col 1:16) as well.

To the urgent question "Who is God?" many contemporary persons would never think of speaking God's triune name. "I am God" or "God is me" falls naturally from the tongue because it is so entrenched in the heart. The history of religion demonstrates this propensity toward the creation of numberless gods. The apostle John addressed this confusing abundance of names. For him the question "Who is God?" had only one answer: "God is love" (1 Jn 4:8, 16). But what kind of love is God's love? God's love is trivial and sentimental, no better than any love from any other divinity, unless it is radically risked. Along all God's ways with us we see risk: creation, incarnation, crucifixion. If the blood of goats and bulls, mixed with the ashes of a heifer, sanctifies the defiled and purifies their flesh, "how much more will the blood of Christ, who through the eternal Spirit offered himself without blemish to God, purify our conscience from dead works to worship the living God!" (Heb 9:14). This verse encapsulates "the shortest expression of the Trinity, [which] is the divine act of the cross, in which the Father allows the Son to sacrifice himself through the Spirit."[101] God's triune name speaks unambiguously through God's triune cross. The Father speaks to us, the Son for us, and the Spirit in us.

2

GOD'S
NAME
ROOTED

*G*OD'S PRESENCE WITH US is God's gift to us and in us. The history of Israel, pointing toward and culminating in Jesus Christ and the sending of the Holy Spirit, is a history of grace. As an incarnational and historical faith, Christianity makes the bold claim that in Jesus Christ "the whole fullness of deity dwells bodily" (Col 2:9), an event that transpired precisely "when the fullness of time had come" (Gal 4:4). The enfleshment of God's eternal Word opens new horizons for humankind: knowing, willing and living in God. "We claim to be sharers in the divine life of the Blessed Trinity not because we are capable of realising what it means, but because we believe that in the Incarnation God entered into the course of this world's history in order to initiate us into this way of life."[1] Sharing God's life is possible only because God the Father has first given his very life to us in Jesus Christ. Arrogance begins and futility ends any quest for God that is not incarnationally driven. God gives and we receive. The Triune God, writes Donald Bloesch, is the "living God who reaches out in love, who becomes incarnate in human flesh."[2]

What happens cosmically and universally is also accorded to us personally and intimately. There can be only one Incarnation, but each new birth is a small reminder of God's gracious intentions toward the world. Prosaic, perhaps even preachy, but nonetheless true is the sentiment captured in calligraphy and presented by my mother upon the birth of our first child: "A baby is God's opinion that the world should go on." The first Advent and Christmas graced by our daughter Rebecca Louise Leupp was a time of theological deepening and personal recognition for me. Sporadic surges of evident development—for example, the suddenly attained ability to pull herself up to a standing position by grasping the railing in her crib—underwrote the slow, gradual, and unseen progress from infancy to childhood.

It is dangerous and potentially idolatrous to equate exactly the triune drama of salvation history with the singular development of one baby. God's love inhabits cradles but also skyscrapers, barns, schools and markets. Nevertheless, the principle of development, so evident in one so young as our firstborn, is necessary for understanding the doctrine of the Trinity. Here we must carefully differentiate between the Triune God in himself and the human work of theologizing about him. Any theological effort is necessarily tentative, unfinished and even groping. We are keenly and painfully aware that the greatest human minds, even when fully surrendered to the task and constantly imploring God's help, will fall short of a full disclosure of God. Should, therefore, the theological shop be altogether shut down? Should theology cease?

Christian Doctrine: A Faithful and Fluid Witness

Theology should not and will not cease as long as there are human minds to inquire into God's ways with the world in creation and redemption. If life in all times and places were identical, then conceivably there could be only one theology. Since life is not an abstraction but is real to us only in the concreteness of living things,[3] it follows that theology, which seeks to elucidate the living God, is also, so to speak, a living organism. There can be no final theology because there is no final human situation. Theology is the study of God, but because God is not a colorless absolute but rather the dynamism of love set on redeeming the world, theology that is true to the Triune God must take serious account of the human context.

"Great acts take time."[4] So said John Henry Newman. The great act of the establishment of classical trinitarian doctrine from the beginnings of Christian history through the time of Augustine is the subject of this chapter. To recognize that our thoughts about God are inevitably hedged in and colored by the particularities of our own histories is to say that Christian doctrine develops. Doctrine does not drop from the sky, ready-made, fully stated, impervious to further insights. Rather, as Jaroslav Pelikan says, Christian doctrines grow "from simple beginnings, through all kinds of vicissitudes, finally to emerge in mature form."[5] And even "mature form" is not the final word. Scripture is fixed in a canon, but the interpretation and application of Scripture cannot be done once and for all times and places. The reality of theological development means that "a static mechanical" metaphor must give way to "a dynamic organic" one.[6]

Any country that aspires to international athletic greatness in any given sport, for example, soccer, knows that it must develop its talent from the bottom up. A fledgling professional sports franchise knows that its fans will not tolerate perpetual losers, so it must decide how to develop: building slowly, refining the skills of young players, or trying to be immediately competitive through the purchase of established stars from other teams. The development principle is applicable everywhere in life, from culture to family to geology to economy.

The development of Christian doctrine may have things in common with other developmental trajectories. What sets it apart, however, is that in theological expression we are not dealing with anything merely human, with any monument to human creativity, but with the revelation of the Triune God. A full understanding of God's revelation is not possible on human terms, and what is possible—a faithful witness to God's presence in Jesus Christ in the power of the Holy Spirit—takes time and special care. Even a teetotaler can appreciate the truth of the advertising slogan: "We will sell no wine before its time." The time of the classical formulation of the doctrine of the Trinity is approximately four centuries. Because "great acts take time," we are not surprised that "it took four hundred years before what was eventually deemed satisfactory expression could be found for the conviction that, without jeopardy to the singleness of [sic] simpleness of God, God's *whole* self is given in begotten Son and breathed in outpoured Spirit."[7] To a brief investigation of this developmental process we now turn.

Jesus and His Father

Immanuel, God with us, is the reason for the doctrine of the Trinity. Those disciples who became the first Christians sensed—and confessed—that Jesus was the Christ (Mt 16:16; Mk 8:29; Lk 9:20), the one in whom God's reign was inaugurated. The developed doctrine of the Trinity would come later, but its source is here, in "the outlook of One who thought of Himself as finding and doing His heavenly Father's will through the indwelling Spirit by whom He was one with the Father."[8] In Jesus the disciples were confronted with the claims of God the Father upon their lives. If Jesus were truly one with the Father (Jn 10:30), as he said, then to know the Son was to know the Father. The God of Abraham, Isaac and Jacob was made known in Jesus of Nazareth. "God's utterance of life finds focus in one Jew, in whose particularity everything is said."[9] The primal Christian confession is that "Jesus is Lord," which cannot be spoken "except by the Holy Spirit" (1 Cor 12:3). To make this confession "is to confess that what is seen, in him, is God's complete appearance. . . . There is, in God, nothing else to see but Jesus Christ."[10]

The Son's unfailingly constant communion with his Father is where we must look to find the headwaters of the doctrine of the Trinity. The disciples *experienced* God, but Jesus *communed* with his heavenly Father, a difference not merely of degree but of kind. Being "the pioneer and perfecter of our faith" (Heb 12:2), Jesus came to teach his disciples how they too could address God as their Abba. The bold familiarity with which Jesus addressed his Father must mean that in Jesus the Father is fully present. In Jesus, God does not turn in a mere cameo performance, saving his best for later. There is no casual resemblance between the Son and the Father, but a full disclosure of the Father's essence spoken in his eternal Word. "The Gospel does not say that Jesus Christ is *like* the Father, but, rather, that, in Jesus, God *appears*."[11] The New Testament bears a steady and reliable witness to God's manifestations in Jesus Christ. Especially in John 1:1, Romans 9:5, Titus 2:13 and Hebrews 1:8, the best reading of the evidence is that "Christ is called 'God' in the fullest sense of the word."[12]

Among New Testament writers, John shows the greatest sensitivity of what the Trinity teaches: not that God is one in isolation or three in multiplicity, but that God is triune in completeness.[13] John 14 offers "a fairly clear statement by Jesus on the trinitarian Godhead."[14] We learn therein that the Father will send the Holy Spirit in the Son's name (vv. 16-17), the Spirit of truth who "will teach you everything" (v. 26). The baptism of Jesus, found in all four Gospels (Mt 3:16-17; Mk 1:9-11; Lk 3:21-22; Jn 1:32-34), is one occasion in Jesus' life where "the threefold-ness of God is definitely affirmed."[15] John's account especially under-scores the baptism as a signal event in salvation history. We observe here that "all three persons of the Triune Family are in complete harmony in placing themselves, through the representative person of the Son, at the disposal of sinners who need salvation. . . . The divine Community acts as one to redeem a fallen creation and draw it back into fellowship with the higher Family."[16]

John's incipient trinitarianism would provide much grist for later explorations. Jesus' speech in John conveys at least three realities, which must be read dialectically, because to attempt to force them into a final synthesis saps all life and vitality. For one, Jesus is equal to the Father (10:30; 14:9, 11; 17:11, 21). Yet, second, Jesus is keenly aware that this equality is not self-generated but granted by the Father (5:26). Furthermore, God the Father does not lord it over his Son, but rather "he listens to the Son, grants his requests, bears witness to him, and glorifies him (8:18, 50, 54; 12:28; 14:16, 26; 15:26; 16:13-15; 17:1, 5)."[17]

Where later trinitarianism would take its stand on the coequality of Father, Son and Spirit expressed through their mutual indwelling and service to each other is intuited in John's Gospel. Throughout chapter 17, as Royce Gruenler sees it, "Jesus prays the paradoxical prayer of sovereign equality with the Father which at the same time entails his conscious and willing service to the Father and his disposability on behalf of the new community."[18]

A paradox, like a parable, is meant to unhinge assumptions, dislocate prejudices and even jolt one to action. A paradox is not a final resting place, but the tension that fuels life. The trinitarian paradox—that God is one and yet three, three and yet one—is not a paradox about the thinking of thought but rather the living of life, the life of God. For Jesus "sovereign equality with the Father" is not "something to be exploited" (Phil 2:6), not a bargaining chip, but is rather the occasion for offering himself spotlessly to God, "through the eternal Spirit" (Heb 9:14).

Before the Council of Nicea

The man who is widely reputed to be the greatest popular singer of the twentieth century has three names: Francis Albert Sinatra. And he has at least as many nicknames: "The Chairman of the Board," "Old Blue Eyes" and simply "The Voice." These nicknames, colorful and descriptive though they are, do not tell the curious everything there is to know about Frank Sinatra. Was he born in 1915 or 1917? Was he a front man for the Mafia? Did he really get his start at the Clam Broth House in his hometown of Hoboken, New Jersey? Was he chronologically old when his eyes were so named?

God's triune name, spoken by Father, Son and Holy Spirit, is the only name whose speaking tells us all we need to know about its owner. No one's name except the thrice-blessed name of God is able fully to reveal the essence of what is named. I agree with Emil Brunner's assessment that "these three Names—Father, Son, and Holy Spirit, in their unity and in their difference, are the content and the meaning of the New Testament. The Primitive Christian Church lived on the fact that through the Son it had the Father, and that it was united with the Father and the Son through the Holy Spirit."[19] Surely it was the overwhelming sense of the lordship of Jesus Christ that "compelled early Christian thinkers to formulate the doctrine of the Trinity."[20] Equally certain is that no one could speak the Son's name unless it was unto the Father, in perpetual remembrance of the Son's sufferings, enlivened by the Holy Spirit.

Overall, as our brief survey of John's overtures toward trinitarian doctrine indicates, it was Jesus' relationship to his Father that evoked in the first Christians the enduring question: "What is the relation of the divine in Christ to the divine in the Father?"[21] Furthermore, Jesus was no longer present in the body. Did the Holy Spirit whom Jesus had breathed on the gathered disciples (Jn 20:22) share the same divinity as the Father and Son seemed to enjoy? These central questions soon rapidly multiplied: Was Jesus of Nazareth related to his Abba intrinsically or only through good deeds by whose virtue the Father had chosen or adopted him? Was the Son eternally a Son, or had he been created by the Father, before all other creatures, but a creature even so? Was the Holy Spirit the personal term of mediation between Father and Son from all eternity, equal in divinity, or only an impersonal, convulsive force? Or was the Holy Spirit perhaps really only the highest of the angels or the voice speaking through Old Testament prophets?

These are representative, but by no means all, of the questions early Christian thinkers had to negotiate along the way to trinitarian clarity. The Father, who was "always and everywhere," the Son ("there and then") and the Spirit ("here and now") seemed to be arrayed along a continuum of time and function.[22] But—and this is the crucial question—were the Son and by extension the Holy Spirit *truly* and *essentially* and *eternally* one with the Father, or only briefly, episodically and accidentally?

The very manner of our posing the questions, holding up God the Father as the "standard of divinity" against which the Son and Spirit are to be measured, is a realistic depiction of how the theologians of the subapostolic period saw the matter. They never doubted the centrality of God the Father. Jewish monotheism was very much alive. The Father's position was unassailable. Until about the middle of the second century, little if any progress was marked beyond New Testament formulations. Christ was held to be preexistent, but as an angel and not as the only begotten Son of the Father.[23] *Shepherd of Hermas*, an early-second-century document, probably of Jewish Christian origin and nearly included in the canon of the New Testament, shows confusion between the Son and the Spirit, seemingly concluding that they are identical: "I wish to show thee all things that the Holy Spirit, which spake with thee in the form of the Church, showed unto thee. For that Spirit is the Son of God."[24] Ignatius of Antioch (c. 35-c. 107), one of the apostolic fathers, depicted believers as the building blocks God the Father would fashion into a holy temple. The cross of Jesus Christ is the crane lifting the devout into place, and the Holy Spirit the rope.[25]

Throughout this literature the functional prevailed, and formulas employed were more triadic than truly trinitarian. The need to find internal coinherence among Father, Son and Spirit was little appreciated. Undeniably, however, there was exhibited among the apostolic fathers a strong soteriological sense. If Jesus was truly to show them the Father, those who are found by the Son are indeed ushered in to the Father. Clement of Rome's second epistle requires Christians to esteem Jesus as highly as the Father, and the reason is linked to salvation: "For if we think any less of him than this, then we expect but little of him."[26]

The growth of the Gentile mission meant that second-century Christians had to take account of a newly emerging thought world that was no longer predominantly Jewish in outlook; they had to factor in Greek philosophy and pagan religions. It thus "became urgently necessary to produce some sort of a coherent doctrine of God which should be neither purely Jewish nor obviously polytheistic but specifically and recognizably Christian."[27]

The Apologists, active between 140 and 200, made the first effort toward a Christian doctrine of God.[28] For all of them, whether the most famous, Justin Martyr, or Tatian or Theophilus or Athenagoras, to say "God the Father" meant not the first among equals, not the source of the Son's and Spirit's divinity, not the first Person of the Trinity. God the Father rather meant "the one Godhead considered as author of whatever exists."[29] The Father was supreme but not alone. To express the Father's relationship to his Word, Justin Martyr employed what is often called the "two-stage theory of the Logos." Immanent within the

Father's mind was his Word, or Logos. Although thought logically precedes speech, unexpressed thought is unrealized potential. The Father must speak; his speech is the Word. The Word present within the Father's mind is stage one; the uttered Word is stage two. R. P. C. Hanson describes how the Apologists typically viewed God, developing the story in a salvific way and showing how this Logos comes to teach and to redeem:

> God, the absolute Being beyond all being, as recognized by the Greek philosophers, always had immanent within himself a principle of energy which could be called his Reason (or Logos): when he desired to make himself known he first caused this Reason to become separate, though not divided, from himself, so that it formed a separate entity which could be called (at least, in Justin's thought) a second or another God; then through this Reason he created the world, and the human race in it; then this Reason instructed the wisest and the greatest of the men of the chosen race in most of the details of Christianity, by appearing to them personally in various temporary forms; finally this Reason himself became a man in order that the Proof should appear along with the Truth. He overcame demons, taught righteousness, offered himself as a sacrifice on the Cross, died, rose again, and now offers eternal life, or incorruption, to all who believe in him.[30]

The principle of immanent reason within, which must express itself, is a flexible one that served the Apologists well as they sought to defend the Christian faith against its sophisticated detractors. Justin Martyr employed a fine analogy to the same end, that a spreading flame in no way diminishes the original while being a true and fit expression of it: "When one fire is kindled from another," he noted, "the fire from which it is kindled is not diminished but remains the same; while the fire which is kindled from it is seen to exist by itself without diminishing the original fire."[31] Since Justin did not extend his analogy to the Holy Spirit,[32] his effort toward trinitarian theology can be judged as no better than "a thinly disguised Binity"[33] of the Father and the Son. His ordering of Father, Son and Holy Spirit within the Godhead "lacks coherence and clarity."[34] Is the thinking of thought strictly equivalent to the saving of souls? Justin's imagery owes more to the history of philosophy than to the history of salvation.

In Irenaeus of Lyons (130-202) we meet with the most advanced trinitarianism before Tertullian.[35] Since much of his theological work was a response to Gnosticism, which held to many orders and economies of salvation, Irenaeus remained strong in his belief that God is one and that there is only one economy of salvation.[36] Irenaeus was less inclined to speak in philosophical than in biblical language, which set him apart from the Apologists. He was influenced by the Logos Christology of the Apologists, which distinguished between "the immanent Word" and "the expressed Word,"[37] yet refused to speculate as to precisely how the immanent Word became the expressed Word. Thus he did not reproduce the Apologists' analogy of human speech issuing from the mind.[38] To Irenaeus this metaphor suggested too casually that while the Father remained hidden from view, the Son became visible. But in the words of Jean Danielou, for Irenaeus "the Father and the Son are equally inaccessible to human scope, and equally accessible, if they will to reveal themselves."[39]

The Father and the Son are willing to reveal themselves. How else, aside from God's willingness, can God be made human? Here again Irenaeus went beyond his immediate theological predecessors, accenting soteriology, the doctrine of salvation, and minimizing cosmology,[40] the seemingly endless speculation as to why there was anything at all and not a blank void. God the Father was one but not alone. "For with Him," Irenaeus confesses, "were always present the Word and Wisdom, the Son and the Spirit, by whom and in whom, freely and spontaneously, He made all things."[41] Elsewhere Irenaeus refers to the Son and the Holy Spirit as God's "hands," who had created humankind in the divine image.[42] A fragment attributed to Irenaeus sees the Word ever present in Old Testament history: "it is He who sailed along with Noah, and who guided Abraham; who was bound along with Isaac, and was a wanderer with Jacob."[43]

Irenaeus's trinitarian theology is subordinationist, but it is a functional subordination in the economy of salvation rather than an essential or ontological subordination within the Godhead itself. Other theologians coming after Irenaeus would inquire into the Godhead's inner recesses, but he was more interested in the continuity between God's creation of the world, which was the work of the entire Triune God,[44] and its eventual redemption, which was already happening, prompted by the indwelling, eschatological Spirit.[45] If it is true that "God and his 'hands' are inseparable,"[46] it is equally true that God desires that all of his creatures—human and nonhuman alike—should return to him. The return to God happens through Irenaeus's renowned doctrine of "recapitulation," wherein God in Christ reverses the sin of Adam so that all creation can be returned to God. Irenaeus believed that

> there is therefore only one God the Father, and one Christ Jesus our Lord, who has come through the whole "economy" and who has gathered together [recapitulated] all things in himself. [Humanity] is also included within this "all," that paradigmatic work of God. He has, then, also recapitulated humanity in himself, by the invisible becoming visible, the incomprehensible comprehensible, the impassible capable of suffering, and the Word being made [human]. He has recapitulated everything in himself so that he might draw all things to himself at the proper time.[47]

Throughout the process of our finding our way back to God—our being "deified" or "divinized" as Eastern Orthodoxy would phrase it—God's enabling and limitless love is the operating motive. Irenaeus said, and many would repeat it, that "in his unbounded love, God became what we are that God might make us what he is." Our return to God is not self-propelled but grace-endued. "This leading into [the vision of God] is a work that God does directly, but of course with the help of the divine hands!"[48]

Moments before our baby was born, I could see her blood-splotched head making its way down the birth canal, convulsed along by my wife's pushes. Head and shoulders, seeing their first light, were gently supported by the hands of the Filipina doctor. If life is the goal of the fetus, might not those two cooperating agencies—my wife's pushes and the doctor's waiting hands—be roughly analogous to the two hands of God? Birth labor and receiving hands equal life.

The Word of God and the Wisdom of God cooperate to bring the soul back to the fullness of God. This is true life—God's glory willingly imparted and rooted in the entirely capacitated soul. "The glory of God is the living human person, and the life of the human person is the vision of God."[49]

Tertullian of Carthage (160-225) traveled further along the road pioneered by Irenaeus. He was the first to use the Latin *trinitas*, translated into English as "trinity." His formula, "one substance in three persons," indicated that much more than his forerunners, Tertullian was willing to talk about the Trinity within, or the immanent Trinity. Substance does not mean that which is material, but rather the divine essence that is found in Father, Son and Holy Spirit. Like that of Irenaeus, Tertullian's thought begins with the Triune God who is active in the world, making and then saving it. R. P. C. Hanson notes that Tertullian's theology means that "the Trinity is still for him a strategy devised by God for purposes of creation and revelation."[50]

The Father's Word and Wisdom have accompanied him from all eternity, Tertullian was convinced, but there was even so a kind of hierarchy within the Godhead. The three Persons were equal in status or quality but not in rank,[51] making the Father "first among equals." Son and Father are not to be confused; they are distinct but not divisible, discrete but not separable. The Logos is eternally begotten or generated by the Father,[52] an idea anticipated by Irenaeus and developed more fully by Origen. The Holy Spirit was sent by the Father through the Son.

Tertullian used images and analogies from the created world to indicate that while God is one, there are yet "distinguishable individualities"[53] within the Triune God. The headwaters or source of a river produce a brook and then the river itself. The sun emits rays that cause reflections. Tertullian had a legal background, and for him these triads in nature, if approached with eyes of faith, could compel belief in the Trinity:

> If one thing comes out of another, it is necessarily a second thing, different from that out of which it came, but it is not on that account separate from it. But where there is a second [person], there are two

[persons], and where there is a third, there are three. For the Spirit is third, with God and the Son, as the fruit is third, coming from the root and the shoot, and the stream is third, coming from the sun and the beam. Nothing, however, is exiled from its source, from which it draws its properties. This conception of the trinity, as moving out from the Father in closely connected sequence, is in no way opposed to the monarchy, and it preserves the order of the divine economy.[54]

If Irenaeus's theological foes were the Gnostics, Tertullian contended with modalism and the sort of subordinationism that made the Son and Spirit inferior to the Father. Modalism teaches that there is a single divine essence that appears, successively, as Father, Son, and Holy Spirit. It depicts God as "an agent acting in three episodes."[55] Regarding it Nicholas Lash writes:

> Modalism comes in many shapes and sizes, but common to them all was the conviction that, in the Godhead, the only differentiations are transitory, episodic, a matter of successive ways (or "modes") of acting or existing. Beneath the play of light and colour, before and after the episode of incarnation, the rock of God endures, unalterable and unmoved. For the modalist, in other words, the three ways we know God are of the nature of appearances, transitory forms, "beneath" which the divine nature, unaffected, stands.[56]

At times Tertullian admittedly sounds like a modalist. Sabellius, a teacher at Rome early in the third century who gave his name to Sabellianism, used the same solar analogy as Tertullian: one sun puts forth heat and light. Yet within Lash's definition quoted above is the reason Tertullian is not a modalist. God's Word and his Wisdom are not for Tertullian merely episodic; they are real and intrinsic to the Godhead. Sabellius reduces the entire Godhead to God the Father, the Son and Spirit being relegated to his self-expressive modes.[57] Because the Son and the Spirit are coeternal with the Father and are not his transitory appearances, "Tertullian counts as being the initiator of a trinitarian solution of the problems in the Christian doctrine of God which were thrown up by subordinationism and modalism."[58]

While Tertullian's trinitarian theology, cognizant of the immanent Trinity as authentically available in the economy of creation and redemption, was a marked advance beyond the crude literalism and triadic schemes of earlier days, the entire scene was unsettled and in flux. "One substance in three persons," Tertullian's formula, influenced the Western part of the church, but confusion still reigned over the exact relationship between the Father and the Son, to say nothing of the Holy Spirit. Origen's trinitarianism was the next major contribution, and it was highly influential both for good and for ill.

Origen (c. 185-c. 254) is well described as "scholar, apologist, speculative thinker, and fountainhead of subsequent doctrinal and spiritual development."[59] Excelling in preaching, teaching, biblical exegesis and defending the Christian faith against its learned and pagan detractors, Origen was "the most many-sided of all the early Christian writers."[60] To him the honor of being the first systematic theologian, represented by his treatise On First Principles, is accorded. Dominating the theological thought of the church's Eastern segment in particular, Origen was the giant of third-century theology, setting the agenda from his lifetime until the Council of Nicea in 325.

The sincerity of Origen's Christian commitment cannot be doubted. Origen's parents were both Christians, and at one point Origen wished to emulate his father, who was imprisoned and eventually martyred. Only his mother's hiding of his clothes prevented the young Origen from offering himself for martyrdom.[61] Therefore Origen had every reason to present and argue for what could be called, using later designations, a very high Christology. The Son of God had simply always been.[62] He had no beginning. Regarding the Son, Origen confessed that "there was not a time when He was not."[63] Since no father can lay claim to that title without offspring, if God is eternally Father, then the Son is eternally Son. Origen's doctrine of the eternal generation, or begetting of Son from Father, was captured in images of the union of husband and wife and the reflection of a mirror.[64] When Origen writes that "it is an eternal and ceaseless generation, as radiance is generated from light,"[65] his meaning is unmistakably clear: the Son is coeternal with the Father. It is because of the Son's very nature as God, and not by any outward act of infusing breath or bestowing honor by the Father, that the Son is coeternal with the Father, eternally begotten from him.[66]

As a speculative thinker, Origen believed not only that God had always been, existing from all eternity, but also that souls were eternal. As the very source of rationality, God was compelled to communicate his rationality with these eternal and indestructible souls. God's very nature is to communicate, and he must do so with rational souls. These souls, not created by God but nonetheless clinging to God, gradually fell from the truth through the abuse of their free will. At this point, for the purpose of winning back these errant souls, God created the physical universe. Only one soul had stayed true to God, and this soul, taking a human body, was Jesus Christ. Through Christ's ministry, all souls, including even that of the devil, would eventually find their way back to God.[67] Origen's vision of the universal restoration of all things, dramatic and sweeping though it is, was later condemned as heresy, as was his notion of the eternality of all souls.

Picture a pristine and elevated lake. This lake is pure beyond measure or imagination. It expresses itself in a cascading waterfall, which in turn produces a second waterfall. In crude outline, this is Origen's view of the Trinity. The Father, who is "the absolute One, beyond all being, simple, untouched by becoming or change or transitoriness or multiplicity,"[68] desires to communicate and reveal himself. This he does through the Son, or Logos, who is from the Father as the waterfall is from the lake, yet not equal in status to the Father, hence lower than the Father. The Son is eternally generated by the Father, and the Holy Spirit is described by Origen as "the most honourable of all the beings brought into existence through the Word, the chief in rank of all the beings originated by the Father through Christ."[69] If the Holy Spirit originates by the Father through Christ, we are clearly dealing with the immanent Trinity. But Origen's admission that there is rank within the Triune God, the Holy Spirit occupying the chief rank of all that originates from the Father through the Son, demands the conclusion of subordinationism within the Triune God.

This is in fact the case in Origen's thinking. Jesus Christ and the Holy Spirit may be God, but they are not "*the* God."[70] This title, indicated by the use of the definite article in the Greek, is the Father's alone. The three Persons are coeternal but not coequal, and this is Origen's most telling weakness in trinitarian theology.[71] Coequality means that Father, Son and Holy Spirit give and take from each other without barriers. Each knows the other two perfectly and in turn is known fully by them. But in Origen's hierarchical handling, the Father's perfect self-knowledge is his alone. The Son knows the Father less thoroughly than the Father knows himself.[72] Bernard Lonergan explains that Origen saw in Jesus' speech "the Father is greater than I" (Jn 14:28) a "universal application: the Son and the Holy Spirit are incomparably more excellent than all other things, but between them and the Father, in turn, there is at least as great a gap, if not a greater one."[73] Christ is good beyond all human comparison, but God the Father is goodness itself.[74]

It is an open question whether marginal role-players and bench riders get quite the same charge out of a championship season as do a team's bankable stars. Sometimes after winning the World Series a team will even quibble as to whether an injured player or one joining the team late in the season should get a full share of the winnings. We cannot press this analogy too tightly upon God, but clearly there are gradations within Origen's Trinity. Only God the Father is a first-rank player, so to speak. Friedrich Schleiermacher captures the dynamics well: "The Father is God absolutely, while Son and Spirit are God only by participation in the Divine Essence."[75]

To participate in is to take part in. On Origen's terms, how can we fully share in God's triune life if that life is itself marked by inequality and hierarchy? True to his logic, believers were instructed by Origen to pray only to God the Father.[76] Such prayer should be directed through the Son as the Spirit gives utterance, but to pray to the Son or Spirit outright is mistaken and might even be sinful. Thus Origen fails the doxological test where praise rises in equal measure to Father, Son and Spirit, because being coequal, they are equally praiseworthy. Origen's Trinity may be philosophically compelling, but it is not religiously and devotionally available. As the One to whom all prayer must be directed, God the Father's range of activity is unlimited. His action extends to the entire cosmos, whereas the Son's activity is limited to only rational beings. The Holy Spirit's sphere of influence is still more circumscribed. Only the holy and the sanctified—saints in the church—can be ministered to by the Spirit. The Spirit's specialization among the saints would seem to limit his role in creation. Origen thought that the gift of God's breath in Genesis 2:7 was not for all people, but only for the saints.[77]

Origen advances beyond the typically economic trinitarianism of Irenaeus and Tertullian by analyzing for the first time a truly immanent Trinity. All things come from the Father through the Son.[78] Irenaeus and Tertullian believed in a sort of immanent Trinity, but it was mainly if not purely functional. For Origen, however, the three Persons "are of the eternal mode of God's being and not just determined or evoked by the needs of the economy."[79] Origen's immanent Trinity is "a picture of the very nature of the eternal God himself" and not "a strategy adopted at one point by God in order to create and reveal."[80] But is Origen's ranking of Son and Spirit below the Father too high a price to pay for an articulated doctrine of the Trinity? Subsequent Christian orthodoxy judged it to be.

The Arian Crisis and the Orthodox Response

Great acts take time—especially a true comprehension of God's full presence in Jesus Christ. Origen, teaching the Son's eternal begetting from the Father, was the first theologian with more than a shadowy understanding of God's being eternally triune.[81] Yet Origen's thought implied, if not outrightly declared, a ranking within the Godhead. For Origen the Son was always Son, from all eternity, and therefore not a creature, but the Son's being a creature was certainly a possible interpretation of his thought. The Alexandrian priest Arius (250-336) followed Origen's subordinationist path. He agreed with Origen that if the Son was "the firstborn of all creation" (Col 1:15), then he must be God but not *the* God.[82] The Logos was divine *(theos)* but somehow less divine than the Father, who was *the* highest God *(ho theos)*.[83]

Arius's ideas were neither sophisticated nor subtle. They were, however, popular, so much so that the first ecumenical council was convened at Nicea in 325 to address the crisis. Perhaps the clarity of his logic accounted for his popularity. "Where only the light of natural reason is operative," writes Bernard Lonergan, heresy is found. Progress and advance in theology happens "where reason is illumined and strengthened by faith."[84] Athanasius (c. 296-373), the champion of what came to be known as Nicene orthodoxy, faulted Arius with choosing a philosophical idea of God over the true biblical portrait of a God who willingly and lovingly extends himself to a sinful world in Christ and lives in human hearts by the Holy Spirit.[85] No, Arius's God is by definition unable to share his divinity with anyone, not even his Son. Arians acknowledged "one God, Who is alone ingenerate, alone eternal, alone without beginning, alone true, alone possessing immortality, alone wise, alone good, alone sovereign, alone judge of all."[86] Can this God possibly communicate any of his essential nature to mere humans? It would seem not, so alone is this God. Some have equated the Arian God with the Muslim God because he is so remote and transcendent and seemingly unknowable.

In simpler language, Arius taught that "the Son . . . is not equal to God in any way, but is made out of nothing by God. The Father, who is alone without cause and without beginning and who therefore is alone God, is completely alien to the Son in essence."[87] The Son, in short, is a creature, admittedly the highest of all creatures, above the angels, but still a creature.

Arius made a serious charge against the Son that had grave consequences. J. N. D. Kelly discusses three corollary charges beyond the initial charge of the Son's being a creature. For one, the Son, while created before time, even so had a beginning. The Arian slogan "There was when He was not" implied that the Father had created the Son before time was created, yet the Father had always been, which was not true of the Son. Second, the Son is God's Word and Wisdom but not the Father's essential Word and Wisdom. Thus the Son cannot know his Father directly. Without knowing the Father directly, can the Son possibly introduce humans to the awareness of God? This question agitated those gathered at Nicea. Being not of the Father's essence, third, the Son is liable to sin.[88]

The English word *heresy* comes from the Greek *hairesis*, whose fundamental meaning is "choice," which leads to the further meanings of "party" or "party spirit."[89] Clearly Arius chose a philosophical God, a God closed in upon self, an incommunicable God. Arius thought he was choosing the biblical God, the omnipotent God. Arius's God was without question superior to his Son, as Arius took pains to prove through citing texts demonstrating the Son's ignorance and weakness or pronouncing the Father greater than himself (Prov 8:22; Jn 14:28; 17:3; Acts 2:36; Rom 8:29; Col 1:15; Heb 3:2).[90]

Some have seen Arianism as the chief example of what is called "godalmightiness." Karl Barth said that "the person who calls 'the Almighty' God misses God in the most terrible way."[91] G. A. Studdert Kennedy feared that God's being almighty would obliterate the central biblical affirmation that God is love (1 Jn 4:8, 16): "God, the Father God of Love, is everywhere in history, but nowhere is He Almighty. Ever and always we see Him suffering, striving, crucified, but conquering. God is Love."[92] Arius's God is naked and unrestrained power, a God who cannot suffer, and therefore a God who cannot become fully incarnate in the Father's only begotten Son.

God's power is indeed real, but it is assuredly not arbitrary. God exercises his power—and restrains it—for human salvation. God's power is thus in some sense a "needy powerfulness,"[93] for it does not ride roughshod over human freedom. Even in becoming incarnate in Jesus Christ, God limited his own power. The obstacle here is that far too many Christians only want Arius's God, turning a deaf ear to the true power of suffering love and the discipleship it engenders. Arius's God is truly "God Almighty," but the God who meets us in Jesus Christ is the God whose weakness is stronger than human strength (1 Cor 1:25).

Jürgen Moltmann assesses Arianism as "monotheistic Christianity in its purest form." Not salvation history, but rather moral clarity and logical explanation characterize monotheistic Christianity. As a result, the work of Jesus Christ "cannot provide any foundation for the redemption that makes full fellowship with God possible; it can only offer the basis for a new morality, for which Jesus' life provides the pattern and standard."[94]

The emperor Constantine was greatly displeased by the Arian ruckus, and he convened the Council of Nicea in hopes of restoring relative theological calm to the empire. Some have even suggested that to break the theological logjam, Constantine introduced the Nicene key word *homoousia*. This Greek word is the one technical theological term every Christian should learn, for its meaning ("of the same substance") is crucial to the Christian proclamation that God is authentically present in Christ. Because the word is not in the Bible, many were reluctant to admit *homoousia*, but finally it won the day as "being the only available means of excluding Arianism."[95]

Athanasius steered the conversation from metaphysics and ontology back to soteriology, the doctrine of salvation. On Arian terms, who could be saved? No one. The Nicene key word meant that the Son was "consubstantial" with the Father, with no hint of inferiority at all, and therefore able to bring penitent hearts boldly to the Father's presence. Athanasius affirmed Origen's idea of eternal generation but without Origen's diminishing the Son to secondary status. "It is entirely correct," wrote Athanasius, "to call Him the Father's eternal offspring. . . . Since God is eternal and He belongs to God as Son, He exists from all eternity."[96]

Wolfhart Pannenberg explains Athanasius's contribution to trinitarian orthodoxy: "Defending the Nicene belief in the *homoousion* of the Son (and Spirit) with the Father, their equal deity, Athanasius vanquished subordinationism, insisting that we cannot think of the Father as Father without the Son and Spirit. He left no place for causally related gradations in the fulness of divine being."[97] The incomprehensibility of the Father without his Son, or, to state it positively, that Fatherhood requires Sonship, was Athanasius's "decisive argument for the full deity of the Son."[98] Athanasius could even argue, on the basis of Jesus' declaration "I am the way, and the truth, and the life" (Jn 14:6), that "the Son was the truth and life of the Father, too."[99] The Father cannot be Father without his Son. Pannenberg explains that "the Son is a condition of the deity of the Father."[100]

Wanting to be rigorously monotheistic, Arius had in fact reintroduced polytheism into the church, because the Son was a lesser God. Athanasius called him on this and pointed out that on Arian terms it would be foolish to continue praying to the Son in worship, because the Son was not truly God.[101] Theology that can be prayed without loss or dilution of meaning is true theology. Calling Jesus Christ Lord and God as a courtesy to him, as Arius suggested, without believing it borders on blasphemy. Yet the telling blow against Arianism was one every Christian could appreciate. Reconciliation with the Father is possible only through One who is himself coeternal as well as coequal with the Father, existing with the Father from all eternity. Speaking trinitarianly, the defender of Nicene orthodoxy, Athanasius, concluded that "there is a single grace, which is fulfilled from the Father through the Son in the Holy Spirit."[102]

In a justly renowned statement, Athanasius pointed to the real reason for Christ's incarnation and why Arianism was totally insufficient as a plan of salvation. Speaking of the Father's eternal Word, Athanasius declared, "He, indeed, assumed humanity that we might become God."[103]

This theme of participation in the very heart of God's triune life is common in early Christian thought, especially among Eastern theologians. Irenaeus also held to the real possibility of our becoming by grace what God alone is by nature. Because of God's unbounded love, confessed Irenaeus, God became what we are so that he might make us what he is.[104] Technical theological language knows this ever more perfect conformity to God as deification, divinization or the Greek word *theosis*.[105] Some Christians describe much the same phenomenon as Christian perfection or entire sanctification. However it may be known, the New Testament admonition to "become participants of the divine nature" (2 Pet 1:4) is not exalting mere humans into the Godhead.

Jesus' command to be perfect (Mt 5:48) is not "idealistic gas," C. S. Lewis tells us.[106] It is God's highest calling and at the same time our heart's deepest cry: to be conformed to God. Everyone beginning this pilgrimage "must realize from the outset," urges Lewis, "that the goal towards which [God] is beginning to guide you is absolute perfection; and no power in the whole universe, except you yourself, can prevent Him from taking you to that goal."[107] Irenaeus and Athanasius might quibble with Lewis's use of the adjective *absolute*, since only the Triune God is absolutely perfect. In more sober and chastened language, Catherine LaCugna nevertheless holds high the invitation to become like God. For her, deification "means being conformed in our personal existence to God's personal existence, achieving right relationship and genuine communion in every respect, at every level."[108] Right relationships—with ourselves, with others, with all parts of the created order—are possible only through God's triune life in us. *Deification* is simply a theological term for the course that every Christian life must take. Since we were created by and for God, the call of deification returns us to our divine origin.

Timothy Ware notes the close connection between deification and Trinity: "Behind the doctrine of deification there lies the idea of the human person made according to the image and likeness of God the Holy Trinity. . . . Just as the three persons of the Trinity 'dwell' in one another in an unceasing movement of love, so we humans, made in the image of the Trinity, are called to 'dwell' in the Trinitarian God."[109]

Thomas Carlyle never spoke more truly than in saying, "If Arianism had won, Christianity would have dwindled into a legend."[110] Arianism very nearly did win. It was forced underground after the Council of Nicea but regained its momentum to a point that Jerome wrote in the middle of the fourth century, "The whole world groaned and marvelled to find itself Arian."[111] The second ecumenical council, held at Constantinople in 381, finally routed Arianism for good.

There remains a perpetual temptation toward Arianism because of our grasping for power and our indifference toward suffering love. Grace alone prevents Arianism from reasserting itself. Every Christian should consider it an honor, privilege and duty to contend for the Nicene faith. "Holy, Holy, Holy! Lord God Almighty!" is sung to a tune called "Nicea" and is probably the leading hymn in honor of the Trinity. God at Nicea did not surrender his essential mystery. But neither, as Arius would want it, did God hoard his mystery. God's divinity is shared equally and fully among all three Persons, so that Father, Son and Holy Spirit are alike, in the hymn's words, "perfect in power, in love, and purity!" God's being "almighty" in Nicene terms means God's life being offered to us in his only begotten Son, Jesus Christ, breathed within us by the Holy Spirit.

The Cappadocian Fathers and Augustine

Prior to the Council of Nicea, God the Father enjoyed unchallenged supremacy as the source of divinity within the Godhead. The Father as fount of divinity can be construed orthodoxly, because beginning with the Father need not automatically consign Son and Spirit to a lower status. But pre-Nicene trinitarianism typically moved toward subordinationism, evident in Irenaeus and Origen among others. The Nicene decision, while rejecting Arianism's philosophical view of God as unknowable in his inner being,[112] established positively that the entire Trinity—not just God the Father—was the fullness of God.[113]

Basil the Great (330-379), Gregory of Nazianzus (329-389) and Gregory of Nyssa (330-395), Basil's younger brother, are collectively known as the Cappadocian fathers, or the Great Cappadocians. They defended the Nicene position in the Eastern part of the church. Jaroslav Pelikan notes that the Nicene faith was officially established in church and state via the council's rulings, but trinitarian orthodoxy "owes its intellectual standing above all to the defense and exposition of the Nicene decrees first by Athanasius of Alexandria (c. 296-373) and then by the three Cappadocians."[114] If Arianism was the misappropriation of the thought of Origen, then the Cappadocians reclaimed Origen for orthodoxy.[115] Following Origen, the Cappadocians clearly distinguished between the Son's being begotten, and hence coequal with the Father, and the Son's being created, which Arius took as evidence of the Son's creaturehood.[116]

The Cappadocians were not subordinationist in the least; they held to the equal divinity of Father, Son and Holy Spirit. In this they advanced beyond Origen, who, as we have already observed, held the Son to be a lesser god than the Father, even though eternally generated out of the Father. Echoing Athanasius, but more decisively, the Cappadocians argued unreservedly for the divinity of the Holy Spirit, an issue left unresolved by the Council of Nicea. The Son and the Holy Spirit, while fully God, are not the source of their own divinity in Cappadocian thought. That source is God the Father. The Father, and he alone, is the fount of divinity. For this sort of trinitarianism it can be said that "the Father has a certain priority not of time, causality, dignity or power, but of origin."[117] Gregory of Nyssa identified the Father as "the source of power, the Son as the power of the Father, the Holy Spirit as the Spirit of power."[118]

God the Father is therefore "first among equals" in Cappadocian thought. The Father is first, however, not standing free of the Son and Spirit. The Cappadocians, notes Pannenberg, should have exercised greater caution in employing their metaphor of the Father as fount of deity. They neglected to add decisively that "the Father is the principle of deity only from the perspective of the Son,"[119] meaning that even as the Son is eternally generated from the Father and is thereby constituted as the Son, so also the act of generation, and only that, constitutes the Father as Father. Given this qualification, it is permissible to name the Father "first among equals," because the Father's divinity is dependent on his relations with the Son and Holy Spirit.

Only within the Triune God is "first among equals" really possible, for everywhere else the "first" would seek to solidify his or her position at the expense of the others. But within the fellowship of the Trinity there is no lusting after power and position. No trinitarian Person considers himself better than the other two, but in loving deference esteems the other two more highly. Gregory of Nyssa compared the Trinity to three torches, the Father's light igniting the Son and in turn the Holy Spirit.[120] This implies no secondary status for the Holy Spirit or the Son, for there are no "degrees of divinity" within the Godhead. Gregory of Nazianzus rejected the hierarchical approach to the Trinity that had been typical prior to Nicea: "To compare the Trinity of Great and Greater and Greatest, as if of Light and Beam and Sun . . . makes a 'ladder of deity' that will not bring us into heaven but out of it."[121] The three divine Persons were, in Gregory's paradoxical language, "separately one and unitedly separate."[122]

The only real distinction among the three was that of causality, the eternal generation of the Son and Spirit originating with the Father. Cyril Richardson writes that "the only distinctions in the Trinity are those of causation. The Father is uncaused, the Son and Spirit are caused, the Spirit being caused from the Father through the mediation of the Son."[123] Not along with an eternal creation, as Origen maintained, or coming after the Father had enjoyed his own divinity in solitude, as in Arius's thought, but from all eternity Spirit and Son had come from the Father. "The first Person must guarantee both the unity of the Godhead and the threefold character of the Persons," as Moltmann explains.[124]

The Cappadocians' most famous trinitarian analogy is that of three individuals—Gregory of Nyssa used Peter, Paul and Barnabas—who share a common essence of humanity.[125] This insight was sealed in their trinitarian formula of "three *hypostases* in one *ousia*," the Eastern equivalent of the West's "three persons in one substance." *Ousia* means "being, nature, substance, essence," and the Nicene use of *homoousia* meant that the Son was "of the same substance" with the Father. The Greek word *hypostasis* originally had much the same meaning as *ousia*, but over time it came to signify "the notes of distinguishability and identifiability,"[126] in short, individuality—not in the commonly accepted definition of "rugged individualism," in which everyone charts his or her own destiny, but as a certain and distinguishable identity. For Basil the Great, *ousia* stood for the universal and *hypostasis* for the particular.[127] Basil illustrates the difference between the universal and the particular by speaking of a different biblical triad—Paul, Sylvanus and Timothy. Basil writes that because these three men share humanhood in common,

> no one will give one definition of essence or substance in the case of Paul, a second in that of Sylvanus, and a third in that of Timothy; but the same words which have been employed in setting forth the essence or substance of Paul will apply to the others also. Those who are described by the same definition of essence or substance are of the same essence or substance (*homoousios*).[128]

But, Basil continues, an essence fully shared does not preclude differentiation:

> That which is spoken of in a special and peculiar manner is indicated by the name of *hypostasis.* . . . It is customary in Scripture to make a distinction of this kind [between *ousia* and *hypostasis*]. . . . Transfer, then, to the divine dogmas the same standard of difference which you recognize in the case both of essence and of *hypostasis* in human affairs, and you will not go wrong.[129]

Any perceptive reader will note how quickly the Cappadocians' human analogy breaks down when moving from the human to God. The Cappadocians have been accused of being veiled tritheists, and clearly no three people could ever be one in the sense that Father, Son and Holy Spirit are united. In what, then, does the divine unity consist? The source and origin of the Godhead's divinity is the Father, and the three are united in the giving and receiving of divinity, yet distinguishable in the precise way in which each Person gives or receives. Basil the Great spoke of Fatherhood, Sonship and Sanctification as distinguishing properties; and Gregory of Nazianzus affirmed the ingenerateness of the Father and generateness of the Son and the Holy Spirit's procession.[130] Robert Jenson paraphrases Gregory of Nyssa thus: "God is the Father as the source of the Son's and the Spirit's Godhead; God is the Son as the recipient of the Father's Godhead; and God is the Spirit as the spirit of the Son's possession of the Father's Godhead."[131] This means, as Jenson concludes, that "the different ways in which each is the *one* God, for and from the others, are the only differences between them."[132]

The Cappadocians are not tritheists as has sometimes been alleged. They are possessed by a vivid sense of dynamism within the Three-in-One God. Their theology begins in wonder and ends in adoration. In the words of Gregory of Nazianzus we find the heart of trinitarian testimony:

> No sooner do I conceive of the One than I am illumined by the splendor of the Three; no sooner do I distinguish the Three than I am carried back to the One.[133] . . . For to us there is but one God, the Father, of whom are all things; and the one Lord Jesus Christ, by

whom are all things; and the one Holy Spirit, in whom are all things; yet these words—of, by, in, whom—do not denote a difference of essence . . . but they characterize the *hypostases* of an essence which is one and unconfused.[134]

Calling the Father the one God may seem to relegate the Son and Spirit to a lesser realm, yet Gregory is clear that Jesus Christ and the Holy Spirit are cocreators with the Father. "All things" are predicated of all three. Perhaps Gregory has in mind Romans 11:36, "For from him and through him and to him are all things," which can be interpreted to refer not just to God the Father, but to the entire Trinity.

The thoughts of Augustine (354-430) on the Trinity are among the most penetrating and luminous in the history of Christian doctrine. His wisdom concerning and valuing the Holy Spirit as the principle of unity between Father and Son, as well as his enlightening trinitarian analogies, is among his greatest contributions.[135] Unlike the Cappadocians, who started with the Father as the source of divinity for the Spirit and the Son, Augustine began his trinitarian work with the whole of the Trinity, the Godhead as such. Fearing tritheism, Augustine was suspicious of the Cappadocian analogy of three persons sharing in a common human nature.[136]

Augustine, who has been accused of being a modalist who denied any distinctions at all within God,[137] said that all that differentiated the divine Persons from each other is their relations to one another. He believed that "what the Father is in relation to himself is God. What he is in relation to the Son is Father."[138] The same holds true for the relations between the Spirit and the Son, and the Spirit and the Father. God is, for Augustine, indivisible, so each of the divine Persons is fully and completely God. "Not only is the Father not greater than the Son in respect of divinity, but Father and Son together are not greater than the Holy Spirit, and no single Person of the Three is less than the Trinity Itself."[139]

A diagram (see figure on page 78) from medieval Christendom well captures Augustine's trinitarianism.[140] The Father (P=*Pater*) is not *(non est)* the Holy Spirit (S=*Spiritus Sanctus*) or the Son (F=*Filius*). Likewise, neither the Holy Spirit nor the Son is other than himself. All three must be distinguishable from one another, but in all the fullness of divinity dwells equally, totally, completely, perfectly, magnificently. Each of them is God *(est Deus)* without dilution or diminution. Augustine declared that "each is in each, all are in each, each is in all, all are in all, and all are one."[141] Cyril Richardson summarizes Augustine's trinitarianism by saying that "God is one according to essence, and three according to relation."[142]

If asked to define the nature of God using only one word, most people would describe God as love (1 Jn 4:8, 16). Augustine's best-known trinitarian analogy captures God as "lover, beloved, love itself," or "he that loves, and that which is loved, and love itself."[143] The doctrine of the Trinity, for one contemporary commentator, affirms that God is "the radiating event of love."[144] No one has expressed this better than Augustine. The Holy Spirit unites the Son and the Father in perfect love. "This eternal *love in God Himself*," says Barth, "is the Holy Spirit."[145] The nature of God is to love, for love is what God is. For both Augustine and Barth, "God cannot *not* be God."[146]

The presence of memory, understanding and will within each rational creature is another noted Augustinian analogy. Each of these three must imply the other two, for none of them operates in isolation from the other two.[147] In employing one's understanding, one wills to do so, and recalls past adventures in thought. Memory is exercised and completed only through understanding and will, and likewise will is necessarily fixed to memory and understanding to form a psychological trinity. The exercise of memory, understanding and will happens simultaneously in every person. If these capacities functioned separately, Augustine would have trouble demonstrating even a triad, to say nothing of a trinity. As Raimundo Panikkar explains Augustine's meaning, "We *are*, we *know*, we *will* (or *love*): I *am* knowing and loving, I *know* myself as being and loving, I *will* to be and to know."[148]

The whole of Augustine's psychology is God-centered and hence trinitarian. Because God had formed the self and marked it decisively, to know the self and to know God are the same reality. Sin, of course, could and did intervene, blocking the vision of the holy. But humanity is framed and formed expressly for divine filling, as in Augustine's heart's cry that his heart would be perpetually restless until at last finding its rest in God. His psychological analogies, including that of the mind coming to the true knowledge and love of itself,[149] work only as the self is pointed toward and grounded in God. As the soul contemplates its true nature, it cannot help but remember, understand and love God.[150] In Augustine's thought, *psyche logos* (psychology), wherein the mind or soul sends forth and interprets its own word, is possible only because God graciously enables. Reflection on God's grace becomes *theos logos* (theology), the glorification of the Triune God. All human potential psychologies would be anathema to Augustine because they cut themselves off from the infinite horizon of grace available only in the Triune God.

Augustine's psychological analogies are refreshing and inviting, yet they must not be seen as equating the human with the divine. It is true that God cannot *not* be God, but humans, simply by being human, do not necessarily reach their full potential. In fact, they never do.

Richardson helpfully reminds us that "these trinities are *in* man; whereas the Trinity is not *in* God, but God *is* the Trinity."[151] Human trinities are present only through God's grace and operate only through God's mercy.

Not all theologians are totally impressed with Augustine's zeal for demonstrating the Trinity within human consciousness. Such theologians wonder if the seeming interiorization of the Trinity does not defeat the purpose of God's outgoing and overflowing love, which by nature seeks the unlovely. But a perfectly contented Trinity of memory, will and understanding has no motivation for finding and loving the other outside of the circle. Colin Gunton asserts that Augustine "is unable to conceive true otherness in the Trinity" because of his "inadequate conception of love as love for the other as other."[152] He further cautions that "Augustine's quest for the Trinity within the soul, the inner Trinity, risks reducing the Trinity to theological irrelevance, for it becomes difficult to ask in what way the doctrine of the Trinity may in other ways throw light on the human condition."[153]

Once one begins to find analogies of the Trinity, it is difficult to know where to stop, when to rein in the project. Trinities, or perhaps more accurately triads, can be found in culture and history in addition to expected appearances in psychology and the history of religions.[154] Neoplatonic philosophy, too, with its triads of principle-wisdom-ray or principle-intelligence-emanation might also be taken in a trinitarian way.[155] Augustine was likely influenced by Neoplatonic thought, but his doctrine of the Trinity never forsook biblical realism. Aside from his psychological analogies, Augustine also looked for the Trinity in the created realm. If, as Augustine believed, the Trinity was found on every page of the Bible, then in every scenic panorama its glory was also not to be denied.

Karl Barth rejected any approach to the Trinity not launched from the Word of God. While Barth was truly Augustinian in seeing the Holy Spirit as the bond of the eternal love between Father and Son, he would not allow the *Vestigium Trinitatis*, vestiges of the Trinity in nature, culture or philosophy.[156] For Barth, God spoke exclusively through Jesus Christ, the Word of the Father. To claim anything else fatally wounded God's finality and freedom.

As noted above, it is often said that the Cappadocian fathers began their trinitarian theologizing by naming the Father, who is not ontologically superior but logically prior to Son and Spirit, as the fount and source of divinity. Augustine's launching point, on the contrary, was the entire Godhead conceived as one. Not everyone agrees with this analysis; at least one scholar finds this dichotomy not in the ancient writings of the Cappadocians and Augustine but in modern interpretation of them. Systematic theologians seem attracted to "categories of polar opposition."[157] Most theologians, however, accept the reality of divergent starting points between the Cappadocians and Augustine. Is this a real issue, or is it just more evidence for those who dismiss the doctrine of the Trinity as fanciful and unnecessary?

Because outcomes and finalities are always linked to beginnings and presuppositions, this is a real issue. The Cappadocians' theology springs from the economy of salvation that unfolds in the Bible, whereas for Augustine, according to a commentator, "it seemed better to begin with the unity of the divine nature, since this is a truth which is demonstrated by reason."[158] Because Augustine, as another commentator sees it, did not adequately link the "eternal intra-trinitarian relations" with "ordinary human relations," his view of God is after all "rather static" and his concept of humanity "individualistic."[159] Where Augustine errs for these critics is in his relative neglect of the biblical economy of salvation. Instead of grounding his thoughts about the Triune God there, Augustine conceives of God's triunity according to "a threefold mind" and "neoplatonic philosophy."[160]

In light of these perceived weaknesses of Augustine's thought, those recent writers who express an opinion tend to favor the Cappadocians' outlook over Augustine's. Karl Rahner finds "the biblical theology of the Trinity" to be the Greek or Cappadocian approach, whereas the later Latin explanation started "from the *one* God whose *one* essence subsists in three persons."[161] To stress God's unity, as Western or Latin theology did beginning with Augustine and accelerating with Thomas Aquinas in the thirteenth century, tends to suggest that whatever needs to be said about God can be said through his oneness. The dynamism of Father, Son and Holy Spirit among them-selves, which spills forth in a world that must then be redeemed, pales to relative insignificance. Since Moltmann promotes a social under-standing of the Trinity, his methodology is to begin "with the trinity of the Persons and . . . then go on to ask about the unity."[162]

Donald Bloesch identifies himself with the Augustinian tradition[163] yet also appreciates the centrality of the Trinity in salvation history. The following analysis shows his belief that the three Persons indwell one another perichoretically, an emphasis of Eastern theology, yet that he is not comfortable proclaiming the Father as the source of divinity. Perhaps Bloesch comes as close as possible to harmonizing Eastern and Western traditions.

> No person of the Trinity is the underlying principle that sustains and undergirds the others. No person can exist by itself in splendid isolation from the others. Yet there is still an order of succession within the Trinity. The Father has a certain priority in that his creative action anticipates the creative and receptive activity of both Son and Spirit. The Father is not the source of the creative energy that constitutes the divine, but he is the first of three expres-sions of this energy. While the Son and Spirit are not ontologically inferior to the Father, they are dependent on the Father for their identity, but the Father too is dependent on them in order to realize his purposes.[164]

Having now concluded our brief tour of early trinitarian doctrine and its development, I feel confident in concluding, with Moltmann, that

> the patristic doctrine of the Trinity does not originate in an absorp-tion of the philosophical doctrine of the Logos, and of neo-Platonic triadologies, as has often been maintained. Its source is to be found in the New Testament witness to the trinitarian history of the Son, and in the church's practice of baptism in the name of the triune God.[165]

The only tenable trinitarianism is the one of the Father's bestowal of his Son, which, through the Holy Spirit, makes us participants in God's life-giving nature. Daniel Migliore speaks truly in saying that "the doctrine of the Trinity is far from an exercise in speculative curiosity. It is, if anything, antispeculative in intent."[166]

If humans had named God triune, then the ridicule vented on Christians for believing in the Trinity would be understandable and maybe even justified. But it is God who has called himself triune, because that is who God is, and through grace that name and its benefits have been offered to humankind. God's single name, spoken in the distinct but inseparable accents of Father, Son and Holy Spirit, is an invitation, a communion, an inclusion. Since we know and are known by God, what can we do but offer our praise?

Holy Trinity, thrice-blessed Name
Age to age ever the same
Father of unbounded love
Depth of depths, Source of life
Speaker of the Eternal Word
God incarnate, God here, God now
From the Father, in the Spirit, the Son for us
Holy Spirit, consuming fire
Dwelling amidst and joining
Father to his Son
Speaking praises through us
Showering love upon us
Working faith within us.

3

GOD'S NAME BESTOWED

A STRONG AND NECESSARY correlation exists between theology ("who is God?") and anthropology ("who is man?"). If the reality of God is denied, if God is thought to be dead, then as the Russian writer Dostoyevsky bleakly predicted, everything is permitted. An empty universe leads directly to an empty soul; a godless world means a purposeless life. Atheists can often be identified by their fallen countenance and hopeless outlook.

Augustine, who probably has influenced Christian thinking more decisively than anyone since the apostle Paul, came to faith in the living God through a tortured path. Never an atheist, he was attracted for many years to a sub-Christian philosophy that there were two eternal principles in the universe, one of light and one of darkness. After much struggle in overcoming a bent toward sensuality, Augustine's "restless heart" finally found peace. His heart found itself not in two combating principles but in the one Triune God.

As I said earlier, Augustine held that every page of Scripture testified to the Trinity. This witness extended to the created realm, where "vestiges" of the Trinity could be seen by eyes of faith. Every tree threw out branches and then twigs from its trunk; there were three, and these three were one. As the master designer of all that is, God added his signature to every inch of the world.

Propelled into God

God's greatest art was performed in fashioning humanity. If God's triunity could not be found within humans, then what good would it do to find it in trees? None whatsoever. But humanity's very essence was indelibly marked by God's triunity, so that, for Augustine, true self-knowledge inevitably led to deep God-knowledge. Since humanity was shaped and molded in God's triune image, any real insight into self had to be at the same time an adventure in knowing God. Augustine's deep appreciation for humanity's indebtedness to God at once established him as the founder of Christian psychology and contradicted modern liberalism, which overturns Augustine's equation. People today are most inclined to probe their own depths as humans and to call the final end of their searches "God." Augustine insisted that it was only because of God's creative graces that anyone could lead a reflective life at all, and that searches toward the true self were successful only as they uncovered what God had already hidden there.

The human mind thus contains revealing "footprints of the Trinity."[1] As we observed in the preceding chapter, every human being is capable of memory, understanding and will. If any one of these three capacities is isolated from the other two, that capacity no longer functions in a human way. Everyone exercises his or her will based on choices made and remembered from the past, and no one exercises his or her will in an irrational way that contradicts the understanding. What is true of the will, that it needs both understanding and memory to perform optimally, is true also of memory and understanding.

Every mind also demonstrates the related trio of love, reason and memory. Each of these three is the special province of one of the divine persons. The Father is the source of love for the entire Godhead. "God is love" (1 Jn 4:8, 16). The Son, as John's prologue (Jn 1:1-14) makes plain, is the eternal Logos or reason. The Holy Spirit's role is to "remind you of all that I have said to you" (Jn 14:26).[2] These mental capacities are, however, inseparable, even if they can be distinguished one from another. The same is true of Father, Son and Holy Spirit; they are distinguishable yet inseparable.

Augustine's astute psychological insights and analogies do not mean that humanity is equal to divinity. The image of God in humankind remains a representative image, full of promise, yet broken and tarnished beyond human repair in the Fall. What is mere image in human beings is full actuality in God, so that it can be truly said (as already noted in chapter two): "God cannot *not* be God."[3] Only in God, but never in a human being, is potentiality fully actualized. No humans ever exhaust their full potential. They must forever strive but will never arrive.

Augustine's psychological analogies of the Trinity impressed upon humankind's very essence are subject to the same limitation every analogy faces: comparing one reality to another never yields exact coinherence between the two. God's triunity is the only project of thought where the many are one in essence and yet at the same time distinct in identity. The Triune God is not in the end a project of thought at all, but the living God who has fashioned humankind after himself. So whatever trinities Augustine finds as defining humanhood—memory, understanding, will; or knowing, willing, loving—are within human beings as planted there by God. Humans are sown with trinitarian seeds, but the seeds themselves are gifts from God, as is the capacity for growth and fruition enabled by the Holy Spirit. Understanding this, we may repeat Cyril Richardson's insightful analysis, lest human explorations of their implicit trinities forget the relation between creature and Creator: "these trinities are *in* man; whereas the Trinity is not *in* God, but God *is* the Trinity."[4] The image of God in humanity is complete so far as God is concerned, because God's original intent for humanity remains firmly and soundly in place in God's mind. We have strayed from God, not God from us.

For John Wesley, "the great end of religion is to renew our hearts in the image of God, to repair that total loss of righteousness and true holiness which we sustained by the sin of our first parent."[5] Only through God's grace fully present in Jesus Christ is this necessary renewal possible, and only as we are renewed into God's image can memory, understanding and will function properly within the mind and soul.

God's image in humanity can be illustrated by the question every small child is sure to hear when developing and maturing: "What do you want to be when you grow up?" The discerning parent knows better than to derail the child's sense of wonder that arises from the promise of growth and finding a new world every day. The Holy Spirit gently yet decisively asks this same question of every Christian and, if they are listening, of all people, because it is the Spirit who encourages and implements our growing conformity to the holy God. Our best visions for "the meaning and promise of human life"[6] are those visions given and sustained by the Triune God. Augustine's discovery was that God's triunity is itself the measure of human potential. Because humankind was marked in its inner recesses by the Trinity, only by returning to the Trinity can God's image be restored. Other Christian writers after Augustine have also keenly sensed this. "The Trinity is the heart of . . . human nature," said one. "No place or position can be found or conceived where the Trinity is not present and in every being; but hidden as the essence of it," another one declared.[7]

The Trinity is hiddenness and the Trinity is heart. The Trinity is God's heart, God's depths, under whose impress humanity was lovingly fashioned. The Trinity's hidden heart becomes known, and God's power becomes available through the Holy Spirit. The Spirit of God "searches everything, even the depths of God" (1 Cor 2:10). In exploring the depths of God, the Holy Spirit at the same time bestows God's gifts of discernment and interpretation on those who will accept them. "Launch out into the deep, and you shall see."[8] God's energy, the Holy Spirit, propels us into God's fullness and at the same time into our own true self-knowledge. The Holy Spirit is not only the "bond of love" between the Father and Son, but also between us and God. An ancient hymn to the Holy Spirit, traditionally sung on Pentecost Sunday, calls us to worship the third person of the Trinity, because, by implication, the Spirit unifies not only the divine, but also the human:

Through Thee may we the Father learn
And know the Son, and Thee discern
Who art of both; and thus adore
In perfect faith for evermore.[9]

Over the past four centuries, the learning, knowing and discerning undertaken by humankind have assumed an increasingly secular disposition. Freedom has been redefined as the actualization of strictly human potential, not the disciplined freedom of serving God through taking up the cross. The knowledge of God, once thought of as foundational to freedom, no longer matters as it once did. Immanuel Kant, an eighteenth-century German philosopher, represents this trend. "Dare to know!" was Kant's motto and the motto of many of his fellow thinkers during the Enlightenment (1650-1800).

Kant framed four questions with which any philosophy or worldview must grapple along the way toward understanding humankind: (1) What can I know? (2) What ought I to do? (3) What may I hope? and (4) What is man? Kant's proposed answers to each of these questions demonstrated him not to be an atheist, and probably not even an agnostic, but, nevertheless, as someone with little interest in revealed religion or classical Christian confession.

The Holy Spirit is no longer the middle term, the point of contact, between God and humanity. Kant replaces Holy Spirit with human spirit. Human knowledge is limited to what arises in the human senses, and these sense data are in turn cataloged and understood by the structures of the rational mind, for example, time and space. Revelation is not subject to empirical verification by human perceptual ability and is therefore beyond the scope of human concern. Regarding what people ought to do, Kant does allow that God is the moral lawgiver who issues the directives of duty to each rational soul. Kant said he really only wanted to know two things, the starry heavens above and the moral law within. But Kant, if a theist, is not a trinitarian, and God as lawgiver is a single, solitary God. Kant stated plainly that "nothing whatever would be accomplished for moral betterment" by believing in Trinity.[10]

If knowledge begins and ends with humankind, and morality is focused on obligation, what about Kant's third question: What may I hope? Religion answers this question, but it is religion that is fenced in on all sides by reason. Kant had no answer for Paul's question to the Romans, "For who hopes for what is seen?" (8:24), because hope had little if any transcendent basis or eschatological pull. Because humankind is made for itself, hope is limited to what human beings can produce.

What a difference it makes—an eternal difference really—if one takes Kant's four questions and answers them in the spirit of Augustine. Kant's culminating question, "What is man?" is always secondary for Augustine. "Who is God?" is the question that frames and anticipates all other questions. Augustine's psychological trinity of memory, understanding and will coincides with Kant's first three areas of concern, if not in exact sequential order. Memory is hoping, understanding is knowing, will is doing. Kant's questions and conclusions are, however, humanistic, whereas Augustine's are trinitarian.

A humanistic trinity—for example, Kant's knowing, doing and hoping—that defines the boundaries of human thought and life, is always the grasp for personal attainment, never the humble reception of divine bestowal. Human boasting has no use for divine condescension, and human speech will not silence itself before God. Immanuel Kant stood for values whose total absence from life would make it intolerable. Idealism, progress, fairness, tolerance, liberality— who could find fault with these? As sterling a catalog as these values are, they must be "transvalued" and "revalued" according to the Triune God. The triune perspective is that from atop Calvary's cross, which represents the foolishness of God at its widest reach (1 Cor 1:18-25). The answer to the query "What is man?" is knowing ourselves as God knows us. Everyone who adopts as his or her own the perspective of the crucified Christ, who when elevated above the earth will draw all people to himself (Jn 12:32), will be able to answer penetratingly Kant's final question. The cross of Jesus Christ, because it is the cross of the Triune God, is the great clarifier. We see there not tarnished human possibility but divine forgiveness.

The Fullness of Personhood

Augustine insisted that the entire world is created in the image of the Trinity. Humankind, as the culmination of creation, bore a special impression. Humanity's triune endowment was humbling, because God was the measure and span of the human, not the reverse. Divinity is sovereign and defining; humanity should be grateful and receptive. Augustine said, "Only two things will I seek to know, God and the soul, the soul and God."[11] His meaning is clear. One cannot truly know God without at the same time knowing one's own soul. The two knowledges—of God and of the soul—are intertwined but not equal. If they were absolutely equal, it would make as much sense to say that the soul created God as it would to say that God created the soul. But this is absurd. The search for the true self erupts differently in everyone. Augustine knew that as well as anyone, so arduous had been his own quest for self-definition and discovery. The search for the self is simply part of being human; it "comes with the territory." That territory soon turns to briars and thorns unless the self is relinquished to the leading of the Holy Spirit. Augustine—as well as everyone—was prone to wander forever unless and until he was found to be in God. He confessed to God, "You have made us for yourself, and our heart is restless until it rests in you."[12] In his sermon "Spiritual Worship," John Wesley paraphrased Augustine: "This one God made our heart for himself; and it cannot rest till it resteth in him."[13]

Spiritual worship for both Wesley and Augustine was the presentation of the body as a living sacrifice according to the mercies of God (Rom 12:1). It is true that Augustine believed in predestination[14] while Wesley strongly opposed it,[15] but that is not the point. Ephesians 3:14-15 is the point: "For this reason I bow my knees before the Father, from whom every family in heaven and on earth takes its name." Because it is God who has named us, the only fitting response is adoration, beginning with the knees and ending with the entire self.

God created our entire beings and accordingly pursues us with renewing grace. God remains intent on humankind's full participation in the divine life. Finding one's true self in God involves the decision to accept God's mercy and grace. The word *decision* means, quite literally, a cutting off of that which has gone before. "Love slays what we have been, that we may be what we were not,"[16] said Augustine. Because God has formed us, God alone knows the fullness of our potential. And God aims to enable our reaching our full potential, underwritten by divine grace.

Human potential is given by God and therefore measured by God. For Karl Barth, "the problem is not whether God is a person, the problem is whether we are."[17] Barth asserts that God is "a Person in a way quite different from that in which we are persons," and that God alone "is a real, true and genuine person."[18] What can it possibly mean to say that personhood is only complete in God and exists but fragmentarily in man? It is immensely humbling yet tremendously relieving as well—humbling, because human arrogance builds its own universe, and relieving, because God's call upon our lives, even God's demand, is a "covered promise." What God expects, God will surely enable.

What God already is, humans are striving to become. Human effort must itself be open to God in a radical way. Human effort must be pointed toward grace and receptive of grace.

Did we in our own strength confide
Our striving would be losing,
Were not the right Man on our side:
The Man of God's own choosing.[19]

The Man in Martin Luther's classic hymn is of course Jesus Christ. Not simply divinity nor humanity alone is present in Jesus Christ, but full divinity and full humanity perfectly conjoined in one person. "In Jesus Christ," Catherine LaCugna writes, "God and a human being have come together in total love for each other and now exist as one for all eternity."[20] This divine and human union is not static, going into hibernation once it has been accomplished. In Jesus Christ, God's love condescends so that human love will no longer be merely human, but will be charged with divine possibility.

If Augustine's affirmation is true, if all of creation bears the mark of the Trinity, then surely any adequate theory of personhood must itself bear the Trinity's impress. Let us examine LaCugna's six qualities of personhood in this light.[21] We must ask whether these qualities are already perfectly accomplished in the Triune God. If they are, then Barth's insight that God is the only true person can be substantiated.

1. *Persons are, in their essence, interpersonal and intersubjective.* Every person who is open to his or her own depths must at the same time be open to others, because no one can reach one's own depths alone. Even monks who live alone are not really alone. They live according to great monastic traditions that have gone before them and toward which they exist as grateful heirs. Truly, "a self-existent life is a contradiction in terms."[22] The triune life of God is not self-existent. Each of the three divine Persons is in constant communication with the other two. Each dwells richly and freely in the other two and is in turn indwelt by them. The God of absolute monotheism can easily become an isolationist God, but God as three-in-one is the only perfect manifestation of interpersonal relationships.

2. *Persons are unique and unrepeatable.* Persons are unfathomable mystery. Father, Son and Holy Spirit are each perfectly present in and totally available to one another. This intercommunion does not suggest that the three are not distinguishable one from the other. Each is unique while each contains the total fullness of divinity. As fully divine, each is fully mysterious. Augustine captured the Trinity's uniqueness in relationality when he named the Father as source of love, Son as object of the Father's love, and Holy Spirit as love itself.

3. *For humans, the exercise of freedom is a balance between self-realization and service to others.* Human personhood, because it is always in the process of perpetual deepening and maturing, "requires the balance of self-love and self-gift." LaCugna's insight rings true for humans, but is it also true of the Trinity? All of the triune members perfectly accomplish the act of self-gift. Each of them is pure gift to the other two. The love within the Trinity overflows and bathes the world in love. Humans soon deplete their reserves of love if they only give love to others and do not receive love in return. Yet this give-and-take and ebb and flow of love is a testimony not to human sincerity but to our being created in the image of the Triune God. All love comes ultimately from God, and whenever anyone gives or receives any love

whatsoever, its originating source is God. We must recognize, as LaCugna surely does, that self-love manufactured and generated by the self is a huge falsehood. The true exercise and application of self-love is always a testimony to the Trinity, even if this witness is not acknowledged by the one loving oneself.

Since all is love within the Triune God, there is no need (and in one sense not even the possibility) for the balance between self-love and self-gift. This balance is necessary in humans, because humans are incapable of loving each other as the divine Persons love each other. Within the Trinity there is no distinction between gift to self and gift to other, because there is no selfishness, no egocentricity, within the Godhead. Because Father, Son and Holy Spirit are not in the least self-seeking or self-serving, self-realization on human terms is unknown to the Triune God. There is only perfect self-gift, of the kind Jesus Christ exhorted all to imitate: "No one has greater love than this, to lay down one's life for one's friends" (Jn 15:13). Each of the three persons gives himself in total freedom to the other two, and in the very act of giving receives his life back again, life that is endless communion among and within the three. The love shared among Father, Son and Holy Spirit is a seamless impulse of love, not two separate motions of first giving love and then receiving love in return, but one moment of love infinitely enacted as perfect bliss. This is the paradox of the gospel, and it is rooted deeply within God himself. Self-giving love of the sort that sent Jesus to Calvary is triune love. Father, Son and Spirit do not cling to their separate lives, because in fact none has his own life, if by "his own life" a separate identity is meant. Humans cannot fathom a life of total self-gift to others, but this inability does not negate the possibility of total gift-love, for this is the love characteristic of the Triune God. In the words of Jesus, "If anyone would come after me, he must deny himself and take up his cross and follow me. For whoever wants to save his life will lose it, but whoever loses his life for me and for the gospel will save it" (Mk 8:34-35 NIV).

Living arrangements in the Philippines may faintly and haltingly illumine the total availability of Father, Son and Spirit one for the others. Families are large and living quarters small in the Philippines, and privacy comes at a premium. Should one be fortunate enough to have one's own bedroom, a closed door is an emphatic sign: "Privacy requested! Do not trespass!" God lives not in a house but everywhere, but if the Triune God indwelt a house, no closed doors would intervene to block the full triune communion. If God is open to humans sharing his life, it can only be because God is himself untrammeled openness and love.

4. *Becoming a self demands discipline, sacrifice and exertion.* God is already fully accomplished and totally realized in his being. God will not grow and deepen through discipline and sacrifice. Much like the preceding criterion, in which the Trinity was seen as being complete self-gift, in this criterion there is no room for improvement within God. God does not need practice at being God, as if to suggest a deficit within the Godhead. From everlasting to everlasting, God is a God of sacrificial love. God's heart has eternally carried a cross.[23] God's eternal sacrifice was the impossible risk of fellowship, the invitation to intimacy with God—impossible, that is, for humans, "but not for God; for God all things are possible" (Mk 10:27). From the human side, simply knowing God is the greatest impossibility; from God's side, this is the greatest risk and sacrifice, God's gift to humankind.

5. *As people mature, they become deeper, richer and freer.* Jesus Christ underwent a normal physical and psychological development from a human perspective. He "increased in wisdom and in years, and in divine and human favor" (Lk 2:52). Furthermore, while "in the days of his flesh," Jesus was a perpetual learner. His chief lesson was to become submissive to his Father: "Although he was a Son, he learned obedience through what he suffered" (Heb 5:8).

The writer to the Hebrews was careful to qualify Jesus' obedience to the time of his being in the flesh. Jesus was never a wild and rebellious prodigal whose independent impulses needed to be reigned in. Yet the Son, while in the flesh, needed to offer himself up in "reverent submission" (Heb 5:7) to the Father. Enthroned at the Father's right hand, even "standing at the right hand of God" (Acts 7:55), the Son is still in a sense submissive to the Father, for "the Son himself will also be subjected to the one who put all things in subjection under him, so that God may be all in all" (1 Cor 15:28).

The human view of submission is the denial of freedom and potential, but the triune understanding of submission is "reverent submission" of each to all and of all to each. This is the way the Trinity lives. There is no preeminence among the three Persons, only perfect beatitude and communion. Even Paul's statement "that God may be all in all" in no way implies the Father's superiority over the Son and the Holy Spirit. The Father may be the originating source of divinity within the Godhead and "first among equals," but the Father's being first does not elevate him above Son and Spirit. There are not three perspectives in the Trinity and not simply one vision in triplicate, but one vision carried forth triunely: from the Father, through the Son, in the Holy Spirit.

Perfect submission within the Trinity is both a gift and a challenge—a gift from God and a challenge to all to become more submissive toward God and by extension to one another. Although blind from the age of six weeks on account of being mistreated by an errant doctor,[24] hymn writer Fanny Crosby keenly saw the benefits of total submission:

Perfect submission, perfect delight!

Visions of rapture now burst on my sight!

Angels descending bring from above

Echoes of mercy, whispers of love.[25]

Human submission to God may end in delight, but only if it goes the way of the cross, the way of Jesus Christ's submission to the Father.

6. *The ideal of Christian faith is persons living in communion with themselves, with others, with the created world and most especially with God.* Indeed, living in communion with God can never be a mere afterthought or an unnecessary appendage that persons should outgrow as they mature, the way a tadpole loses its tail in becoming a frog. The reverse is true. Communion with God is the only avenue, the only bridge, toward a life lived communally. "I am the vine, you are the branches. Those who abide in me and I in them bear much fruit, because apart from me you can do nothing" (Jn 15:5).

Christian personhood strives toward full fruition, toward full realization of implicit potential. What is ideal for humans is actual in the Triune God. What is hoped for among men and women is accomplished among the Father, Son and Holy Spirit. Because God has created us in the Trinity's fulsome image, we are able to hear God's self-identification as triune. Hearing, we must obey. The hearing and the obeying are not purely academic or intellectual. Hearing that God is triune is itself a testimony to the Trinity within us, and obeying means that we allow God's Spirit to pull our hearts ever closer to God's heart. Karl Rahner has written that "the Trinity is not merely a reality to be expressed in purely doctrinal terms: it takes place in us, and as such does not first reach us in the form of statements communicated by revelation. On the contrary these statements have been made to us because the reality of which they speak has been accorded to us."[26]

In no way is Rahner discounting the importance of revelation. Unless God has first stamped his image on us, Rahner contends, no amount of revelation will mean anything. God's triune gift to each soul is far deeper than statements of revelation. The gift is God's own essence. The prayer of the hymn writer, "Stamp Thine own image deep on my heart,"[27] was answered through creation yet subsequently forfeited by Adam's original sin. Now God desires to restore his triune image through the Son's sacrifice and the Spirit's sanctifying presence.

Persons in Community
God, and only the Triune God, has been shown as the sole full and complete representation of what it means to be a person. Karl Barth's judgment that God alone "is a real, true and genuine person"[28] is therefore a true assessment. Donald Baillie agrees with Barth and gives a somewhat fuller description of the divine personhood: "God is always and wholly and in every respect *personal*. Nothing in God is impersonal. His Word is personal. His Spirit is personal. Personality in God must indeed be a very different thing from personality in us. But that is because we are far from being perfectly personal. God is the only perfectly personal Being."[29]

How, specifically, does God's vision of personality stand apart from the human vision? How can God's view correct ours? American culture values the single and the solitary. Youth are admonished to "make your mark on the world," with reference to their personality. A strong personality is thought automatically to cover a multitude of sins: faulty reasoning, lack of compassion, selfishness, lust for power. Is it any coincidence that a military dictator is often called a strongman? American culture is not alone in setting up a cult of personality. When former Philippine president Ferdinand Marcos's body was returned to be buried in the land of his birth, a few Filipinos actually believed Marcos to be some sort of god, returning to erect a celestial reign.

No one can deny the need for a strong and centered self. But the typical American prescription for mature selfhood—symbolized by the cowboy, the mountain man, the business mogul, the entertainer who "did it my way"—is flawed and skewed. A forced choice between the individual and the communitarian is a false choice. There are not two distinct paths, the personal and the social. There is not even one path with a partition down the middle. All those within the "cloud of witnesses" (Heb 12:1) are unaware of any gap between the singular and the communal. They have not succumbed to this false dichotomy, because they are not even looking at each other, let alone themselves. It is on Jesus, "the pioneer and perfecter of our faith" (Heb 12:2), that all eyes are set. Jesus is no pioneer in the mold of rugged individualism. Jesus is a pioneer of salvation and the perfecter of our faith, because Jesus gave himself up for a cause infinitely richer than his own personality development, namely, to save the world.

It is an awesome thing to become a self. It is an unfinished task. It may even be an unfinishable task. John Wesley speculated that even in heaven one's likeness to God needs continual deepening and purifying. Christian perfection, thought Wesley, may go on for all eternity. On this side of eternity, the suggestion is sometimes made that one is first a human being and only then a Christian. Humanhood, in short, defines Christian existence. Presumably, then, human needs must always be chosen ahead of Christian requirements.

Imagine if God said, "First I will be God, and only then will I be triune." No, God is God, God is truly God, only as triune. Likewise, any human is truly human only inasmuch as he or she draws life from the Trinity. One is not first human and then Christian. Neither is one first Christian and then human, as if to say that Christianity limited and ultimately defeated human potential. As God's Spirit infuses divine life into human life, the proper equation is: as one becomes more conformed to God's likeness, one becomes more human, so that it can be said that Jesus Christ, not Adam, is the truly representative human. In other words, as a physician well put it, "Jesus Christ was the only perfectly mature man who ever lived."[30]

Within God, there is never a forced choice between the personal and the communal. Triune life is the life of pure relationality. "To be is to be related"[31] is both an apt description for God's inner life and an inescapable judgment on our own shortsighted view of personhood, which would exalt the individual over the communal. God's triunity offers a stern and needed corrective to our unceasing individualism, because "in the Trinity, community and person are strictly correlative."[32] John Zizioulas, the contemporary Greek theologian who has articulated an entire ontology of relationality, elaborates the point that true being is being-with, being-for, and being-through: "Because the Father, the Son and the Spirit are always together, the particular beings are the bearers of the totality of nature, and thus no contradiction between 'one' and 'many' can arise. In trying to identify a particular thing, we have to make it part of a relationship, and not isolate it as an *individual*."[33]

The modern view of the person is heavily reliant on the ancient definition given by the philosopher Boethius early in the sixth century. A person is an "individual substance of a rational nature."[34] Today, since "substance" typically means something material, "person" is more apt to be defined as ego, bent on fullest possible self-awareness and development. Because our view of personhood is so fixed on the ego, and because there is no egocentricity in the Trinity, some have thought that the word *person* is no longer adequate to define the members of the Trinity. Augustine believed that *person* should be retained, and his assessment is classic. We cannot say there are three

beings in God, and we certainly cannot say there are three Gods. What
then shall we do? How then shall we speak? We affirm there are three
Persons "so that we are not simply reduced to silence when we are
asked three what, after we have confessed that there are three."[35] Karl
Barth was very sensitive to this issue and believed that *person* falsely
conveyed entirely too much individualism to the mutual indwelling
that characterizes the life of the Triune God. Instead of three Persons,
Barth preferred to say "three 'modes (or ways) of being' in God."[36]
Karl Rahner, too, thought that the common understanding of person
could lead one away from a true comprehension of who the Triune
God really is. Rahner preferred to say that "the one self-communication of the one God occurs in three different manners of given-ness"
or, in terms of the immanent Trinity, that "the one God subsists in three
distinct manners of subsisting."[37]

Not every theologian applauds this move away from the concrete
language of persons to the at least potentially nebulous language of
modes of being. Clark Pinnock, for one, claims that "given the fact that
Father and Son are persons and that the Spirit is spoken of in personal
terms in the Scriptures, it is appropriate to speak of God as a community of persons rather than as modes of being."[38] This dispute regarding the proper description of the Triune God's "component parts,"
whether "persons" or "modes of being," may be more semantic than
real. Barth founded his trinitarian investigations squarely and wholly
on God's unrepeatable revelation in Jesus Christ. While the evidence
is perhaps less clear in Rahner's case, at no point in his thought do
philosophical categories completely overwhelm biblical truth.

The fact that love has today often degenerated into sensuality has
not provoked too many people to abandon the use of the word *love.*
Rather, efforts to clarify what love truly is are continually being made
by making comparisons with God's gift of love. God's love as standard is winnowing and chastening, so that lesser understandings of
love drop by the wayside. "God is love" is a strikingly different
pronouncement from "love is God," which is all too often the modern
version. Similarly, God's idea of personhood is worth fighting for. We
have already noted that Barth believed that God was the only true

Person, and thus his preference for "modes of being" is not a rejection
of personhood as conceived by God, but just the corruption of personhood in the direction of overblown individualism. Thomas Weinandy
perceptively states that anchoring *person* in God's triune depths not
only protects against God's being thought of subpersonally but also
humanizes our world in the right direction, toward God:

> Granted that the contemporary notion of "person" as a subjective
> self-conscious, autonomous, free individual must be nuanced
> when applied to the Trinity, the specifically modern insistence that
> personhood necessarily implies unique subjectivity is actually an
> advantage, and not a hindrance, to our present understanding of
> the Trinity. The stress on subjectivity better enables us today to
> grasp that within the inner being of God there are truly three
> subjects and not three impersonal "things." It further deepens and
> clarifies, it radically "personalizes" for our time and culture, the
> traditional Scholastic notion of person as an individual substance
> of a rational nature. Rightly, the emphasis is now fixed upon
> subjectivity and not on substance. Thus, to say that there are three
> persons in God may not do full, or even adequate, justice to the
> truth of who God is, but it would be deceptive and wrong to say
> anything less.[39]

Egocentricity is different from ego awareness. Every person, even
every divine person, must be aware of his or her uniqueness. Father,
Son and Holy Spirit are each aware of being fully God. Divinity is not
divisible by three: the Father is totally God, the Son is totally God, the
Spirit is totally God. If it can be said that each divine Person first knows
himself, it cannot be said that each one knows himself better than the
other two know him. The gradation of good, better, best can be applied
to human knowledge of other people, or else the phrase "best friend"
is without meaning. But the love and knowledge shared among
Father, Son and Holy Spirit are perfect and complete and can admit
of no increase. Each triune Person does have his own identity and in
that sense first knows himself. This knowledge may in some way be
considered as logically prior, but it is not a deeper knowledge than the
other two have of the third. The mystical intercommunion present

between Christ and the church and toward which every human marriage intends, is fully consummated among Father, Son and Spirit. Thus there is no egocentricity in God, even though all three Persons have distinct, if truly inseparable, identities. As Augustine taught, the Father is not Father to himself but only to the Son. To himself the Father is God. The same is true for Son and Spirit. The Son did not beget himself, and the Holy Spirit is not in love with himself, but with the Father and the Son. Humanistic psychology says "first love yourself." The triune premise is that love is completed when it is invested in the other. Love that is given away does not impoverish, but enriches and perfects, the giver.

Triune life is thus both deep and wide. Each divine Person understands his own depths but finds fulfillment only in the company that is three yet one. Employing Augustine's psychological analogies of memory, understanding and will, we have already observed how triune life is deep life. No self can even be a self apart from the exercise of memory, understanding and will. Memory, however, is at least partially communal memory, remembrance of family, classmates, vacations and so forth. Understanding and will are likewise seldom, if ever, isolated from the stream of social life. This suggests that a second class of analogies, the social, is needed to fill in the gaps left by all psychological analogies.

The Cappadocian fathers, three Greek-speaking theologians of the fourth-century Eastern church, worked out the social analogy of the Trinity. Peter, Paul and Barnabas, so reasoned Gregory of Nyssa, are one in that they all share a common essence of humanity.[40] Yet undeniably each of them is also his own person. Daniel Migliore explains how the Cappadocians' insight completes Augustine's thinking: "The 'social analogy' of the Trinity is needed to correct and complement the psychological analogy. In distinction from the psychological analogy, which focuses on the dynamic unity of psychic activities, the social analogy looks to the phenomenon of persons in relationship for a clue to the mystery of the divine life."[41]

No analogy ever conveys all it intends, as is especially true of analogies that presume to describe God. Regardless of how intimate and complete their knowledge is of each other, no three people are ever one in the same sense that Father, Son and Spirit are one. If an analogy can never hit the bull's-eye straight on, a good one will at least hit the target. Both analogies, psychological and social, are ancient, well attested in Christian literature and capable of new formulations. One woman, integrated in her own person and at the same time carrying forth three relational roles—for example, attorney, board member and wife—would seem to combine the insights available in both analogies. She is one person yet multiple in relationality.

A word of caution, however, is appropriately sounded whenever the social and psychological analogies are made to say too much, are made uncritically to transport ideas to our time that are patently geared for another time. Every analogy must remain an "empty vessel" to be filled with the particularities of time and place. Reified and frozen analogies cannot hold the new wine of fresh examples. The broad and general forms of the psychological and social analogies may be ongoing, but there is always a need for new content to be analyzed and applied. Otherwise these analogies are dead and deadening, and they become "highly inadequate."[42]

Human speech has also been mined for its trinitarian possibilities. Language seems to have a three-in-one structure: I-you-we. The very act of speaking requires thought, utterance and the hearer's reception. These three aspects of thought, vocalization and hearing work only in a single, unifying act. The whole constellation of language is clearly both individual and social. Pressing this example more specifically, one scholar sees the Father as the I-relation, the Son as the you- or thou-relation and the Holy Spirit as the we-relation.[43] This is essentially Augustine's insight seen in linguistic terms. The Father's "I" must be spoken in love, spoken to the Father's "eternal thou," his Son. The Son receives the Father's "I" in the communion of the Holy Spirit, who joins the "I" and the "thou" in a perfect "we."

Human endeavors beyond the strictly theological can thus benefit immensely from the model of God as triune. Psychological investigations into personhood are enriched by Augustine's intrapersonal analogies, and political promptings toward the ideal society cannot possibly improve on the Cappadocians' social analogy. Reflections on the linguistic analogy would enable everyone to speak with greater caution and understanding.

The Trinity's marked utility as an explanatory device should not be underestimated. Yet not explanation but salvation (forgiveness of sins) and participation (God's image restored) is why the Word became flesh. Approaches to the Trinity that push toward problem solving and slight the mystery of revelation and the urgency of salvation are preliminary but not final, and analytical prowess as its own end is dangerous and misbegotten. The Trinity is the strongest statement God can make to us, for us and in us. God's triune life is offered to us because Jesus Christ died for us, enabling the Holy Spirit to live within us and bring us to fellowship with God the Father and God the Son. "Solving" the problem of how, logically speaking, three can be one and yet remain three, while neglecting the Trinity's pervasive spiritual pull and address, is much like gaining the whole world at the expense of losing one's soul (Mk 8:36). Like the star over Bethlehem that led the wandering magi to worship the Christ child, any analogy, to be edifying, must point beyond itself to confession and adoration. An analogy must be transparent to luminous grace, because, in Catherine LaCugna's words, "the doctrine of the Trinity is not above all a theory about God's 'internal self-relatedness' but an effort to articulate the basic faith of Christians: In Jesus Christ, the ineffable and invisible God saves us from sin and death; by the power of the Holy Spirit, God continues to be altogether present to us, seeking everlasting communion with all creatures."[44] An analogy may be like a check drawn on the bank of the imagination. God, who created all things, created every imagination.

The Contours of Grace

To what, then, may the grace of the Triune God be compared? Does its sheer infinity, its awesome profusion, preclude from the outset any analogical comparison? For how can the inherently limitless reality of grace be circumscribed by the fences of sifting, weighing, working and locating that any comparison must erect? The story of the bishop, the boy and the sea hints at the immensity of God's grace and our inability to appreciate this fully.[45]

Augustine, bishop of Hippo, was walking along the shore of the Mediterranean Sea pondering his classic work *The Trinity*, as well he might, taking as it did more than fifteen years to compose. Spotting a small boy pouring seawater into a hole in the ground, Augustine puzzled over this activity and then asked the boy what he was doing. Believing that no explanation was necessary for such an obvious project, the boy replied that he was pouring the Mediterranean into the hole. "That's not possible," Augustine rebuked him. "The sea is too vast and your hole too small." The boy, theologically precocious, had the perfect rejoinder: "No less possible is your attempt to write a book about the Trinity."

Throughout our entire inquiry we have placed the burden of proof on God. That is to say, God as triune is God's own book, his own telling of his own story. Three eternally equal and completely in love characters tell the one story that constitutes them as one God. One plot line unites Father and Son and Spirit, and from start to finish that is grace. They are not "three characters in search of a story," unfulfilled until they happen somehow upon the one note all of them can sing well. To say that would subordinate the three Persons to an alien process that was imposed on them from without. Father, Son and Holy Spirit are one God precisely because all of them are united in the one symphony of grace. Within the Triune God there are not three divine wills or three divine essences. There is only one will and essence, so that Bernard of Clairvaux is absolutely correct that within the Triune God there is "not a union of wills but a unity of will."[46] This single will is realized in perfection within God as total love and becomes grace when extended to humanity and the world.

The best path to the Trinity, therefore, does not lead to the library, the lecture hall, the psychoanalyst's couch or even the pastor's study. The best path leads to the prayer closet, the sanctuary, the chapel and—what validates and sustains all of these—the cross. More than any other religious symbol, the cross invites (and really requires) participation with one's whole being, for in it God's entire being is exposed to the world. Study and cogitation can bring one into the cross's neighborhood, yet by themselves show only the polished surfaces and not the rough, pulsating center. In the cross is overflowing, drenching grace, and grace is how God seeks to engage our attention. Grace is God's introduction, his calling card. Grace illumines the path to God and energizes God's search for us. In one sense there is no path to God at all, if by path is meant hacking through jungles of religious curiosity to God. Left to merely human devices, our stabs at God are stabs into darkness. God has not left humankind to its own devices, but "has shone in our hearts to give the light of the knowledge of the glory of God in the face of Jesus Christ" (2 Cor 4:6). Grace is light that brings knowledge of God's glory.

Some of theology's most strenuous battles have been fought on the terrain of grace. Can grace be resisted? Can grace be canceled and forfeited once one has known and tasted of its benefits? Can one be "in grace" and not know it? Will grace ever return once someone has self-consciously and emphatically rejected its overtures? Is fallen humanity totally without grace? To what degree, if at all, can human freedom cooperate with grace?

The puzzles of grace do not have to be solved in order for the benefits of grace to be applied. God's grace is in that sense like the Trinity: both are necessary for salvation (if it is even possible to think of them apart from each other), but their exact workings are mysterious. John Wesley, while admitting that no one can fully comprehend the Trinity, asserted that no Christian could ever deny the sheer fact of the Trinity.[47] The same is true for the workings of grace.

The best synonym for grace is love. Gustaf Aulén writes that "Christian faith knows of no other grace than that which consists in the self-impartation of divine love, or, in other words, the fact that God gives himself."[48] Grace and love are not complete without mercy. The meanings of these three words are so intertwined that a sort of triune dynamic is at work: the three are three yet virtually one in meaning. Mercy is "forgiving love," grace is "mediated mercy,"[49] and love is "the greatest of these" (1 Cor 13:13). If God is "the great ocean of

love,"[50] then grace pulls us in like the tide, and mercy is the sheer
enormity—the horizon-to-horizon expanse—of God's care.

> The steadfast love of the LORD never ceases,
>> his mercies never come to an end;
> they are new every morning;
>> great is your faithfulness. (Lam 3:22-23)

Although they came down on different sides of the issue of predestination, Augustine and John Wesley were both held captive to grace.
Augustine was a dire predestinarian, asserting that the human will,
created free, was now so bound by sin as not to be able to make even
the most preliminary of motions toward God. Salvation was all of God
and all of grace. Wesley denied natural free will, it being a casualty of
Adam's sin, but believed that "every man has a measure of free-will
restored to him by grace."[51] Wesley started his sermon "Free Grace"
with the certain affirmation: "The grace or love of God, whence
cometh our salvation, is free in all, and free for all."[52]

Given his firm reliance on that efficacy of grace alone, with the
resultant predestinarianism, Augustine surprises us by his well-
known saying: "He that made us without ourselves, will not save us
without ourselves."[53] Wesley, who quotes this statement in his sermon
"On Working Out Our Own Salvation," concedes that Augustine "is
generally supposed to favour the contrary doctrine."[54] What could the
great doctor of the church from North Africa mean?

The first half of the statement is clear. The orthodox Christian view
of creation, to which Augustine adhered, stresses that God creates
freely, of his own sovereign choice, and that God creates out of
nothing. God does not create out of already existing stuff, because
then that material stuff would be a rival to God. God does not even
create the world and all that dwells within it out of his own being and
essence, because that would tend toward pantheism. There would be,
if God created all that is out of himself, no final separation between
Creator and creatures.

The world and humankind, if created out of nothing, are even so
created for a definite purpose. "You have made us for yourself,"[55]
testified Augustine. Not only was humanity made under God's ex-

press intent of the desire for divine-human fellowship, but the entire creation is also thus oriented. In the midst of his notably trinitarian eighth chapter of Romans, Paul confesses:

> For the creation waits with eager longing for the revealing of the children of God; for the creation was subjected to futility, not of its own will but by the will of the one who subjected it, in hope that the creation itself will be set free from its bondage to decay and will obtain the freedom of the glory of the children of God. We know that the whole creation has been groaning in labor pains until now; and not only the creation, but we ourselves, who have the first fruits of the Spirit, groan inwardly while we wait for adoption, the redemption of our bodies. (vv. 19-23)

God's making us for himself means that we have been created in the triune image, that God's indelible stamp has been placed on us. Augustine's psychological analogies, seen in their proper light, mean that no one need look any further than his or her own soul to find the Trinity.

God, therefore, did make us without ourselves, but he so molded us after his triune nature that everyone bears the Trinity within. Sin, however, has blocked both our view of God and our view of our own true selves. Sin has so polluted our vision that looking within confronts us only with our perverted selves, not the self as God intended. We are getting closer to understanding Augustine's meaning that God "will not save us without ourselves." Although grace may for Augustine be irresistible, at which point he and John Wesley would part company, the grace that God gives is the grace that enables the self to return to its true home in the Triune God. "Our heart is restless until it rests in you,"[56] confessed Augustine. Grace is what enables rest. Grace acts upon the waiting soul so that it may remember and acknowledge its having been created in the triune image. Our remembrance of God, our understanding of God, our love for God is another of Augustine's psychological analogies.[57] None of those three—remembrance, understanding, love—is possible without grace. The mind, its irrefutable self-knowledge and necessary self-love are also highlighted by Augustine as proof of the Trinity.[58] Grace clarifies the

mind and allows the mind to become transparent to the indwelling
Holy Spirit. Because grace brings us at long last to our true selves,
Augustine can meaningfully assert that God "will not save us without
ourselves." It is not some inert putty that God saves, but the human
self, and God does this through grace.

Musing about grace may seem a strange way to close a chapter
whose chief concerns have been to assert our creation in God's triune
image and to understand its implication for our own growth toward
wholeness. The chapter title is key: "God's Name Bestowed." Grace
is bestowal. Without grace there can be no human transformation into
God's image. Paul Tillich believes that "it would be better to refuse
God and the Christ and the Bible than to accept them without grace.
For if we accept without grace, we do so in the state of separation, and
can only succeed in deepening the separation. We cannot transform
our lives, unless we allow them to be transformed by that stroke of
grace."[59]

Charles Wesley's verse identifies the necessary connectedness between Trinity and grace. Aside from the bestowal of grace by the
Triune God, there is no grace. Aside from grace, our knowledge of God
is limited, warped and perhaps even nonexistent. As Wesley sees it,
grace flows and fills, and we as grace's grateful recipients can only
stand amazed.

Let the Spirit of our Head
Through every member flow.
By our Lord inhabited
We then Immanuel know.
Then He doth His name express,
God in us we truly prove,
Filled with all the life of grace
And all the power of love.[60]

Grace, like the Triune God himself, is a mystery and will remain so
until mortals put on immortality. Even if, as for John Wesley, God's
grace must in one sense be released by human freedom, it is only by
God's grace that we are able to exercise our freedom. An inheritance
left by a departed parent is not increased at all through the children's

acceptance of it. Nor can anyone add one cubit to the awesome edifice of grace by accepting grace. Grace is not an abstraction, not a palace that God constructs for his exclusive use, limiting us to the adjoining dog kennel.[61] No, the palace is for us, but the palace is also cruciform, in the shape of a cross. With all the other pilgrims encircled by mercy, drawn by grace and compelled by love, let us sing:

Holy God, we praise thy Name,
Holy Father, Holy Son, Holy Spirit:
Three we name Thee, though in essence only one;
Undivided God we claim Thee, and adoring
Bend the knee, while we own the Mystery.[62]

4

GOD'S NAME RESTORED

WHEN PAINTERS AND SCULPTORS have tried to depict the Trinity, they frequently have demonstrated a redemptive wrestling of the artistic and the theological. Artists of the ancient and medieval church typically pictured God the Father as the venerable "Ancient of Days," with foreboding gaze and resplendent beard, often atop a throne. God the Son is resting in the bosom of the Father, sitting on his lap, or else descending from the cross under the Father's watchful care. The Holy Spirit, invariably a dove, flutters in the midst of Father and Son, a biblical symbol that Augustine called the "bond of love" between Father and Son. Because the Trinity is best understood as "the incarnate expression of sacrificial love,"[1] any artistic rendering must emphatically point toward the fact that "Christ Jesus came into the world to save sinners" (1 Tim 1:15), an event in which the entire Triune God participates.

Images of the Triune God
Images, whether in life or in theology, are much more important than we commonly acknowledge. God the Father seated on a throne is an image capable of multiple meanings, running the gamut from aloof

and domineering potentate to judicious governor and merciful over-
seer. It is even possible to say, "First you have the images, then come
the words."[2] Images are not idols but are windows into reality. Jesus
Christ is "the image of the invisible God" (Col 1:15). Jesus Christ is
also the Word of God (Jn 1:1), but here "Word of God" is to be taken
symbolically, as itself an image, and not literally.[3] As the Father's
Word, Jesus Christ is not letters on a page but the essential utterance
of God's nature.

As well intentioned as they were, ancient and medieval artists
could never fully succeed in committing to canvas or chiseling from
stone what they knew in their heads and felt in their hearts. No one
can. At best a kind of tritheism emerged, showing three Gods who
were not yet fully realized and related as one God. A perfect portrayal
of the Trinity truly "is as impossible as touching the sky with one's
head."[4] No image of the Trinity could ever fully disclose the triune
mystery, and we must denounce and discard as idolatrous any image
making such a claim. But some images ring truer than others. Images
that are biblically grounded and part of the church's ongoing inter-
pretive tradition are much superior to those that are not.

For example, the Trinity has conveniently been described as being
like water. Water, since it is capable of existing in three states (vapor,
solid and liquid) seems compelling as a symbol of the Trinity. Without
question, water is a powerful religious symbol. Jesus told Nicodemus
that "no one can enter the kingdom of God without being born of
water and Spirit" (Jn 3:5), which seems to many to be Jesus' mandated
endorsement of baptism.[5] Jesus Christ himself came "not with the
water only but with the water and the blood" (1 Jn 5:6). When a soldier
pierced the crucified Christ's side with a spear, both blood and water
flowed forth (Jn 19:34).

This evidence, impressive though it may be, does not lead us into
the presence of the Triune God. As a symbol, water appears signifi-
cantly—but only sporadically—when surveying the whole drama of
salvation. A true image must be manifest throughout the entire history
of salvation, not just in certain episodes. Furthermore, the Bible does
not suggest that ice, water and water vapor can meaningfully be

attached to Father, Son and Holy Spirit or any combination thereof. The Spirit and the water and the blood all agree (1 Jn 5:8), but there is no hint that the Holy Spirit should be thought of as water in a literal sense, although on the Day of Pentecost the Holy Spirit was poured out on all flesh (Acts 2:17).

The point is that no image ought to be stretched beyond a plausible interpretation, for all images must answer to logic and rationality. Symbols, religious or otherwise, may well be above and beyond the strictly rational, but symbols cannot simply be absurd, lunatic or contrary to all reason.

Symbols of the Triune God must also be universal, not necessarily having the same meaning in all times and places, but at least being universally present in all cultures. Bread and wine are universal symbols, for every culture has these or their equivalents. Water in three states fails this test, because (at least before modern refrigeration) some cultures knew nothing of ice.

The symbol of water, then, has a limited utility when applied to the Trinity. Of considerably greater promise are fire and light. Justin Martyr explained the relationship between the Father and his Word using a fire analogy. When one fire is started from another, "the fire from which it is kindled is not diminished but remains the same; while the fire which is kindled from it is seen to exist by itself without diminishing the original fire."[6] When the Father speaks his Word, the Father's divinity is in no way reduced or compromised, even as starting a new fire from an existing fire does not lessen the intensity of the original flame. Regrettably, Justin, like others among his second-century contemporaries, placed the angels before the Holy Spirit[7] and did not extend fire to the Holy Spirit.

Light, too, could be a friendly insight into the Trinity, although some took light metaphors to mean that the Son and the Holy Spirit were subordinate to the Father. Two fourth-century theologians, Gregory of Nyssa and Gregory of Nazianzus, took opposite positions. The first Gregory saw the Trinity as three torches, with no secondary status for the Son or the Spirit, because there can be no "degrees of divinity." The Father's light ignited the Son, who ignited the Spirit.[8] But Gregory of Nazianzus rejected this analysis because he took it to be a hierarchical approach to the Trinity. He said that "to compare the Trinity of Great and Greater and Greatest, as if of Light and Beam and Sun . . . makes a 'ladder of deity' that will not bring us into heaven but out of it."[9] Every living symbol must be capable of differing and even seemingly contradictory interpretations. The two Gregorys well document this, as Nyssa sees light as an equalizing metaphor but Nazianzus sees it as a hierarchical one.

Fire and light are more appropriate symbols for the Triune God than is water. Yet they share the liability with water of not being present throughout the entire narrative of salvation. There was no light when Jesus hung on the cross. It was night (Jn 13:30) when Judas left the company of Jesus and the disciples, and it was not fully light again until the resurrection.

The Triune Cross

The only true, direct and real image of the Triune God is the cross of Jesus Christ. If the image of the cross is exalted, then the appropriate words will follow, words that speak the realities of praise, thanksgiving, fellowship, communion and salvation. The Triune God comes to fullest expression in the triune cross; each is meaningless without the other. Apart from the cross, the Trinity could conceivably remain the center of Christian theology, but it would not be the center of Christian faith.[10]

Because theology seeks to clarify God's revelation so that people may respond to revelation through the totality of their beings (faith), theology that leads away from faith will soon lose its very reason for existence. Faith does not depend on theology, for faith is a total orientation of the self toward the object of faith, to where the one exercising faith becomes united with the object, and it is no longer an object on which one may or may not decide; rather, it is totally present, becoming, in the language of Paul Tillich, an "ultimate concern."

Faith may not depend on theology, but a faith uninformed by the fruits of theological labor will not stand up to scrutiny. Faith can never make its final decision based solely on theological analysis, but a faith without theology is not worth exercising. Faith and theology must always exist in a reciprocal relationship: theology is disciplined reflection on God's revelation, and faith is existential commitment to what revelation requires of us. Theology does not create or invent its own data, for those data are symbolically given in revelation. Faith is not aimless commitment to commitment; it stakes its very life on the truth and trustworthiness of its object. Revelation is the middle term between theology and faith. Theology organizes and analyzes revelation; faith decides for and commits to revelation. Because humans are finite and can neither analyze perfectly nor engage themselves entirely, theology and faith will never exactly overlap. In a totally redeemed world, however, there would be complete identity between theology and faith.

The chief criterion of an image or a symbol is that it must point beyond itself and really engage in the reality that it symbolizes.[11] This means at least two things in our present discussion: First, the Trinity viewed as only a doctrine may be interesting and fascinating on its own terms, even infinitely so, but it remains the Trinity of curiosity and not the Trinity of transformation. Douglas John Hall has wisely said that "the doctrine of the divine triunity, like that of the incarnation, is misconstrued as soon as it becomes interesting in itself."[12] All theology, and especially that which focuses on the Trinity, should never be an end in itself, but "always a means for understanding and developing transformed living."[13] Second, even as the Trinity is not a doctrine closed in upon itself but is God's decisive revelation to us, for us and in us, the cross can likewise not be isolated off by itself, for the cross is God's chosen instrument for imparting triune life to us.

The cross marks Christianity off from all other religions, persuasions and worldviews. Hans Urs von Balthasar believes that "Christianity remains without analogy" because Jesus Christ "remains an unsplittable atom" in the "unity of claim, cross and resurrection."[14] In the cross of Christ we meet not one-third of the Trinity (if it is even possible to divide the Trinity), not Jesus Christ acting alone, but the fullness of God. In the cross we see plainly, as nowhere else, that the Trinity is not abstract and speculative, but an evangelical urgency.[15]

The blood of Christ washes away all abstractions and all pretense, especially our relentless quest for self-salvation. "The place of the doctrine of the Trinity is not the 'thinking of thought,' but the cross of Christ,"[16] Jürgen Moltmann confessed.

Really there should be no division or separation between Christian thought and Christian faith. Faith in Jesus Christ begins at the cross, not in an intellectual journey into the back pages of God. It is exactly in the cross, so trinitarian theology claims, that we learn everything about God that we need to know, or even that is worth knowing. The theology of the cross is the theology of the Triune God, and vice versa. Theology must be critical reflection on the necessity of salvation. There is no salvation apart from the triune cross.

The cross of Golgotha has perhaps not been as sentimentalized as the manger of Bethlehem. The cross can be seen as "old" and "rugged" without being sugarcoated. Søren Kierkegaard was one who would, if he could, rub his hand against the grain of the cross, for the splinters would prick his soul and rouse it from lethargy. Kierkegaard's understanding of theological vocation seems impossibly harsh: "To be a Professor of Theology is to have crucified Christ."[17] He simply means that real theologians must confess that their sins are responsible for the death of Christ.

Kierkegaard asks us to imagine a child thumbing through a picture book or rifling a deck of picture cards. Here is a clown, here is a tiger, here are uncounted sights to amuse and delight. What if, Kierkegaard counters, a crucifixion card is slipped into the deck, unknown to the child? Not the empty tomb, the rejoicing disciples, the resurrected and ascending Christ—no, the raw and brutal crucifixion. Will not the child turn away in grief, in horror, in despair? Will not the child cry for his or her mother?

On the cross, Jesus Christ cried out for his heavenly Father. We have not wanted to hear this cry. Viewing God as less than triune not only will stop our ears to Christ's cry but will stop the cry itself. It was the Son, and not the Father, who was crucified. The Father and the Son are not identical and interchangeable so far as the cross is concerned.

The teaching of the Father's being crucified was rightly condemned by the early church, a heresy called patripassianism, the passion of the Father.[18] The Father does not belong on the cross itself, but neither must the Father be banished from the scene of suffering only to return at the resurrection. The cross is not a one-act drama of the Son alone. It was an angel, and not God, who stayed Abraham's hand from sacrificing Isaac (Gen 22:10-12). God, if watching, watched from a distance. At Calvary, God the Father did not merely watch the death of his Son as a curious onlooker. The Father was in many ways the initiator of the drama, the Son was the focus of the drama, and the Holy Spirit was the One who completed and consummated the drama. From first to last, either the cross is the triune cross or it is the meaningless cross.

Moltmann further states that "the content of the doctrine of the Trinity is the real cross of Christ himself. The form of the crucified Christ is the Trinity."[19] No life is possible without form and content. Form gives life structure, and content gives life depth. The form and content of the Christian life is inescapably triune, and living the cruciform life, in full cognizance of the triune cross, is the life God desires for every human being.

The New Testament clearly teaches that God the Father "hands over" and "delivers up" his Son for our benefit. The Greek word for "deliver up" is a strong word meaning to give over, to betray, to cast out.[20] The Father's delivering up of the Son "is one of the most unheard-of statements in the New Testament,"[21] made by Paul in Romans 8:32: "He who did not withhold his own Son, but gave him up for all of us, will he not with him also give us everything else?" God desires to give us all things, which means sharing totally in the triune life, and only Jesus' death on the cross will suffice to reconcile us to God the Father. Paul is clear about the Father's motivation in subjecting his Son to the cruelest of all deaths: "For our sake he made him to be sin who knew no sin, so that in him we might become the righteousness of God" (2 Cor 5:21). If the Father willingly crucifies his Son, he takes absolutely no pleasure in the death. God the Father is no sadist. God the Father has not cut a deal with the devil, handing over his only begotten Son to the powers of darkness. Some versions of the ransom theory of the atonement have suggested a divine-demonic transaction. God does not deal with the devil, for the devil is a liar.

The Father's motives in subjecting Jesus Christ to death cannot be questioned, nor can the Son's receptivity to the Father's wishes. Not joyfully, but willingly, the Son became a curse for humanity, that all might be redeemed from the curse of the law (Gal 3:13). The Son was unspeakably generous, becoming poor for our sakes, so that we can own all of God's riches in Christ Jesus (2 Cor 8:9). Rejection and abandonment become transformed into acceptance and inheritance at Calvary. The Son is rejected, forsaken and abandoned by his Father. Having worked briefly for a passion play, having seen the crucifixion reenacted two dozen times, the only moving moment for me personally was the agonized cry captured in Mark 15:34: "My God, my God, why have you forsaken me?" Why indeed?

The only possible answer to this question is the one given by the Nicene Creed: "for us and for our salvation." The Father abandons his Son—which is unprecedented in God's entire history and being—*so that we might be saved.* Many Christians will accept with the greatest reluctance John J. O'Donnell's assessment, but accept it we must: "The cross is an event between God and God. . . . The cross is an event in which we see an abyss in the divine life, a division between God and God."[22] Even John Wesley, who, because he believed that true religion means happiness and holiness,[23] might be expected to ignore the triune cross, could not overlook the clear scriptural warrant. It is in fact only through the cross that happiness and holiness will come and will remain. Wesley understood Christ the Son as the fulfillment of the Suffering Servant of Isaiah 53. God the Father is he "'who spared not his own Son,' his only Son, but 'wounded him for our transgressions, and bruised him for our iniquities.' "[24]

The cross is God's wound, given by the Father, received by the Son, overseen by the Holy Spirit. The suffering of the triune cross encompasses the entire Trinity. If an earthly parent is moved by a child's suffering, how much more the infinitely merciful and compassionate Father? It must be the case that, in the words of Daniel Day

Williams, "incarnation involves not only the suffering of the man Jesus, but also the suffering of God the Father. How can we speak of love between Father and Son if the Father is unmoved by the Son's suffering?"[25] God's passionate love for us is God's suffering love for, with and in us. This claim is fundamental for Moltmann's entire theology: "God suffers with us—God suffers from us—God suffers for us: it is this experience of God that reveals the triune God."[26]

The theme of the "crucified God" is well attested in Christian tradition, beginning with certain church fathers and continuing to the present day. Gregory of Nazianzus[27] did not blink at the scandal of the crucified God, and neither did Martin Luther.[28] Charles Wesley followed his older brother John in the frank admission that the cross of Christ must be understood as the cross of the Triune God:

Endless scenes of wonder rise
From that mysterious tree,
Crucified before our eyes,
Where we our Maker see:
Jesus, Lord, what hast Thou done?
Publish we the death divine,
Stop, and gaze, and fall, and own
Was never love like Thine!

Never love nor sorrow was
Like that my Saviour showed:
See Him stretched on yonder Cross,
And crushed beneath our load!
Now discern the Deity,
Now His heavenly birth declare!
Faith cries out: 'Tis He, 'tis He,
My God, that suffers there![29]

"When I Survey the Wondrous Cross" was the commentary Isaac Watts made on Galatians 6:14: "May I never boast of anything except the cross of our Lord Jesus Christ, by which the world has been crucified to me, and I to the world." Watts's poetry transports us to the foot of the cross:

See from his head, his hands, his feet,
Sorrow and love flow mingled down;
Did e'er such love and sorrow meet?
Or thorns compose so rich a crown?[30]

The Triune God is the "crucified God" to whom Dietrich Bonhoeffer witnessed not long before his martyrdom: "God lets himself be pushed out of the world on to the cross. He is weak and powerless in the world, and that is precisely the way, the only way, in which he is with us and helps us."[31] When placed on Jesus' brow, the crown of revulsion—as the world saw it—became the crown of reconciliation.

The values so richly evident in the triune cross are the values of God's kingdom. What the world scorns as weakness and lack of power is the point of entry into the kingdom. God's love at Calvary is sharply at cross-purposes with the hierarchies and structures of worldly wisdom. When we look at the cross, we see love given, received and sustained forevermore. We see love that begins with the Father's wounding of the Son, with the Father's delivering up and handing over his Son, an action the Son experiences as forsakenness. This forsakenness, while decisive, is by no means final. Union. Separation. Reunion. The rhythms of the triune cross are the rhythms of life. "The Father is crucifying love, the Son is crucified love, and the Holy Spirit is the unvanquishable power of the cross."[32] The power of the cross is finally the power of reunion and reconciliation. The Father and the Son are rejoined in the "bond of love" that is the Holy Spirit, and this same Spirit testifies to human hearts that they too can know the abundant life that springs from the triune cross. Our hearts can rest only when "God the Holy Ghost witnesses that God the Father has accepted [us] through the merits of God the Son."[33]

The apostle Paul pronounced simply and compellingly, "I have been crucified with Christ" (Gal 2:19). Paul knew that the only way of attaining resurrection from the dead was conformity to the cross (Phil 3:10-11). The life of suffering was the life of glory—glory hidden now under suffering, awaiting its full manifestation. John of the Cross, a

Spanish spiritual writer of the sixteenth century, lived up to his name
when he wrote:

O sweet cautery
O delightful wound!
O gentle hand! O delicate touch
That tastes of eternal life
And pays every debt!
In killing you changed death to life.[34]

The wound, the hand and the touch are all given through love and
applied to human hearts through love. A poet declared there to be
three sorts of love:

Love that caused us first to be,
Love that bled upon the tree,
Love that draws us lovingly:
We beseech you, hear us.[35]

Causal love, bleeding love, drawing love—these three loves together
are the gospel. Creating love became saving love and indwelling love.
The triune cross is "rooted and grounded in love" so that we "may be
filled with all the fullness of God" (Eph 3:17, 19).

The Son's Benefits, the Spirit's Presence

Philipp Melanchthon, a Lutheran theologian of the Protestant Reformation, believed that "to know Christ means to know his benefits.
. . . For unless you know why Christ put on flesh and was nailed to
the cross, what good will it do you to know merely the history about
him? . . . Christ was given us as a remedy and, to use the language of
Scripture, a saving remedy (Luke 2:30, 3:6; Acts 28:28)."[36]

We have established that Christ's benefits can best be known—really can *only* be known—through the triune cross, just as God himself
is best known as triune. Knowing Christ through his cross means that
a saving knowledge is a suffering knowledge.

Any employee joining a company hears all about its benefits: day
care, maternity leave, pension plan, health insurance. The benefits of
Christ are differently accented: cross-bearing, persecution-enduring,
righteousness-hungering and—finally—eternal life. Anyone who

sees only the outcome of eternal life and ignores the path leading to it knows neither Christ nor his benefits.

As has often been said, the cross is the intersection of heaven and earth, the point of contact between the human search for the divine and the divine search for the human. The two searches are neither equal nor identical—not equal, because God is God and humankind is human; not identical, because God's search for humankind is always prior to the human quest for God. That is the meaning of prevenient grace, grace that initiates and goes before. Poetically put by Søren Kierkegaard, God is "a spring that itself seeks out the thirsty traveller, the errant wanderer: who has ever heard the like of any spring!"[37] Many gods play hide-and-seek with those who try to find them, and even when found, their resources are soon drained and exhausted. Only of the Triune God can it be said: "Thou dost not remain, like the spring, in a single place, but Thou dost follow the traveller on his way."[38] The Triune God not only follows the thirsty traveler but goes before and walks alongside also. "Where can I go from your Spirit?" (Ps 139:7 NIV).

The first Christians knew the Triune God more by proclamation and declaration than by investigation and interrogation. Their grasp of God was that God had grasped them in Jesus Christ. It was in the name of Jesus Christ that the earliest Christians were washed, sanctified and justified (1 Cor 6:11). Jesus Christ put a face on God and a claim on those who recognized that face for what it was: "the reflection of God's glory and the exact imprint of God's very being" (Heb 1:3). The act of recognizing the face of God is the work of the Holy Spirit within. It is the Holy Spirit who opens the eyes of our hearts (Eph 1:18), who guides our hands to touch the face of God. The name of Jesus Christ is the only name whereby we can be washed, sanctified and justified, but Paul makes it clear that we can pronounce this name only "in the Spirit of our God" (1 Cor 6:11). If Jesus Christ is "the exteriorization of God," then the Holy Spirit surely must be "the breathing forth of [God's] *inner love*"[39] or even, stated picturesouely, "the Flower of the Divine Tree."[40]

The benefits of Christ Jesus that Melanchthon wanted to know above all else must be applied by the Holy Spirit. In his sermon "The Means of Grace," John Wesley stressed that whatever means of grace are used, the solitary purpose is to "seek God alone. In and through every outward thing look singly to the *power* of his Spirit and the *merits* of his Son."[41] No Christian can focus spiritual vision through a sheer act of the unaided human will. Looking to the cross can never be a random glance, but is the ministry of the abiding Holy Spirit. The power of the Holy Spirit winnows and makes single, making all aware that salvation is only through the Son's merits.

To be founded wholly and without exception upon God is the essence of sanctification. This is the special province—and providence—of the Holy Spirit. Sanctification is simply bearing the full likeness of God within and without, and only God the Holy Spirit can introduce us to and encourage us toward such a complete identity with God's original intent for us. God's desire, in Charles Wesley's preaching, is "that total renovation, that sanctification of spirit, soul, and body, 'without which no man shall see the Lord.' "[42]

The great mystery and uncertainty surrounding the Person and work of the Holy Spirit has caused many to view the Spirit as the personification of every religious hunch and urge ever known to humankind. The Holy Spirit is said to be the religious germ lurking within everyone, which can take root and grow. This assessment is partially true, but in its falseness it is dangerously false. The diagnosis and description are true: God has not left himself without a witness. Implanted within every heart is the craving for the divine. God has placed it there through creating us. Yet correct diagnosis is one thing; true satisfaction of our religious need is quite another. "The longing of the human heart is so immense and so profound that only God is great enough to fulfil it," says Walter Kasper.[43] To know the religious need, and even to feed the religious hunger that is powerfully and innately felt, can be very far from God's provision: "Blessed are those who hunger and thirst for righteousness, for they will be filled" (Mt 5:6).

Righteousness is not a haphazard concept, capable of being bent and twisted to please whoever is defining it. Righteousness is woven over, around and through the triune cross. Sin repulsed and offended the righteousness of God the Father. Jesus Christ the righteous assumed the world's debt to the Father and paid it. Through the Holy Spirit all can know God's righteousness firsthand. For Charles Wesley, the definition of a Christian is transparent: "He is a Christian who hath received the Spirit of Christ. He is not a Christian who hath not received him. Neither is it possible to have received him and not know it."[44] The Holy Spirit undoubtedly is at work when anyone feels a pulling or inclination toward God. Faithful attendance upon the Spirit's ministrations will lead the soul to God's righteousness won for humanity by Jesus Christ. In other words, the yearnings provoked by the Spirit can be met only by Jesus Christ. The fact that Father, Son and Holy Spirit are fully engaged and working toward our full salvation from first to last is amply shown by Paul's letter to Titus:

> But when the goodness and loving kindness of God our Savior appeared, he saved us, not because of any works of righteousness that we had done, but according to his mercy, through the water of rebirth and renewal by the Holy Spirit. This Spirit he poured out on us richly through Jesus Christ our Savior, so that, having been justified by his grace, we might become heirs according to the hope of eternal life. The saying is sure. (3:4-8)

The Holy Spirit channels innate religious curiosity toward Jesus Christ, its only possible fulfillment. The "living water" offered by Jesus not only cleanses the palate of sin, so to speak, so that one appears blameless before the Father, but also produces in one a more discriminating palate, where the realities of God nourish and sustain as never before. "As this life of Christ is deepened in us by the Holy Spirit, there is created in the Christian a 'sense of Christ,' a taste and instinctual judgment for the things of God, a deeper perception of God's truth, an increased understanding of God's dispositions and love toward us."[45]

Could one ever develop an "instinctual judgment" for God? Yes, if instinct means a return to what God had intended for humankind—namely, life "from him and through him and to him" (Rom 11:36), and we must add "in him." Life in the Triune God is what Augustine meant in declaring that the soul is by nature Christian. "Natural" life is triune life, the life of God's primal call, the life of fresh grace. What passes for a "natural" life in the world of media and influence is really perverse. It is self-driven and not God-seeking. God's reality is that "in the Spirit we have access through Christ to the Father, so that in this way we may share in the divine nature."[46]

The Holy Spirit is rightfully called the Spirit of God and the Spirit of Christ.[47] The Spirit's traditional depiction as a dove suggests a fluid presence in the midst of Father and Son. Because of this fluid identity, where the Spirit is of God (Gal 3:5) and of the Son (Gal 4:6), in the same book in adjoining chapters, detractors have impugned the Spirit's identity. Some have gone so far as to say that Christianity is about Jesus and the Father only, since the Holy Spirit is obviously not a distinct divine Person.

Corporate America is discovering that true leadership is servant leadership. The Triune God has known eternally that servant love is transforming love. In love the Holy Spirit offers himself to serve the Son and the Father. The Spirit offers to serve not because of any lesser status, but because he is the "bond of love" between the Father and the Son. The Holy Spirit has been called "the shy member of the Trinity," because it is the Spirit's special calling to focus all thoughts on the Father's disclosure in Jesus Christ. Perhaps the Holy Spirit is rather like a narrator in a stage drama. The narrator is absolutely essential for the continuity of the production and in that sense is vitally a part of the drama, yet the narrator would think it presumptuous to upstage the actors. The Holy Spirit assuredly *is* an actor in the drama of salvation, but an actor behind the scenes, not demanding top billing or his name up in lights. The Holy Spirit's deepest desire is for our learning, knowing and discerning.

In his maturity, approaching his eighty-sixth year, John Wesley understood the impulses of the Holy Spirit. The Spirit reveals Father and Son to each other and kindles love in our hearts: "As soon as the Father of spirits reveals his Son in our hearts, and the Son reveals his Father, the love of God is shed abroad in our hearts; then, and not till then, we are happy."[48]

The Depths of God

The Holy Spirit searches all things, even the depths of God (1 Cor 2:10). The act of searching is often thought to indicate a lack, a confusion or an emptiness. Searching heated by zeal and singed by intensity can only be called "frantic." Searching can be a quest for some viable middle ground, as when warring factions in a labor dispute are "searching for a compromise solution." AIDS researchers are assiduously "searching for a cure," because in fact millions of lives stand to be lost. Many an adolescent has set out on a "search for self" that may never end.

Searching seems an odd fit with God. From the human side, God's evangelical thrust toward humanity, the making known of "the gospel of God" (1 Thess 2:2), could be called a "search and rescue" mission. The forces of evil are bent on a "search and destroy" calamity, but God in Christ Jesus has overcome the world. "Search and rescue" fits the human need, but does it fit the divine character? Atheists have hooted that if there is a God, this God is so out of touch with modern reality and historical energies as to be a bumbler, incompetent. An atheistic reading of the Spirit's searching the depths of God would mock, as Friedrich Nietzsche did, that God must be lost. The prophet Isaiah lamented his own lostness (Is 6:5); how can a God perpetually lost hope to help Isaiah—or anyone?

Why does the Holy Spirit search the depths of God? Paul suggests an analogy. Only the human spirit within each person can begin to fathom what is truly human. Humankind can be known only by humankind, Paul says. Deep calls out to deep; like resonates with like. Paul immediately elevates the conversation from humanity to God: "So also no one comprehends what is truly God's except the Spirit of God" (1 Cor 2:11). The Holy Spirit's search is therefore not one of futility, but one of truth and comprehension. "Why would anyone search for what he already has?" someone may ask. Jesus Christ confessed himself to be the essence of truth (Jn 14:6). The Holy Spirit is the Spirit of truth (Jn 14:17) given by the Father. The Triune God is the God of truth and the one true God.

The Holy Spirit's search is not a search *for* truth. Pilate's question to Jesus, "What is truth?" (Jn 18:38), ranks as one of the most presumptuous questions ever. Kierkegaard believed that the outcome of Pilate's question was his condemning of Christ to be crucified.[49] When the truth incarnate is standing before you, it is absurd to raise the question "What is truth?" Here *is* truth! The Holy Spirit's search is one *of* truth and *in* truth. It is a truthful search, a search planned in truth, conducted in truth, ending in truth. The glory of the Son of God is the glory of his being filled with grace and truth (Jn 1:14).

The depths of God are not murky and clouded like the bottom of a muddy river. God is not a source of puzzlement and confusion to himself. God's depths are infinitely pure and crystalline, far surpassing the cleanest, clearest lake. The Holy Spirit's searching of God's depths is not to introduce God to himself. God's triunity ensures that from all eternity there has been reciprocity and give-and-take within God. Father, Son and Holy Spirit all have perfect knowledge of one another. God needs no guided tour of his own depths. God lives within his own depths. Would the president of the United States of America stand in line to take a tour of the White House? He may perhaps do so to make a political statement of humility and equality, but not to learn anything new.

God, to extend the analogy, needs no tour of heaven. If a U.S. president offered to conduct a tour of the White House, that is a dim approximation of the Spirit's searching of God's depths, because the Spirit's search is motivated not by God's felt lack, but by God's hunger to share triune life with humankind. No common tourist would expect to see the White House living quarters of the president and his family. Anyone making this attempt would be charged with trespassing. Yet in searching God's depths, the Holy Spirit opens God's depths—every millimeter of divine presence—to human participation. God would have it no other way.

The Holy Spirit's journey into God is therefore really for human benefit. The Spirit's motivation is directed squarely toward this outcome: "that we may understand the gifts bestowed on us by God" (1 Cor 2:12).

Parents can become frantic during a gift-giving season if money is tight. They anxiously search for extra money to expend toward their children's happiness. The Father's perfect bestowal is Jesus Christ, a costly gift of free and infinite grace. This gift having been given at Calvary, the Holy Spirit understands the Father's great cost and the Son's flawless sacrifice. God's depths reveal the fullness of love, and the Holy Spirit elevates human understanding and teaches by divine wisdom, "interpreting spiritual things to those who are spiritual" (1 Cor 2:13). Membership among "those who are spiritual" is not cliquish or clannish, for the Spirit's search of God—conducted in freedom and conducted for us—is God's openness to the entire world.

The human search for God is typically disjunctive. How could it be otherwise? Humankind torn by original sin carries out its search with flawed instruments and skewed perspectives. Paul was paying humanity a compliment in writing that only the human spirit within really knows what is truly human (1 Cor 2:11). The "truly human" was and remains God's primordial design in creating humankind. God wanted and still wants fellowship with those he created. Sin's radical inroads have disrupted God's created harmony, interposing between God's plan and human achievement a perverted and depraved will. Humanity has chosen its own way rather than God's way. Truly human expression must be continually made through God's enabling grace. When the Holy Spirit makes God's depths available to us, they are depths of grace.

If the human quest for the divine is disjunctive, then God's approach to humans is conjunctive. God's search has only one goal: "to sanctify the people by his own blood" (Heb 13:12). "His" blood refers of course to the blood of Jesus. It may be disrespectful to talk of "the blood of God," but as we have seen, the cross cannot be assigned to only the second Person of the Trinity. Sanctification is conjunctive, because it means joining God's kingdom fully, unreservedly and completely. A disjunctive search does not know where to turn next and has no drive toward completion. A disjunctive quest is by definition never-ending. God's conjunctive search is also never-ending, but its dynamism is grace, its provision the cross, its goal the restoration of all people "not only to the favour, but likewise to the image of God."[50]

Sanctification infuses human life with triune life. God's love energizes and transforms human love. Along with infusion, sanctification can and should be discussed under many different aspects. Sanctification is a many-splendored thing, but mostly it is God's life opened to human participation. Cleansing, infilling, making whole and therefore perfect, ingrafting—these are only the most obvious pointers toward God's sanctifying grace. The triune principle of the several acting as one is obviously operative here, for there is much cross-fertilization among these four or five ways of naming sanctification.

For me personally, sanctification as renewal and restoration is the most compelling vision. John Wesley, foremost persuader of and witness to sanctification, saw it thus: "Gospel holiness is no less than the image of God stamped upon the heart."[51] When the hymn writer wished to describe life in conformity to God, he used a similar figure: "Stamp Thine own image deep on my heart."[52] The image of God, relinquished through sin, is reclaimed through sanctifying grace. "Renewing men in that image of God wherein they were created"[53] is for Wesley the special province of the Holy Spirit. The renewed Christian is the simple Christian, shorn of excess and freed from every hint of self-salvation. Renewed Christians can stand up to scrutiny, for "whosoever desires may look into their hearts and see that only love and God are there."[54] Only God and love are there, because the Holy Spirit is doing his purging, cleansing, illuminating work.

True religion is not an empty concept begging to be filled by every wild scheme; it is not, as someone humorously said, what people do with their spare time. The sanctified soul may have spare time but not idle moments, for the sanctified one is continually hungry for fresh supplies of grace. "The great end of religion," said Wesley, "is to renew our hearts in the image of God, to repair that total loss of righteousness and true holiness which we sustained by the sin of our first parent."[55] Wesley's choice of the word *repair* might not seem sufficiently strong to offset what follows—namely, the "total loss of righteousness and true holiness." We must remember, however, with whom we are dealing—God and not a human being—and that with God all things are possible. A wreck of a car deemed hopeless by the average person can be firing on all cylinders after being attended to by a master mechanic. How much more can the Triune God repair wrecked lives!

Cultural images of restoration abound. An antique cannot be fully appreciated until it has been painstakingly restored. An old house or even a once grand train station will similarly languish unless the work of restoration is carefully applied. The labored restoration of Michelangelo's frescoes on the ceiling of the Sistine Chapel sparked enormous debate. Could Michelangelo's original colors be determined? Once determined, could they be retrieved? This debate was not satisfactorily resolved and perhaps never will be. The knowledge and wisdom of art historians is often all too limited. The Triune God has no such limitations. God knows us as we are in actuality, envisions us as we could be in possibility, and works via his grace to close the gap between the actual and the possible. The God who inspired Paul to write, "For this is the will of God, your sanctification" (1 Thess 4:3), will faithfully complete the work once begun (Phil 1:6).

The Triune God is both a restorationist and a preservationist. Directors of museums may see those tasks as distinct, but God does not. A preservationist may be overly scrupulous in the attempt to duplicate every detail of the past, while a restorationist may restore more according to the canons of modern taste than in homage to a retreating past. In God's hands, preservation is never mere nostalgia, and restoration is never shallow trendiness. God both preserves and restores, simultaneously, in one and the same movement. God restores human lives to wholeness to preserve the divine intent of creation. The restored life looks two ways—back to God's foundational plan for that life and forward to the day of consummation and glorification. But preeminently and over all, the restored life looks toward "Jesus the pioneer and perfecter of our faith" (Heb 12:2) and to the God who declared, "See, I am making all things new" (Rev 21:5).

God's act of restoration is a little bit like the great joy that accompanies the discovery of a missing movement of a grand symphony.

However beautiful the work of art may have previously been, when it can be presented in its original glory and power, performers and listeners alike experience a deep satisfaction. Experts might remain divided as to the proper way of playing the newly found movement, the proper nuancing of musical dynamics, but all would rejoice in the discovery. As Paul knew, "when the complete comes, the partial will come to an end" (1 Cor 13:10).

The symphony played without the missing movement will undoubtedly still possess a certain beauty and magnificence, but not so the partial life. Any partial life is bound to be deficient at the point of God's grace, and God's provision of sanctifying grace, with which human effort must surely cooperate, frequently works at its own mysterious pace. Anyone restoring an antique understands that such work is best undertaken from motives of love; great art cannot be rushed. The art of creating a person is God's art alive. No human act of restoration, be it poetic, artistic, architectural or historical, can perfectly intuit the original intent of the creator. Souls conceived by God can be fully realized only by God's care. C. S. Lewis makes clear with whom we have to do: "But the question is not what we intended ourselves to be, but what [God] intended us to be when He made us. He is the inventor, we are only the machine. He is the painter, we are only the picture. How should we know what He means us to be like? . . . But all the time He knew His plan for us and was determined to carry it out."[56]

One of the greatest poetic witnesses to the Triune God and the life he makes available to us is Charles Wesley's wondrous hymn "Love Divine, All Loves Excelling." The whole tenor of this hymn is incarnational and transformational. On one level it appears that the first three stanzas are devoted, respectively, to Son, Holy Spirit and Father, yet the total impression is of the oneness, rather than the triple distinctiveness, of God's work. Wesley's vision climaxes in the fourth stanza with his prayer for God's completion of God's new creation in purity, without spot or blemish, perfectly realized and restored in God. The total effect on the rapt soul can only be "wonder, love and praise!"

Love Divine, all loves excelling,
Joy of heaven, to earth come down,
Fix in us Thy humble dwelling,
All Thy faithful mercies crown:
Jesus, Thou art all compassion,
Pure, unbounded love Thou art,
Visit us with Thy salvation,
Enter every trembling heart.

Breathe, O breathe Thy loving Spirit,
Into every troubled breast,
Let us all in Thee inherit,
Let us find that second rest:
Take away our *power* of sinning,
Alpha and Omega be,
End of faith as its Beginning,
Set our hearts at liberty.

Come, Almighty to deliver,
Let us all Thy life receive;
Suddenly return, and never,
Never more Thy temples leave.
Thee we would be always blessing,
Serve Thee as Thy hosts above,
Pray, and praise Thee without ceasing,
Glory in Thy perfect love.

Finish then Thy new creation,
Pure and spotless let us be,
Let us see Thy great salvation,
Perfectly restored in Thee:
Changed from glory into glory,
Till in heaven we take our place,
Till we cast our crowns before Thee,
Lost in wonder, love and praise![57]

Life, Light and Love

Having shaped us for divine fellowship, God will not rest until human estrangement from him is overcome. God's vision is that every person should become "a bright stainless mirror which reflects back to God perfectly (though, of course, on a smaller scale) His own boundless power and delight and goodness."[58]

God's tenacity and sincerity in carrying forth this restoration can be sidetracked only by human hesitance. All along the way, God has faithfully provided witnesses to his intent for humanity, culminating in Jesus Christ, the light of the world (Jn 8:12). Jesus himself declared John the Baptist to be "a burning and shining lamp" (Jn 5:35), and the psalmist exulted in an implicitly triune thought, "For with you is the fountain of life; in your light we see light" (Ps 36:9). The psalmist understands that God is not alone; God must necessarily express himself in the fountain of life, imagery that suggests both the living water of Jesus Christ (Jn 4:14) and the pouring forth of the Holy Spirit (Acts 2:17). God's light is not self-contained; it illumines everything. The final source of light can only be God, and not humanity, yet God's light is meant to bring everyone to a true self-recognition, even if this is at times a painful one. The light we see is always God's light, and the Holy Spirit invites us within, to step and walk in divine light. In so doing, a vision of God's intent for each soul is held before it. No one can remain in God's light without coming into ever greater conformity to that light.

The Triune God is the God not only of light but also of life and love. Among the many, perhaps infinite, characterizations one could offer of the Triune God, few are more accurate and insightful than God's being the fullness of life, light and love. John's contributions to the New Testament especially explore this triad,[59] which is not surprising considering that of all New Testament authors, John is the most adept at moving beyond the simple triad of Father, Son and Holy Spirit to the profound reality of their interpenetration. In John's Gospel Jesus declares: "The Father and I are one" (10:30). Life, light and love, aside from being intrinsically attractive and adaptable religious symbols, well capture the fellowship among the divine Persons, fellowship the

Triune God wishes to share fully: life that is energized by light and love, light that burns with love and illumines life in a truthful way, and love that engenders life and light in others. It would be foolish and counterproductive to try to separate life, light and love from each other. They are like the rhythms of time that we arbitrarily label as past, present and future, while we intuitively know that time cannot be divided. Earlier I quoted a theologian who described Jesus Christ as "an unsplittable atom," and this phrase well applies to life, light and love. What Augustine said about Father, Son and Holy Spirit seems peculiarly apt when thinking of life, light and love: "Each is in each, all are in each, each is in all, all are in all, and all are one."[60] Each of the divine Persons is himself the perfect fullness of life, light and love. Their love for and fellowship with one another does not increase these qualities, for no triune Person has any lack or deficit whatsoever. Perfectly engaged and realized, the triune community extends itself to all who desire to join it, that they too may abide in life, light and love.

For all of their relatedness and cohesiveness, life, light and love can be distinguished one from the other. These are, after all, three words and concepts and not one. Yet rather like a famous trio of singers such as Peter, Paul and Mary, life, light and love are at their best not as solo performers, but intertwined. The harmony is more compelling than the most polished solo act. In the incarnate Word of the Father, life and light were such an efficacious pair that love was spontaneously generated from the coupling: "In him was life, and the life was the light of all people" (Jn 1:4).

Only when they are acknowledged to spring directly from the very being of God can life, light and love become a functional trinity of three-in-one and not just another triad. None of these three has a life of its own apart from God. It is true that "life and love, by their very nature, are dynamic and overflowing,"[61] but this is true only if life and love emanate from God. They have no nature of their own. They should not be discussed in isolation from the divine nature. They are meaningless abstractions unless infused with divine life.

A versatile trio of singers has presumably at a minimum mastered three-part harmony. Depending on the gender mix and range of voices involved, it is conceivable that different singers could at different times switch off parts for variety, texture and surprise. Subtly varied harmonies could result. However skilled each singer may be, it is likely that each one will retain his or her own unique identity, as in "I am a baritone, not a bass" or "Although I can sing soprano, I am really an alto."

Consider the further example of three-on-three basketball, which is currently a popular format for amateur tournaments. No successful team would want three players with the same skills and attributes. Such a team would never be successful. A team stocked with fancy scorers would lack defense and rebounding. A team of three defenders and rebounders might win a lot of games but would be boring to watch and maybe even boring to be a part of. The best three-player basketball team would have three excellent competitors who each specialized in one of the following areas: (1) ball handling, passing and play making, (2) scoring, (3) defense, shot blocking and rebounding.

Analogies from athletics and music are at best only human, for the Triune God infinitely exceeds the human capacity even to comprehend the infinite distance between God and humanity. The songs of God explore tonal structures unknown to humanity; the sports of God are infinitely exciting and exhilarating but have no losers. Yet even given all conceivable limitations, the Trinity still is vaguely like the three-member basketball squad and the trio of singers. Each of the divine Persons *is* a specialist, not haughtily or competitively so, or to show up the other two. And the specialized work launched by any one of the three is only consummated and perfected through the contributions of the other two.

The Father, for example, may be regarded in some sense as the source of life, but the Father's life is the Son, and the sharing of life between Father and Son is the Holy Spirit. The apostle James called the first Person of the Trinity "the Father of lights" (Jas 1:17), and yet it is precisely Jesus Christ who is the Father's only begotten Light. The reality of God's triunity is that the presence of one, even if a focused

and highlighted presence, is necessarily the fullness of all. Paul understands that the God of creation is at once the God of redemption and
that only triune light can banish the darkness: "For it is the God who
said, 'Let light shine out of darkness,' who has shone in our hearts to
give the light of the knowledge of the glory of God in the face of Jesus
Christ" (2 Cor 4:6). The light of God, which is uncreated because it is
of God's very essence, is sent forth by the Father, becomes incarnate in
the Son, and shines in willing human hearts via the Holy Spirit.

If one accepts John's premise that "God is light and in him there is
no darkness at all" (1 Jn 1:5), whether John means God the Father, God
the Son or God the Holy Spirit is insignificant and quite beside the
point. John means nothing less than that the Triune God is filled with
light. Each triune Person pours forth life, light and love in equal
measure with unceasing passion and perfect execution. Knowing this,
the Christian is edified when Jesus Christ, in Augustine's portrayal,
says this about himself: "I am come as a Word from the heart, as a ray
from the sun, as heat from the fire, as fragrance from the flower, as a
stream from a perennial fountain."[62] The results are no less striking
when Jonathan Edwards shifts the focus from God the Son to God the
Holy Spirit:

> I have many times had a sense of the glory of the third person in
> the Trinity, in his office of Sanctifier; in his holy operations, com-
> municating divine light and life to the soul. God, in the communi-
> cation of his Holy Spirit, has appeared as an infinite fountain of
> divine glory and sweetness; being full, and sufficient to fill and
> satisfy the soul; pouring forth itself in sweet communication; like
> the sun in its glory, sweetly and pleasantly diffusing light and life.
> And I have sometimes had an affecting sense of the excellency of
> the word of God, as a word of life; as the light of life; a sweet,
> excellent lifegiving word; accompanied with a thirsting after that
> word, that it might dwell richly in my heart.[63]

Simply and directly, Jesus Christ said, "I have come as light into the
world, so that everyone who believes in me should not remain in the
darkness" (Jn 12:46). The Holy Spirit, as Edwards so richly believed,
is the warmth of Christ's light illuminating and healing all willing

souls, sanctifying and enlisting them as the children of light. The Word of God, by which Edwards means the Bible, is the record of the saving activity of God in Christ Jesus. It is altogether natural that the Holy Spirit would lead the eager heart into the Holy Scriptures. There, following Edwards, one will discover sweetness and excellence. But every heart must understand that the Triune God cannot compromise with sin and that the Holy Spirit must convict of sin before Jesus Christ can save from sin. Not all will accept the Spirit's rebuke; many will continue to love "darkness rather than light because their deeds [are] evil" (Jn 3:19). The sinner who through grace turns toward God's light will be encouraged and undergirded in the act of turning. As character is changed, dispositions altered and virtue refined, the turning toward God will be immersion in sanctifying light.

God's total presence in the world is light, although sinners refuse to see the light. Sinners create their own universe, centered on self and bent on destruction. In God's universe, divine light perpetually gleams and the Holy Spirit continually invites. The Spirit's merciful prod from human deprivation to divine salvation does not reduce God's mystery or potency. Because even the sun will eventually burn out, and the sun presumably is the closest thing to infinite light we have, we must be careful not to presume upon God's light. It is an inviting light, yet an awesome light, for it is God alone "who has immortality and dwells in unapproachable light, whom no one has ever seen or can see" (1 Tim 6:16). Timothy's reminder of God's unspeakable majesty is never wasted on anyone. God is unapproachable, which is why God has chosen to approach us in Jesus Christ. Sanctification is the desired culmination of God's approach to humankind—that is, the sanctified heart is the heart wherein God's image is being fully restored.

A restoration of similarity, sanctification is also the decrease of dissimilarity between the divine and human hearts. The obvious definition of sanctification is conformity to God, but a differently accented understanding also has much utility and wisdom: sanctification is "becoming less unlike God in one's being and behavior."[64] The accent on overcoming dissimilarity keeps us squarely in God's gracious presence and prevents our believing that sanctification is just a smoothly orchestrated exercise of our natural religiosity. Humans were like God before sin interposed. As sinners, humans are radically unlike God. Jesus Christ is the sinner's only way back to God. Jesus Christ came into the world to ignite divine fires in human hearts. The prophet Malachi, in a phrase many have taken to point ahead to the Christ, believed in the rising "sun of righteousness" (4:2), immortalized in Charles Wesley's Christmas classic:

Hail, the Heaven-born Prince of Peace!

Hail, the Sun of righteousness!

Light and life to all He brings,

Risen with healing in His wings.[65]

The sun of righteousness is sanctifying light. When the Holy Spirit shines the light of Christ, the waiting heart will also rise with healing toward fully joining with God's triune life. It is a flight toward divine likeness and away from unlikeness. Celestial fires are incalculably hotter and more intense than earthbound ones. Campers telling stories around a bristling fire know there is an organic relationship between their local combustion and the starry fires in the heavens. But none would foolishly conclude that the campfire is greater than the fire in the sky. Becoming less unlike God means extinguishing the lingering blazes of pride and ego within and becoming instead totally consumed by Jesus Christ, the Sun of Righteousness.

Life, light and love are among God's best ways of allowing us to experience the divine totality. They are three undeniable ways God has of inviting us to human wholeness and to becoming engrafted into the divine life. They are God's eye on the world, purging and clarifying each soul's vision of God, others and self. "If your eye is healthy, your whole body will be full of light" (Mt 6:22), Jesus assured us. To open oneself to God's life, light and love is to dwell richly in grace. Symeon (949-1032), known to tradition as "the New Theologian," wrote that "those who have not received the light have not yet received grace. Those who have received grace have received the light of God and have received God, even as Christ Himself, who is the light, has said, 'I will live in them and move among them' (2 Cor

6:16)."[66] In John Wesley's understanding, the one reclaimed by grace and restored through the sanctifying Spirit "knows what the peace of God is; what is joy in the Holy Ghost; what is the love of God which is shed abroad in the hearts of them that believe through Christ Jesus."[67]

God's triune life descends from the Father to be perfectly refracted in his only begotten Son. The Holy Spirit energizes and focuses the Father's uncreated Light, so that humankind might hear, see and touch it (1 Jn 1:1). Uncreated because it is eternal, the Light of the World is God's love for the world, and the Holy Spirit is God's abiding presence in the world. Where the Holy Spirit dwells, there is the transforming love of Jesus Christ. Because the Spirit of God is as wide as creation (Gen 1:2; Jn 3:8), God's hope for a renewed creation is equally unbounded. Because God notices when sparrows fall and counts hairs (Mt 10:29-31), God's Spirit penetrates the heart's inner recesses. "Where the Spirit of the Lord is, there is freedom" (2 Cor 3:17), freedom to live continually in the Son's light and the Spirit's love, a life sent from God and destined to return to God.

The Immediacy of God

In many cultures children are impressed at an early age that it is wrong to point at people, especially at strangers. The reason for teaching children not to point is obvious: pointing is rude and obnoxious, for it violates the personal integrity of its target. The pointing child soon becomes disrespectful toward elders and may even try to manipulate parents. What motivates the pointing is surely not all bad; it is the sense of otherness and mystery confronting the child, in whose presence the child feels slightly uneasy. Pointing may be the child's attempt to break the ice of the unfamiliar and experience another person and dimension of being.

My mother tells me that when I was a small child, I once exclaimed, no doubt pointing as I did so, "Who's the man with the black mask on?" My experience with black people had been minimal up until then, and my curiosity was therefore justified, although crudely put in a five-year-old's vernacular.

Humanity's innate religious hunger means that everyone points toward the unknown, hoping to encounter otherness. This inherent urge to meet with the divine—any divine—leaves no stone unturned. However real and sincerely undertaken any religious quest may be, it comes to nothing unless it springs from the Triune God and returns to the Triune God. No one is capable, humanly speaking, of successfully pointing toward God. God remains forever unknown if that is God's choice. It is the Christian affirmation, however, that as Trinity God points to and identifies himself; the Trinity is God's perfect correspondence to and notification of himself. The length and breadth and depth of God's revelation is Jesus Christ, sent from the Father through the pulsating love of the Holy Spirit. Because God has identified himself as triune, Christians have the joyful privilege of bearing witness—even of pointing!—to God's incarnation in Jesus Christ. Every Christian must be a John the Baptist, signifying the Savior, as the Baptist does in Matthias Grünewald's remarkable sixteenth-century painting *The Crucifixion*.

Pointing to the bleeding Savior carries its own certain risks. Those who truly point will be noticed, and their lives will be scrutinized by a curious and doubting world. Their lives will also be scrutinized by God:

Search me, O God, and know my heart today.
Try me, O Savior; know my thoughts, I pray.
See if there be some wicked way in me;
Cleanse me from ev'ry sin, and set me free.[68]

No one who witnesses for God in the world can expect to be ignored by God. God must ensure that those who stand for God are indeed filled by God.

The positive steps taken by Christians toward the goal of God's totally infilling presence are collectively known as Christian spirituality. Kierkegaard used the phrase "training in Christianity" and said that Jesus desired not admirers but followers. Because it is "religious exercise as well as religious experience,"[69] the goal of Christian spirituality is simply to produce followers of Jesus Christ, not fair-weather friends but true disciples. Theologian Geoffrey Wainwright defines spirituality in a trinitarian way, as "an existence before God and amid the created world. It is a praying and living in Jesus Christ. It is the human spirit being grasped, sustained, and transformed by the Holy Spirit. It is the search of believers for a communion that arrives as a gift. It is a present anticipation of the divine kingdom and human salvation awaited in an age to come."[70]

Within Wainwright's definition are many of the practices, attitudes and qualifying factors of any Christian spirituality: prayer, searching, waiting and anticipation, being grasped, living in the created world. These practices and attitudes arise from the Triune God and can be perfected only in him, so that "Christian spirituality is not incidentally but essentially Trinitarian. The Christian must be one with Christ in sonship of the Father and in the Holy Spirit."[71]

Spiritual depth intensifies through sharing in the means of God's grace. John Wesley is typical in listing the following as God's chosen ordinances for the imparting of divine life: "public worship of God; the ministry of the word, either read or expounded; the Supper of the Lord; private prayer; searching the Scriptures; and fasting, or abstinence."[72] Wesley also endorsed what he called "Christian Conference," the intimate acquaintance shared by believers among themselves. Wesley believed that because God's grace is unlimited and effusive, the means of grace "are varied, transposed, and combined together a thousand different ways."[73] Grace's universal availability does not, however, suggest that it comes from any source other than God's unceasing love. In employing the means of grace, Wesley insisted on a trinitarian criterion. "In using all means," he advised, "seek God alone. In and through every outward thing look singly to the *power* of his Spirit and the *merits* of his Son."[74]

Giving praise to God is not often listed as a means of grace. It ought to be. Taking Wesley's advice and looking singly to God is bound to provoke praise. The life of praise is the life of beatitude, the life of doxology. When we are in the presence of the holy God, all of our questions dissolve into the "doxological answer"[75] of the highest praise and broadest gratitude. Praising is to the spiritual life what breathing is to the physical. "There cannot be such a thing as true life without praise. Praising and no longer praising are related to each other as are living and no longer living. . . . Only where God is praised is there life."[76] Like all things that are true, honorable, just, pure, pleasing and commendable (Phil 4:8), praise itself springs from the triune depths. "Praise God from whom all blessings flow" is more than just a worship interlude; it is an entire cosmology. God's love is so effusive that it cannot be contained. Love spills over, and blessings inundate the earth. The creation was conceived in love and born as blessedness, and all creation praises its Maker. Francis of Assisi's entire person was offered in praise to God, and his words encourage the entire realm to join him:

Let all things their Creator bless,

And worship Him in humbleness,

O praise Him! Alleluia!

Praise, praise the Father, praise the Son,

And praise the Spirit, Three in One![77]

The Trinity is not a mutual admiration society. Nothing of the sort is implied when we claim that praise is rooted in God. Triune praise, while certainly expressed in and through creation, predated creation. In fact, praise existed before there was a world, because praise is ultimately generated from within God himself. Wherever the fullness and plenitude of goodness abides, there is bound to be praise. God is perfectly good, and therefore praise exists. Because God's perfect goodness is shared among Father, Son and Holy Spirit, with no hint of jealousy, praise spontaneously wells up when any one of the three offers praise to the other two and in turn receives their praise. God's language is praise language, and praise language is God's language.

Human praise of God elevates God, as well it should, yet God's idea of elevation is not often fully appreciated in our praise life. For Jesus to be elevated meant first the act of emptying himself (Phil 2:6-7) and then being lifted up from the earth on a cross (Jn 12:32). One day thousands of thousands will sing with full voice, "Worthy is the Lamb that was slain to receive power, and riches, and wisdom, and strength, and honour, and glory, and power" (Rev 5:12 KJV). Those who follow the triune cross now will one day join that chorus.

Sincere praise will multiply itself. True praise does not feed on itself and hence devour itself, but rather feeds upon God himself. God's resources are without measure or boundary, as Catherine of Siena, a fourteenth-century Italian spiritual writer, discovered: "You, eternal Trinity, are a deep sea: The more I enter you, the more I discover, and the more I discover, the more I seek you. You are insatiable, you in whose depth the soul is sated yet remains always hungry for you, thirsty for you, eternal Trinity, longing to see you with the light in your light."[78] *Insatiable* is a word whose most common contemporary usage is in reference to the sensual. An insatiable appetite for God is nearly unheard of today, because food, sex and power are the new gods.

Yet praise humbly offered to God will cure more of the soul's ills than any other treatment. The heart in praise of God is open to God, and God can and will work with an open heart, infusing divine life. Through the Holy Spirit, every parched soul can "drink of the river of Jesus' love"[79] and be satisfied eternally. The waters are sweet, not bitter, and partakers are bound to praise their God.

I have insisted time and again that the Triune God is pure mystery—not mystery for its own sake, for such mystery would have no interest in or inclination toward disclosure. God's mystery is that of invitation, participation and encounter. God's mystery is a mystery of enticement and love, a mystery heightened—not diminished—by human penetration and participation in it. Theologically, God expressed this mystery—that God should love humanity—on the triune cross. The cross is the most compact and riveting speech possible about God's triunity.

Praising God acknowledges the mystery, stands in reverent repose before it and admits its finality. Praying to, through and in God is the soul's entry into and penetration of God. No one can pray apart from the Holy Spirit, for in the act of prayer "that very Spirit intercedes with sighs too deep for words" (Rom 8:26). The full force of the Triune God is present whenever anyone prays in the Spirit. Robert Jenson says that "believers *know how* to pray to the Father, daring to call him 'Father' because they pray with Jesus his Son, and so enter into the future these two have for them, that is, praying in the Spirit."[80]

Prayer is the defining act of Christian devotion. The Trinity is the summit of Christian theology. Both devotion and theology can easily be sidetracked by routine formulas that, for all of their correctness, bleed life and vitality from that which they were designed to enhance. Ritual perfection does not always translate into spiritual dynamism. Ritual is important, but not as a thing in itself, for ritual works only when it succeeds in transcending itself. No formula is magic. Like the Pharisees, we all are capable of offering beautiful but empty prayers.

The church father Origen believed that prayers directed to the Son and the Holy Spirit were sinful. Few would agree with that today. Yet most would agree that a prayer lined up with the letter, a prayer sent *to* the Father *through* the Son *in* the Spirit, will not necessarily avail much. Any prayer demonstrates both form and content, but one intuitively senses that God cares more for content than for form.

Still, one should not underestimate form. There is much theological wisdom in the tradition of praying to the Father, through the Son, enabled by the Spirit's power. Adhering to form—out of love and not from fear or mere duty—will remind the believer that every prayer, if uttered in devotion, will necessarily engage all of the Trinity. If God is triune, then prayer must be voiced to the Triune God. C. S. Lewis commended genuine prayer for bringing theology and devotion together. He remarked that "the whole threefold life of the three-personal Being is actually going on in that ordinary little bedroom where an ordinary man is saying his prayers."[81] Metaphorically, Lewis suggested that the Father was the "goal" of prayer, Jesus Christ the "road or bridge," and the Holy Spirit the "motive power" propelling the believer along the way of Jesus toward the Father.

Assigning the prepositions *to, through* and *in* respectively to Father, Son and Spirit can seem to chop the unified act of prayer into three more or less disjointed pieces. The God who experiences time as a whole, as "the eternal now," certainly experiences prayer the same way. Screenwriter, producer and director all pour their energies into a motion picture, but the finished product is one, not three. The specialization of each is merged into the force of the whole. So it is in prayer. When the Holy Spirit intercedes for believers (Rom 8:27), the

Spirit does this "according to the will of God." Since the will of God in any given instance is always one and never three, prayer can never be directed to one divine Person without touching all or be prayed in one's name without engaging all. Some Christians will occasionally single out Father, Son or Spirit and direct a prayer to one isolated from the other two in hopes of finding one listening ear. Such practice not only misses the point of prayer but gravely misunderstands the nature of God.

Praise, as noted above, begins in God, because the history of praise is the history of God. Father, Son and Holy Spirit have praised one another from all eternity. Angels, when created, joined the chorus. Is prayer likewise eternal, rooted in God's essence? If it is defined as communication with God, or better still as communion in God's presence, then prayer is eternal. Creation is God's prayer, uttered by God's sweeping wind, God's eternal Spirit (Gen 1:2). If the goal of prayer is immediacy with God, who can be more immediately in God's presence than God himself? As the Triune God is the fullness of life, light and love, so is intratrinitarian prayer, shared among Father, Son and Holy Spirit, the only truly and perfectly efficacious prayer.

Seldom, and then only with trepidation and reluctance, have we tried to look within the Trinity to discover God's inner workings. While believing that prayer is rooted in the Triune God, we cannot speculate how or what the Triune God prays. After sin's incursion into humanity, for example, did the "heavenly committee" hold a prayer meeting to determine which one of the three would become incarnate? That sort of unwarranted guessing misses the mark. The Trinity's dignity is compromised. The particular manner and exact content of God's internal prayers may be beyond our discerning, but *why* God prays is evident to all who have let the Spirit escort them into the deep things of God. God prays because God loves us. God's creation was God's primal prayer. Our redemption now is the most urgent prayer God could ever utter. Charles Wesley knew that Jesus' work of intercession for us and our sin would be real only within a triune framework. The Son's prayer, conceived in the agony of the cross, ends in the assurance of the believer.

The Father hears him pray,
His dear anointed One;
He cannot turn away
The presence of his Son:
His Spirit answers to the blood,
And tells me I am born of God.[82]

The spiritual life, toward whose understanding we have been driving, is wonderfully expressed in Paul's admonition to the Philippians: "Let the same mind be in you that was in Christ Jesus" (2:5). Paul aims undeniably high, settling not for a similar mind, but expecting through the Spirit's implanting the very same mind of Christ. The mind of Jesus Christ is the essence of God, for Christ's mind is shared fully and perfectly by the Father and the Spirit. A God with three minds would be weirdly like those alleged to have multiple personalities. The mind of Christ implanted within must be activated through the soul's discerning eye. The Holy Spirit enlightens the heart's eyes and extends the heart in hope, and the sanctified Christian life is well described as "training the eye of the heart on the glory of God, and living in such a way that one acquires the habit of discerning the brilliance of God's glory."[83]

As I noted in the introduction to this study, the comedian Groucho Marx once said that he would not care to belong to any club that would have him as a member. The one regret filmmaker Woody Allen confesses to having is that he is not someone else. These sentiments are humorous, existential and poignant, but they are not trinitarian. The triune premise states that God inhabits himself; that is what the act of indwelling among Father, Son and Spirit is all about. Triune life is life "in the midst"—for each divine Person in the midst of the other two giving and receiving in perfect ecstasy, and for each Spirit-driven soul in the midst of God's effusive glory. God has no regrets about his own perfect blessedness, although God is and will remain disturbed by human sin. God inhabits his blessedness not as a fortress but as a banquet hall, to which all are invited. Augustine hinted at this invitation when he wrote that "the Trinity is in us as God in His temple, but we are in Him as the creature in its Creator."[84]

"The Trinity is in us"—what a stunning proposition! Can any other religion support such a claim? The Christian lives within this hope because God lives within the Christian. Because Father, Son and Spirit perfectly love each other, not selfishly but overflowingly, humankind was created in and for love. This is God's love, not mere human love. God's enduring Spirit elevates human love and transforms it into triune love. Bernard of Clairvaux taught that the highest degree of love is "where man loves himself only for God's sake."[85] He elaborated the meaning of this love: "To lose yourself as though you did not exist and to have no sense of yourself, to be emptied out of yourself (Phil 2:7) and almost annihilated, belongs to heavenly not to human love."[86] If one feels uncomfortable with the implications of "almost annihilated," John Wesley means essentially the same in describing the sanctified heart as the place where "only love and God are there."[87] If one reaches the stage of valuing one's own life only because God values it, then one's life will at last be truly and infinitely valuable, and for the right reason: that person will realize that he or she is created to love God and to do so only as the Spirit enables and illumines.

Catherine of Siena had a highly developed sense of God's persuasive love, which stretches from creation through redemption to the consummation of the world and history. "You, eternal Trinity, are the craftsman; and I your handiwork have come to know that you are in love with the beauty of what you have made, since you made of me a new creation in the blood of your Son."[88]

To restore the beauty of what God had made, God in Jesus Christ endured the unspeakable ugliness of the cross. "He himself bore our sins in his body on the cross, so that, free from sins, we might live for righteousness; by his wounds you have been healed" (1 Pet 2:24). Everything that breathes should praise the Lord (Ps 150:6). The Christian's breath, supplied by Father, purified through Son, elevated in Spirit, unceasingly turns to song:

From earth's wide bound, from ocean's farthest coast
Thro' gates of pearl streams in the countless host,
Singing to Father, Son, and Holy Ghost:
Alleluia! Alleluia![89]

5

GOD'S NAME EXTENDED

*G*OD'S NAMING OF HIMSELF AS triune was never intended to be a self-purifying reservoir of the holy. God's love is something like water that perpetually seeks its lowest level, for God's love invites especially the outcast and the marginalized. Jesus came preaching good news to the poor, release to the captives, recovery of sight to the blind and freedom for the oppressed (Lk 4:18). The banquet Jesus came to serve always has room for one more, because Jesus serves humanity in the same way Father, Son and Spirit serve each other: in humility, in hope, in expectation, in gratitude. The arms of Jesus encompass all who would come within them, for the love Jesus shows could not be less than the dynamism of love that is the Trinity. "The relationship of the divine persons to one another is so wide that it has room for the whole world."[1]

The writer to the Ephesians had this sense of God's overwhelming expansiveness when he prayed in a triune way:

For this reason I bow my knees before the Father, from whom every family in heaven and on earth takes its name. I pray that, according to the riches of his glory, he may grant that you may be strengthened in your inner being with power through his Spirit, and that

Christ may dwell in your heart through faith, as you are being
rooted and grounded in love. I pray that you may have the power
to comprehend, with all the saints, what is the breadth and length
and height and depth, and to know the love of Christ that surpasses
knowledge, so that you may be filled with all the fullness of God.
(3:14-19)

To be filled with God's fullness is God's most fervent desire for all of
his children. God's essence is love, and God is not thrifty or stingy
when it comes to pouring forth his love. A god less than triune would
be careful and scrupulous about love, like a child returning from a
well with a full bucket of water taking care lest any spill. But the Triune
God is reckless and effusive in his love for us. "God's economy,"
Catherine LaCugna writes, "is not the austere distribution of meager
resources but lavish grace, a glorious inheritance, bestowed in prodigal good pleasure, foreordained to be consummated."[2]

The Ways God Works

To dwell in God is to live amid love. God's love is singular in quality
but triple in action and application. Augustine said that God's love is
like the same gold covering three statues, although God's love is not
stationary like a statue, but dynamic and questing. The singular love
of God is triply focused and nuanced as source (Father), speech (Son)
and union (Spirit). "God is originatively Love as Father, expressively
Love as Son, communicatively Love as Spirit: three subjects in the
one conscious infinite act of Being-in-love."[3] The Father's love
gives every family in heaven and on earth its name. Nameless,
every family is also without identity. In giving his name, the Father
gives his strength—not the strength of mere outer scaffolding, but
the flexible and resourceful strength of the Holy Spirit living
within. The Son's love is love beyond knowledge reaching to wisdom. Christ lives in hearts through faith, rooting and grounding
them in the Son's love. The Spirit's love is that of union, of self to
God and therefore self to self and self to others. To use an imperfect
analogy, if love is God's dwelling among humankind, a palace
sprung from God and fit for humans, the Father is like the prop-

erty's developer, the Son its architect, the Spirit its builder.

An actual housing development may isolate these three tasks of developer, architect and builder. Other projects may call away the developer and architect before the builder's work is completed. Triune work is fully integrated work so that if each divine Person is in one sense a specialist, all specializations are interwoven and perfectly compatible and complementary one with another. Augustine's insight into God's triune life is evident: "When any one of the three is named in connection with some action, the whole Trinity is to be understood as involved."[4]

Classical Christian theology refers to this vision of specialization working in complete harmony as the doctrine of trinitarian appropriations. This teaching's primary contribution is to identify particular divine activities and connect them with—to appropriate them to—particular divine Persons, while yet believing (as Augustine above) that these activities are in some sense carried forth by God's entire triunity.[5] Father, Son and Spirit are specialists in that each one accomplishes certain duties unique to him in the divine economy, but all of God's work is ultimately centered in God's peerless love for the world. A mission to outer space demands that every astronaut make a distinctive contribution to the mission's overall goals; individual tasks are always pointed toward mission consummation. The Trinity is a little like that.

The classical trinitarian appropriations are power (Father), wisdom (Son) and love (Spirit).[6] Ephesians 3:14-19 seems to support the classic arrangement, with the Father's naming showing forth his power, the Son's wisdom surpassing knowledge, and the Spirit's demonstration of love revealing all of its dimensions—breadth, length, height and depth. The true sense of this magnificent prayer, however, does not allow such a neat dissection of divine functions. The Father exercises his power through his Spirit, and Christ not only conveys wisdom beyond knowledge but in addition grants love. As complementary and overlapping as are the Trinity's duties, the tasks are not interchangeable in a random or arbitrary way. The economy of salvation, while directed toward human salvation, nevertheless remains God's economy, to be planned and executed as God knows best. The Son, and not the Holy Spirit or the Father, became incarnate. "In Christ God was reconciling the world to himself" (2 Cor 5:19) cannot be changed to "the Holy Spirit was in the Father reconciling all things to Christ" just for the sake of novelty.[7] God's triune structure is flexible but not thoughtless, adaptable but not unprincipled.

Appropriating certain functions and tasks to, respectively, Father, Son and Spirit does not compromise the unity of the Triune God. Incarnation, if fully realized only in the Son, expresses the entire range of God's resources. The redemptive work of Jesus Christ was offered to glorify the Father and could be offered and accomplished only in and through the sustaining Holy Spirit. The classical appropriations of power, wisdom and love are fully engaged throughout God's offer of salvation to humanity. They are also to be seen in all of God's creative activity, whether original or re-creative and restorative. Creation begins in the "eternal fecundity of the Father,"[8] or the unsearchable depths of his mystery. Thomas Aquinas likened God to an artist who works through his expressive Son and integrating Spirit: "God is the cause of things through his mind and will, like an artist of works of art. An artist works through an idea conceived in his mind and through love in his will bent on something. In like manner, God the Father wrought the creation through his Word, the Son, and through his love, the Holy Ghost."[9]

Augustine testified that "if the Father, the Son, and the Holy Spirit are a single God, then a single world was made by the Father, through the Son, in the Holy Spirit."[10] If creation's initial surge is in the Father, its multiplicity finds expression in the Son (Jn 1:3; Col 1:16) and continuity in the hovering Holy Spirit. Leonardo Boff writes that "creation is of the Trinity, comes from the Trinity, goes to the Trinity, reflects the Trinity, but is not the Trinity."[11] God's triune appropriations of power, wisdom and love are active in, around and through the entire created realm, made by God out of nothing (ex nihilo), not out of the divine self. Creation is the first and best work of the Triune God. The new creation in Jesus Christ (2 Cor 5:17) will not eclipse the first creation but will restore it to God's original design. The God who is triunely active in creation yearns and groans and longs for its reclamation.

Appropriations within the Triune God are not meant to handcuff or limit God, or to partition one part of God off from any other part. There are no "degrees of divinity" within God. There are no levels of skill and accomplishment within God, like an old-fashioned approach to teaching reading in the elementary grades—advanced, average, remedial. If a committee of three could function perfectly, it would be the Trinity. No human committee will ever reach perfect unanimity, because no humans can finally and convincingly love one another with the same release and intensity burning within God. Love breeds communion. Hence Boff can write:

> God is communion precisely because God is a Trinity of Persons. *Three Persons and a single communion and a single trinitarian community:* this is the best formula to represent the Christian God. Speaking of God must always mean the Father, Son and Holy Spirit in the presence of one another, in total reciprocity, in immediacy of loving relationship, being one for another, by another, in another, and with another.[12]

News media sometimes report on "misappropriation of funds," meaning that someone, typically in the public sector, has abused trust and sought personal advantage. While misappropriation is altogether possible humanly speaking, triune appropriations never misfire, overreach or fall short of the mark. The Father's power, the Son's wisdom and the Spirit's love are not treasures to be hoarded but ministries to be fulfilled. If the apostle Paul became all things to all people, so that at least some might be saved (1 Cor 9:22), then the Triune God is surely at least as flexible in winning back his creation. Only a stuffy doctrinal purist would reprimand John Wesley for applying to the Son what Paul seems to exult about all of God. "For from him and through him and to him are all things," Paul wrote to the Romans (11:36). Wesley explained how this applied to Jesus Christ, the end of all things: "of him as the Creator; through him as the Sustainer and Preserver; and to him as the ultimate End of all."13 The eternal beatitude of Father, Son and Holy Spirit means not that they are competing for supremacy among themselves, for the Trinity is like three sets of eyes with a single vision: human life restored to divine favor.

Love's Demand

Triune appropriations point directly to what God requires of humankind. The doctrine of appropriations does not imply that God is evading his responsibilities—far from it! Rather, God is providing a means for limited human wisdom to begin to appreciate how God works in the world, for healing, making right and bringing God's kingdom to fullest expression. We are able to love only because God first loved us (1 Jn 4:19). God's power, wisdom and love have been offered not only to capture every heart but also that the captured hearts may do God's work in the world. God first worked for us; now we must work for God, always within the Spirit's provisions.

Peter believed that Christians were those "who have been chosen and destined by God the Father and sanctified by the Spirit to be obedient to Jesus Christ and to be sprinkled with his blood" (1 Pet 1:2). The changes wrought in every soul through the triune cross not only are personally transforming, but they enable the Christian to be yeast that will leaven the entire loaf, or the whole world (1 Cor 5:6; Gal 5:9). The Father's choice and destiny are not bestowed carelessly or lightly, but are for the express purpose of receiving the Spirit's sanctifying presence. Choice, destiny and sanctification urge the believer to submit without reservation to Jesus Christ, an obedience made possible and confirmed by Jesus' sprinkled blood. Obedience to Jesus will compel the Christian to serve his or her neighbors, as Martin Luther believed in writing that "a Christian lives in Christ through faith, and in his neighbor through love."[14] That is a simple yet profound definition of Christian ethics: to live in and for one's neighbor through love. All will bring different passions and aptitudes to this task, but the Christian trusts that the God of all will orchestrate human multiplicity toward the end of divine simplicity.

Paul knew that the triune premise must hold sway for human diversity to be coordinated with God's overarching purposes. Gifts launched by the one Spirit, service undertaken through the one Lord, activity under the one God's care—this is Paul's summation of Christian ethics triunely given (1 Cor 12:4-6). It is the Holy Spirit, breathed forth by Father and Son simultaneously, who works in each toward the good of all. "The common good" (1 Cor 12:7) is not an idea to be dominated by social theorists and political philosophers. The primordial common good is the Trinity. All good is triunely given to the world and enacted in responsive lives by the Trinity. But common good originates in God, in the dynamism of love given and received among Father, Son and Spirit.

If Christian ethics is seen as the imitation of Christ, obedience toward Christ's directives must be central—an obedience often contrary to our human desires. Paul put it this way: "For the love of Christ urges us on, because we are convinced that one has died for all; therefore all have died. And he died for all, so that those who live might live no longer for themselves, but for him who died and was raised for them" (2 Cor 5:14-15). Christ's urging love is in other biblical translations Christ's compelling or constraining love. Whatever the key word, the call toward radical discipleship cannot be turned away. Hadewijch, a thirteenth-century writer, in effect commenting on Paul's insight, suggested a dialectic of demand. Whatever God may require of us, God is poised and ready to fulfill in us. "We are now under love's demand toward the Holy Trinity. Therefore we ourselves must make a demand on love, and we must do this with all ardor; and we must demand nothing else but his Unity."[15]

Can love make a demand of us? Viewed sentimentally, romantically or sensually, love is benign and docile. A stroll down memory lane is this love's highest order. But God's love does demand, for Christ's love urges, compels and constrains. God does not, however, demand love of us without creating love within us. That is the reasonable demand we can make of God: show us the way to love truly. Any child reasonably expects his or her parents to offer a convincing demonstration of mature living. The child expects to hear from the parent at minimum, "This is the way; walk in it" (Is 30:21). Christians can make that demand on the Holy Trinity: Show us where to walk, and even how to walk, in the urgency of Christ's love, in the benediction of the Holy Spirit, to the glory of the Father. God welcomes this demand for a demonstration of love in response to God's demand that we be holy and loving people. In explicating John Wesley's hermeneutics, Albert C. Outler comments incisively, "All moral commands in Scripture are also 'covered promises,' since God never commands the impossible and his grace is always efficacious in every faithful will."[16] Love's demand toward us is not impossible, because the requiring God is thoroughly the enabling God.

The great commandment to love God unreservedly and one's neighbor as oneself (Mt 22:37-40; Mk 12:28-31; Lk 10:27) has a built-in triplicity. Love happens, if it happens at all, among God, self and neighbor. Originating in God, love is required of humans—first to love God and then to love others more than one loves oneself. Ethics that are Christian, notes Paul Ramsey, are about "regarding the good of any other individual as *more* than your own."[17] With humans this is impossible, but with God all things are possible (Mt 19:26). For Reinhold Niebuhr the Christian ethic was "an impossible possibility," not possible through any human exertion, but only possible through God's constant graciousness. Christian faith should be hopeful and optimistic, Niebuhr thought, but only as it "places its ultimate confidence in the love of God and not the love of man, in the ultimate and transcendent unity of reality and not in tentative and superficial harmonies of existence which human ingenuity may contrive."[18]

Every culture has rhythms and harmonies all its own. Some Asian cultures seem to be oriented toward events and happenings, events not hemmed in by time's strictures, whereas time dictates days for people in the West.[19] Every cultural harmony, regardless of how ancient, will be "tentative and superficial" unless shaped by God's triune rhythms. No personal existence can ground itself, because mature life can never be strictly from itself and for itself. We are all looking for transcendence, but only God's coming down in Jesus Christ is able to elevate human possibility beyond its own scarce resources. Hadewijch understood this triune fluidity, the only possible basis for Christian ethics:

The Father has poured out his name in powerful works, and rich gifts, and just justice. The Son has poured out his name in revelations of burning affection, in veritable doctrine, and in cordial tokens of Love. The Holy Spirit poured out his name in the great radiance of his Spirit and of his light, and in the great fullness of overflowing good will, and in the jubilation of sublime, sweet surrender on account of the fruition of Love.[20]

The tasks of Christian ethics really cannot be described any better than that: doing "just justice" (Father), offering "cordial tokens of Love" (Son), acting toward all in "great fullness of overflowing good will" (Holy Spirit), ending in the rich harvest of "the fruition of Love." Contemporary Christian social theorist Max Stackhouse says much the same thing in claiming that the Father is intent on building a just and responsive social order, the Son desires personal transformation, while the Spirit ensures the freedom of the redeemed.[21] This is what Christian ethics means when understood as it can only be—that is, triunely. LaCugna writes,

> Living trinitarian faith means living God's life: living from and for God, from and for others. Living trinitarian faith means living as Jesus Christ lived, *in persona Christi:* preaching the gospel; relying totally on God; offering healing and reconciliation; rejecting laws, customs, conventions that place persons beneath rules; resisting temptation; praying constantly; eating with modern-day lepers and other outcasts; embracing the enemy and the sinner; dying for the sake of the gospel if it is God's will.[22]

Virtually all goodwilled people would agree that ethics is about living "from and for others." Ethics is the quest for the good life, the best life of all, and it is to be carried forth among humans. Ethics is human commerce of the good. For the Christian, however, living "from and for others" is empty pantomime without the prior condition of "living from and for God." Consider the nine specific acts and attitudes mentioned above, which taken together are an impressive catalog of Christian duty:

1. Preaching the gospel
2. Relying totally on God
3. Being ministers of healing and reconciliation

4. Refusing to value rules over persons
5. Resisting temptation
6. Praying without ceasing
7. Maintaining solidarity with the marginal and the outcast
8. Loving enemies and sinners
9. Dying for the gospel if God wills it

In the most generous assessment, a strictly humanistic ethic might argue for persons over moral rules, and possibly for standing firm with those whom polite society ignores and wishes gone. Even a humanistic ethic will be unconsciously operating under God's grace if it really loves the "modern-day leper." But humanism will judge the other ethical requirements to be too "religious" and "irrelevant" for the modern person.

Humanism, if it bothers with religion at all, acknowledges only the ethical dimension of it and sees that as "doing good" toward one's fellow human beings. Humanism can accept the criterion of "What would Jesus do?" as defining correct conduct, but it is a Jesus without transcendence, not the Jesus who said, "The Father and I are one" (Jn 10:30). This all-too-human Jesus, Jesus without the Trinity, satisfies humanism's interest in a religiously based morality. Thomas Jefferson, who believed in God but had little use for the Trinity, viewed Christianity's proclamation of the Trinity as "incomprehensible jargon" and "artificial scaffolding." The "very simple structure of Jesus," Jefferson feared, had been hidden under the obscurities and evasions of "the Trinitarian arithmetic."[23] The difference between the simplicity Jefferson found in Jesus and Jesus' true simplicity is like the difference between a mirage and an oasis. The one promises refreshment that turns to illusion, while the other satisfies eternally through Jesus the living water (Jn 4:14). An oasis is nourished by hidden springs, invisible but organically connected to the pool of water. Stretching the analogy somewhat, that desert oasis is not unlike the Trinity: hidden source (Father), living water (Son), invitation to refreshment (Holy Spirit).

Transparency, a word of near-faddish popularity of late, is yet an apt description of the Son's pure relations with the Father. The Son was transparent to the Father's purposes; in that purity is the Son's simplicity. Triune simplicity is much closer to Oregon's Crater Lake, one of the world's most pristine bodies of water, than to the "muddy" Mississippi. A shining singularity of purpose attends each act in God's career of redemption, a singularity Thomas Jefferson mistook for ethical humanism. However refined are humanism's goals, any ethic founders if not anchored in God's triunity.

Immanuel Kant, born in Germany about twenty years before Jefferson, shared many of the latter's intellectual assumptions. Kant, one of the greatest philosophers of the modern era, did not fathom the triune message of his given name Immanuel, "God with us." More incisively than Jefferson, Kant wrote off the Trinity as follows:

The doctrine of the Trinity provides nothing, absolutely nothing, of practical value, even if one claims to understand it; still less when one is convinced that it far surpasses our understanding. It costs the student nothing to accept that we adore three or ten persons in the divinity. One is the same as the other to him, since he has no concept of a God in different persons (*hypostases*). Furthermore, this distinction offers absolutely no guidance for his conduct.[24]

To Kant's credit he does acknowledge the triune mystery; he is convinced that this doctrine "far surpasses our understanding." We would, however, expect Kant to say precisely this, because his understanding was radically tilted toward the rational. Kant's God was a moral lawgiver, not a divine revealer. On practical terms, Kant believed, there had to be human freedom, a law-giving God and an immortal soul for morality to work at all. Yet Kant saw no practical value in the Trinity, and if God were three or ten, it made no vital difference for one contemplating a moral decision.

Let us accept Kant's challenge forthrightly. Let us even accept his terms for the discussion. Of what "practical value" is the doctrine of the Trinity? An adorable mystery, evoking deepest reverence, must not be an irrelevant one, for God's triunity is offered to every human life not only for its salvation but also as the only viable hope of social justice. Jürgen Moltmann says simply and compellingly that the Holy Trinity is *the* Christian social program.[25] How can this be? How can a "mere" doctrine, and an infinitely complicated one at that, hope to transform social ills into a community of redemption? Colin Gunton claims that "everything looks—and, indeed, is—different in the light of the Trinity,"[26] and this everything means not only our ways of thinking the Christian faith but also, importantly, our ways of living the Christian life and answering the Christian call.

From Augustine we have learned that each person is created with the image of the Trinity deeply stamped within. Sin has effaced this image; Calvary's grace restores it. Restoration is a personal reality but is meant to become a community reality, for "the true human community is designed to be the *imago Trinitatis*,"[27] or the image of the Trinity correcting the entire world. Kant assumed that moral living was strictly human effort, never divine bestowal. Grace never entered Kant's moral equation. But triune living is from grace, through grace, toward grace. The Father's gracious depths are limitless, the Son's mediation of grace totally accurate and sufficient, the Spirit's encouragement in grace a visible witness to a world whose profoundest intuition of grace is figure skating. Grace is not a vague divine commodity. It lives in Jesus Christ and encounters the world—builds community *in* the world—through the Holy Spirit. Grace is eminently practical, and perfectly available, for, notes LaCugna, "the life of God is not something that belongs to God alone. *Trinitarian life is also our life.* As soon as we free ourselves from thinking that there are two levels to the Trinity . . . then we see that there is *one* life of the triune God, a life in which we graciously have been included as partners."[28]

The practical value of the Trinity is nothing less than God's making his divine life available to human beings. The infusion of human life with divine life is God's goal for all of his creatures. The realization of this goal, of triune life within, overcomes and unites many of our cherished dichotomies: social *or* personal, understanding *or* mystery, contemplation *or* action, subject *or* object, being *or* doing, engagement *or* observation, involvement *or* detachment. God's life is a seamless whole integrated around a common life shared perfectly among Father, Son and Holy Spirit. Within its recipient, triune life binds up wounds and heals divisions. When people live triunely, no gap re-

mains between orthodoxy (correct thinking about God) and orthopraxis (redemptive action in the world for the sake of God). The
linguistic relation between orthodoxy (right belief and doctrinal formulation) and doxology (the proper praise offered to God) means that
thinking about God necessarily leads to the praise of God. Theology
that cannot be preached, prayed, praised and sung is hollow and
shriveled. Orthodoxy, doxology and orthopraxis—thinking, praising,
enacting—are themselves an efficacious witness to the triune premise.
They are three, yet they become one in any Christian who stands
honestly and expectantly before God.

Divine Koinonia
The most profound idea that trinitarian thought wishes to convey is
in some ways the simplest. It is an idea with enormous implications
not only for Christian ethics but for human psychology as well.
Trinitarian theology lives or dies with the idea of relationality. The
doctrine of the Trinity "is *par excellence* the theology of relationship. Its
fundamental principle is that God, who is self-communicating and
self-giving love for us, is from all eternity love perfectly given and
received."[29] Greek philosophy approached God as a divine substance,
as a thing to be analyzed, not as the giver of covenant who expected
covenantal response from those who loved him. "God as Plato or
Aristotle understood Him to exist cannot be God as Christians understand Him, for He is an abstraction.... But God is supremely concrete
and not abstract"[30] in Christian faith and practice. Trinitarian theology
stresses that "God is a partner in love and not an object to be scrutinized or controlled by the intellect."[31] Christian ethics that hopes to be
triunely grounded must be an ethics of relationality and not of an
abstract and inert divine substance. Christian ethicist James M. Gustafson writes that "it is better to make one's interpretation of the right
and the good primarily in relational terms than in substantive ones."[32]
    The doctrine of the Trinity not only allows, but positively requires,
that God be thought of relationally. As triune, "God exists as the pure
relationality of love given and received."[33] The essence of God is
self-giving, self-sacrificing love. Although we cannot presume to

know everything about God's inner workings, what we have else-where called the immanent Trinity, in confidence we declare that God, in Charles Wesley's evocative phrase, is "pure, unbounded love."[34] Wesley applied this phrase specifically to Jesus Christ, but if true of Jesus it is also true of the Father and the Holy Spirit. God's love is pure and unbounded because it springs directly from the triune depths. Any human analogy—pristine water drawn from a well, pure oxygen breathed for the benefit of health—must stumble, because God's purity is of an entirely different class from any other sort of purity. The question of why God's love is pure is really beyond human ability to answer, and it is a presumptuous question to ask. We are again thrust fully into the realm of unsurpassable mystery, and we are again reminded (as we can never be too often) that while the Triune God is himself utter mystery, the doctrine of the Trinity is not itself mystery but is the human attempt—admittedly nurtured by grace, enlivened by love and extended toward hope—to understand the Trinity.[35]

The unbounded quality of God's love means that God has not erected any boundaries within himself to stifle, dilute or divert love. The negative expression is that there are no walls of hostility within God. Positively, God's unbounded love means that, in the words of Geoffrey Wainwright, "the divine Persons empty themselves into each other and receive each other's fulness."[36] As Father, Son and Holy Spirit give and receive love among themselves as they have in perfect harmony from all eternity, love is not somehow purified or improved or intensified. Each of the three Persons is in himself the height and depth and breadth of pure, unbounded love. But in giving themselves without reservation to one another, they not only demonstrate what love is but offer the most powerful witness to what love ought to be like in the world: selfless, other-regarding, welfare-oriented.

The dynamism of love that is the Trinity means that God's very nature is not divine substance but is rather divine koinonia.[37] *Koinonia* is best defined, according to ethicist Paul Lehmann, as "the *fellowship-creating reality* of Christ's presence in the world,"[38] a presence coming graciously from the Father and sustained by the life-giving Holy Spirit. Furthermore, "a *koinonia* ethic can only be faithful to its messi-

anic occasion and character upon a trinitarian foundation."[39] The
fourth-century theologian Basil the Great well described the divine
koinonia when he wrote that "everything that the Father is is seen in
the Son, and everything that the Son is belongs to the Father. The Son
in His entirety abides in the Father, and in return possesses the Father
in entirety in Himself."[40]

During a time of great intimacy with the Father, Jesus prayed in the
power of the Holy Spirit: "As you, Father, are in me and I am in you,
may they also be in us, so that the world may believe that you have
sent me" (Jn 17:21). As the Father and the Son mirror each other so
that the Trinity is not just "a doctrine of *God of God* but of *God in God*,"[41]
Jesus prays that the witness of total knowledge of Father in Son and
Son in Father will spread to faithful believers, and that this cumulative
witness would ultimately convince the world that Jesus did in fact
come from the Father.

The Christian tradition developed a specialized vocabulary to
express what is really inexpressible—namely, the perfect giving and
receiving of love within the Trinity. Eastern Orthodoxy applied the
Greek word *perichoresis* to this ineffable mystery, whereas the West
employed two similar Latin terms, *circumincessio* and *circuminsessio*.
Perichoresis, which has been likened to a divine dance, suggests continued movement, fluid motion and spontaneous activity.[42] A God
who dances, even within the hidden recesses of the Trinity, may seem
frivolous and irresponsible. The psalmist, however, suggested that
dancing was an appropriate response to God's goodness (Ps 149:3;
150:4), and David declared, "You have turned my mourning into
dancing; you have taken off my sackcloth and clothed me with joy, so
that my soul may praise you and not be silent" (Ps 30:11-12). The
divine dance means, as perichoresis proclaims, that "God is alive from
all eternity as love."[43] The most joyous human welcome or reunion,
shared among intimates and accompanied by delight and glee, frees
the human spirit (if only temporarily) and gives a hint of the
perichoretic union perfectly realized among Father, Son and Spirit.
Perichoretic union means mutual interpenetration of each in all and
all in each. Humans can be reunited after rifts or hurts have separated

them, but aside from the cross, there is no known occasion of upheaval in the Trinity. Perfect union is who God is, which for Karl Barth means that "the divine modes of being mutually condition and permeate one another so completely that one is always in the other two and the other two in the one."[44] Divine joy powers the divine dance.

The two Latin words carry similar, but not identical, meanings. *Circumincessio* captures the active and dynamic sense of perichoresis. It is also continual movement—not random or reckless movement, but movement with focus and purpose. *Circumincessio* "refers to the entry of each divine person into the life of the others in total openness and freedom."[45] How many occasions of human entry—into holy matrimony, into friendship, or even into a room—are marked by "total openness and freedom"? The answer is none. Humans enter to "make a big splash," to gain advantage, to satisfy a personal need, to draw attention away from a character flaw. Humans do not often enter to give selflessly, to practice humility and to expand and refine the sense of community. The triune Persons are selfless, humble and promoting of community, not because they need to practice these virtues, for God is the summit of all virtue, but to invite humans to share in and faithfully extend these traits. God's "total openness and freedom" is an invitation, not a restriction, and can be limited only by human choice.

Circuminsessio also conveys mutual indwelling, but more as a completed act than an ongoing process. It is the rest that each Person feels in the company of the other two, "the welcoming and comfortable dwelling together of the three divine persons."[46]

The mutual interpenetration indicated by all three of these technical terms is a powerful indication toward what Christian ethics is all about. The reciprocity and mutuality practiced by Father, Son and Holy Spirit point to a perfection of purpose, resolve and will within the Godhead. This in turn points toward what God expects of humans who intend to live under God's provisions. General or philosophical ethics is content with a kind of least common denominator approach to morality, summarized variously as the pleasure principle, the happiness quotient, the social contract or the call of duty. Occasionally a general or public ethic will reach as high as some form of the "golden rule," yet without the acknowledgment that this rule is required by God—not mere expediency—and that its performance owes everything to God's grace. Perichoresis and the two Latin words (rendered in English by *circumincession*) go far beyond any golden rule. Because perichoresis means living for others under the canopy of God's grace, it is God's highest ethic. Perichoresis founds human community on its only sustainable base, the Triune God, and his love for the world. The following, spoken by Metropolitan Mar Osthathios, is an expansion and a refinement of this perichoretic vision.

> The unity of humanity is to be modelled on Trinitarian unity. . . . Ultimately all differences and separations between human beings have to be dissolved in a mutual *perichoresis* (embracing, penetrating, not merely sharing) where "thine and mine" are not different in case of property, purpose and will but different only in different personal and group identities with full openness to and penetration of each other. . . . The mystery of the unity of humanity in Christ, patterned on the mystery of the Triune unity in the Godhead, has high significance for our social goals also. . . . Ultimately, parochialism, insularity, division, separation, class, ethnic conflict, political and economic injustice, exploitation and oppression have to be judged by this criterion![47]

Cynics, joined by not a few Christians, would dismiss this ethic as extreme and utopian. Jesus did not see it that way. Jesus believed that the freedom he and the Father felt in each other's presence must extend to all who believe that Jesus is the Christ and that this intimacy would ultimately multiply itself and convince the world of God's love (Jn 17:23). Christian commitment is not cheap or haphazard; it may require one to lay down one's life for one's friends (Jn 15:13).

In serving the Son and Holy Spirit, the Father experiences the deepest joy. Simultaneously with the Father's serving, the Son gives himself unreservedly to the Holy Spirit and the Father, and the Spirit's very life is to please the Father and the Son. Human talk about love without conditions, hidden motives or reservations pales in comparison to the triune demonstration of love. Perhaps Paul knew deep down that only Father, Son and Holy Spirit could totally keep the spirit of Philippians 2:3-4: "Do nothing from selfish ambition or conceit, but in humility regard others as better than yourselves. Let each of you look not to your own interests, but to the interests of others."

Spontaneous generosity so amazes us that the story of a Boston man handing fifty-dollar bills from a limousine at Christmastime is front-page news. But what philanthropist ever gave away his entire fortune? If he did, he would soon be out of the philanthropy business, seeking a new identity. By giving all, the old identity of philanthropist no longer would be possible, for what is a philanthropist without his millions? Jesus, owning infinitely more than millions, and

> though he was in the form of God,
>> did not regard equality with God
>> as something to be exploited,
> but emptied himself,
>> taking the form of a slave,
>> being born in human likeness.
> And being found in human form,
>> he humbled himself
>> and became obedient to the point of death—
>> even death on a cross. (Phil 2:6-8)

The humility Paul earlier urged upon the Philippians is flawlessly demonstrated by Christ's act of self-emptying *(kenosis)* and taking the form of a slave. In so doing, Jesus showed to fullest effect God's heart and nature, for, writes Geoffrey Wainwright, "we might say that the very essence of God is, in Christian eyes, *kenosis:* self-giving love extended also to his creatures for the sake of their salvation."[48] Charles Wesley was moved by kenosis when he wrote:

> He left his Father's throne above,
> So free, so infinite his Grace!
> Emptied himself of all but Love,
> And bled for Adam's helpless race:
> 'Tis Mercy all, immense and free!
> For, O my God, it found out me![49]

I am not asserting that perichoresis (mutual interpenetration) and kenosis (emptying out) are identical, but both do have undeniable truth for Christian living. God's perfectly perichoretic life is a prescription for how people ought to live. Father, Son and Holy Spirit are all continually involved in perichoretic union. Is there also kenosis within the Trinity? Since each of the three lives to serve the other two, it may even be possible to speak of kenosis within the Godhead, providing this does not imply that any of the three has selfish ambition that needs to be purged and emptied out. There are no social climbers or influence peddlers in the Trinity. There is only grace, benediction and beatitude.

Kenosis as Paul understood it refers to the incarnation of Jesus Christ, for he was "born in human likeness." Since only the second Person of the Trinity became incarnate, kenosis in the incarnational sense refers to Jesus Christ alone. But kenosis as the principle of self-giving love applies to everything God is and does.

The reality of divine koinonia and God's desire to enkindle it in human society shows the close relationship between theology (orthodoxy) and ethics (orthopraxis). Theology is not just pious talk, and ethics is not aimless action. Both must be grounded in the Trinity. Divine koinonia begins with the Christmas Immanuel, "God is with us," and culminates in the Easter glory, Christ resurrected for us. In between are faith, hope, love and suffering. Around, over and within are Father, Son and Holy Spirit, distinctly three yet inseparably one.

Conscience: Gift and Requirement

Another means by which God's name is extended is the conscience. Divine koinonia and perichoretic union suggest mutuality and convergence among a group of people, wherein each counts the other better than him- or herself. Conscience certainly has a social function to perform, as when a prophetic voice is referred to as "the conscience of his generation." The fruits of conscience may be social and public, but the roots of conscience are more personal and interior.

What have the conscience and the Trinity to do with one another? Are the workings of the conscience congruent with the workings of the Triune God? The conscience has customarily been defined as God's voice cautioning against some actions and compelling toward others. Does this mean that conscience is to be solely identified with the Holy Spirit, who has always been "the inner light of conscience"?[50] While not denying the centrality of the Holy Spirit for the refinement and execution of conscience, we wish to locate conscience in the whole of the Triune God.

The very meaning of the word *conscience* implies a triune setting for conscience. Understood through its constituent parts, *con-science* literally means "with knowledge" or "knowledge with." We have seen that Immanuel is another "with" word: God is with us. Jesus Christ is Immanuel only as descending from the Father and sustained by the Holy Spirit. What Immanuel means for salvation, conscience means for morality. Jesus' "withness" connects him to the Father and Spirit, and the "withness" of conscience similarly speaks the language of connectedness. As a relational term, *with* means not only privilege and connection but also obligation and responsibility.[51] To whom we are obligated is shown in defining conscience as "the awareness of oneself as a morally responsible being who can be called to account not only by one's fellow human beings, but by one's own inner self, and in religious terms, by God."[52]

Conscience is not created by social forces or psychological needs, as some social scientists and psychologists have recently asserted. The capacity for conscience is implanted within every human by God. "The mind making moral judgments"[53] is how Thomas Aquinas viewed conscience, and no one can create or implant one's own mind. Conscience, like mind, is a gift from God, a gift that assuredly is molded and influenced by social forces but not created by them. John Wesley identified conscience with the true light coming into the world and being given to enlighten everyone (Jn 1:9).[54] Because the light of conscience was given to all, Wesley believed that "no man living is entirely destitute of what is vulgarly called 'natural conscience.' But this is not natural; it is more properly termed 'preventing grace.' " [55] Wesley sees conscience as being between nature and grace but much closer to grace than to nature. A purely natural conscience would ultimately lead to the moral anarchy of "the survival of the fittest." A conscience beholden to and formed by grace can work redemptively in the fallen world. Conscience is not a natural phenomenon, Wesley plainly says; its presence within everyone is God's best witness to the reality of prevenient grace, the grace that goes before and leads willing persons to salvation.

As an endowment from God, conscience works within each person to clarify one's vision of oneself, work that by definition will never be completed. One can never reach the summit of moral maturity. Even as the Holy Spirit searches all things, to the very depths of God (1 Cor 2:10), so the conscience probes the depths of the human soul, investigating motives, examining inclinations and ordering priorities. Simply by being human, everyone will necessarily carry on this interior dialogue of the soul with the soul, at times fully cognizant of so doing, at other times hidden in the unconscious. If conscience, following Wesley, is the presence of prevenient grace within, then that conscience which functions best is the one immersed in grace.

A conscience nourished by grace will soon realize its need for purification. The cleansing of conscience is forcefully set in a trinitarian context by the epistle to the Hebrews: "How much more will the blood of Christ, who through the eternal Spirit offered himself without blemish to God, purify our conscience from dead works to worship the living God!" (9:14). Every human conscience is blemished, and no conscience can present itself faultless before God. That is for the blood of Christ to accomplish through the eternal Spirit. As this purification is being accomplished, the potential for the full and free knowing of God can be realized. Barth sensed this.

If there is concrete fellowship with God the Redeemer, then and only then there is such a thing as conscience. . . . To have a conscience is no more and no less than to have the Holy Spirit. For "no one knows what is in God except the Spirit of God" (1 Cor. 2:11). To have a conscience is to know what is in God, to know his judgment on our conduct. To have a conscience is to look and reach beyond the limits of our creatureliness. . . . A conscience that tells us the truth has to be this conscience that is captive to the Word of God.[56]

168   Knowing the Name of God

Barth's assertion that there is no conscience at all apart from fellow-ship with God is astounding. Barth defines conscience more narrowly than the capacity of making moral choices that is to be exercised by all. Unless it is totally oriented toward the Triune God, conscience is not conscience at all. The proper exercise of conscience is toward the will of God. Christian ethics is not about promoting the common good or following moral common sense. Barth's concern was forcefully put by Dietrich Bonhoeffer. The Christian "must from the outset discard as irrelevant two questions which impel him to concern himself with the problem of ethics, 'How can I be good?' and 'How can I do good?'; and instead of these he must ask the utterly and totally different question 'What is the will of God?' "[57]

John Calvin defined a good conscience as "nothing other than inward integrity of heart."[58] Father, Son and Spirit, if triply distinguish-able, yet share only one heart, and the goal of conscience is the creation of such an integrated heart, integrated with self, others and God. Conscience may begin within, but no conscience will advance in ma-turity without constant interaction with other consciences in the moral universe. Conscience is formed by the constant dialectic between the self and the community, which for the Christian is the church.

The Christian conscience then is a knowing with one-self or an integrity of heart in which the self's integrity or image of itself is constituted in God as he has made himself and true manhood known in Jesus Christ and as this revelation is mediated through the Christian community. The joint authorship of conscience, i.e., the self-in-the-Christian-community and the Christian-commu-nity-in-the-self, points to and is derived from a transcendent theonomous authority.[59]

The ending phrase, "a transcendent theonomous authority," is a com-plicated way of saying "God." Conscience derives from God but matures and develops in the interplay between self and community.

Without inventing data where none exists, it yet seems undeniable that the moral life encompasses and analyzes many groups of three, or triads. Moral living, for example, involves the interaction of spirit, soul and body (1 Thess 5:23), which together constitute a self. The self, in its turn, carries on a moral discourse with itself, with others and with the natural world, and it does so via thoughts, words and actions, which is the traditional Christian division of human happenings.[60] Conscience, for one writer at least, must take into account reason, emotion and will as it comes to "self-committed decisions about right and wrong, good and evil."[61] The Christian exercises conscience in the direction of realizing and perfecting the three theological virtues of faith, hope and love (1 Cor 13:13).

The moral life is often described as the quest for purity. Kierkegaard's famous recipe for Christian living was "Purity of heart is to will one thing." "Purify your hearts, you double-minded" (Jas 4:8) is a direct indictment of moral duplicity, of which the presence of mixed motives may be the leading indicator. The triune premise—that three are three and yet one—suggests that purity does not necessarily exclude and forbid multiplicity, but rather orders and prioritizes many factors according to God's will and in so doing synthesizes the many into the one. Every moral situation may call forth a new synthesis according to the impulses of the Triune God.

The moral agent is not asked to become all spirit and to do without soul and body, but is asked to live an integrated life unto God. Indeed, morality will quite often address bodily questions (abortion, alcoholism, homosexuality, suicide, euthanasia), which is no surprise considering that the Word came into flesh (Jn 1:14) and that God's Spirit dwells within the body as within a temple (1 Cor 3:16-17; 2 Cor 6:16). Likewise, there is nothing to be gained in reducing faith, hope and love to one "supervirtue," or in saying that reason, emotion and will must be collapsed into one. At times God may wish to apply faith to a particular place; at other times he may apply love or hope. Decisions of conscience may be formed more by reason one time, whereas will and emotion may exert a greater influence later.

The Triune God is infinitely wise and everlastingly creative. Mature moral living is never monolithic in the sense of considering only one factor or set of circumstances. The purity demanded of moral activity is purity of intention, and intentionality is purified and clarified as several intentional impulses are fused around a common purpose in the same way that several strands make a cable or a rope. The singleness of vision urged by Jesus (Mt 6:22-23) does not require an eye to gaze perpetually on one thing only. Incessant gazing at the sun would blind a person. Jesus knew there is an infinity for the eye to behold. But multiple visual stimuli do not have to destroy the singleness of vision Jesus commended. Perhaps that is the difference between vision and sight. Vision focuses, refines, hones and narrows, but sight simply absorbs, catalogs and observes.

"In good conscience," then, is in triune conscience. By triune conscience I do not mean that any three factors (for example, memory, understanding and will) are united into one as conscience operates. Saying that would deny the dynamism of the human person. Since many more factors than three work together to form a conscience, no numerical formula defines a triune conscience. By this phrase I simply mean that the Trinity is not only the originating source of the conscience but also the model after which the conscience is to strive.

Recent discussions of conscience have stressed that it is not just one more human faculty or function to take its place alongside of other aspects of humanity. No, conscience is at the core of the person, not a peripheral adornment. In this light, conscience "is not a function of physiological, psychological or sociological factors. It is rather the whole human person characterized by a drive towards and a demand for the realization of value. It is the dynamic thrust towards authenticity and self-transcendence at the core of a person's consciousness, the demand for responsible decision in accord with reasonable judgment."[62]

The Trinity is not one of God's functions. God is the Trinity. The Trinity is God. These two statements are equivalent, for it is only in the Trinity that "God corresponds to himself," as we have learned from Karl Barth. The goal of every conscience should be that it would perfectly correspond to itself. "Training in Christianity" (Kierkegaard) is at the same time training in conscience. "The divine training that is known by faith" aims at "love that comes from a pure heart, a good conscience, and sincere faith" (1 Tim 1:4-5). Charles Wesley yearned for this training.

I want a principle within
Of jealous, godly fear,
A sensibility of sin,
A pain to feel it near.

That I from thee no more may part,
No more thy goodness grieve,
The filial awe, the fleshly heart,
The tender conscience give.

Quick as the apple of an eye,
O God, my conscience make;
Awake my soul when sin is nigh,
And keep it still awake.

If to the right or left I stray,
That moment, Lord, reprove,
And let me weep my life away
For having grieved thy love.

O may the least omission pain
My well-instructed soul,
And drive me to the blood again
Which makes the wounded whole.[63]

God's Name Finally

The doctrine of the Trinity is absolutely central for Christian faith and practice. It is the frame on which Christianity's entire theological and devotional tapestry is woven. By divine design, it is God's intent that every person would find him- or herself woven into this tapestry, for it is God's greatest hope that all would repent and none would perish (2 Pet 3:9). The Triune God is steadfastly and tirelessly laboring toward the hope "that God may be all in all" (1 Cor 15:28), and God labors not alone, but engages humans as covenant partners.

As I have tried to make plain, it is not the *doctrine* of the Trinity on which Christian faith is founded. Faith must be founded on the Son of God, the crucified and risen One, who under the Spirit's anointing intercedes for all creation before the loving and waiting Father. Faith in a doctrine makes as much sense as faith in a national constitution or a flag. It is not a piece of paper or a segment of cloth that excites the passions people feel toward their nation. Passion and loyalty are aroused by what the nation *means* to the people, meaning that is captured by ideas the constitution articulates and the flag continually keeps before the people. A flag symbolizes what a country stands for but works as a symbol only when people clearly recognize that it points beyond itself. The doctrine of the Trinity likewise points ahead to the Triune God, for it is inconceivable that God should reveal a doctrine and yet fail to reveal himself. Any theological doctrine is a human reflection on divine revelation, a human distillation of divine presence, a human recognition of divine purpose.

To say this is not to denigrate doctrine or to consider it unworthy of exploration and refinement. But it is to say that God does not reveal doctrine. God reveals himself. And that self is unfathomable mystery in whose presence many people are manifestly uncomfortable because they want to control and manipulate all variables to their advantage. Ultimate Mystery, however, holds its own. All Christian doctrines, and perhaps especially that of the Trinity, intuitively recognize and respect the limits imposed by mystery, limits not designed to frustrate any intellectual quest, but limits that are the gateway to reverence, the acknowledgment of holy ground. It was in Augustine's words "not that [the mystery] might be spoken, but that it not be left unspoken"[64] that he developed his technical vocabulary for the doctrine of the Trinity.

While a doctrine is not to be worshiped, it is also not to be set aside arbitrarily as of no consequence. A map is not the place itself, but no motorist can successfully negotiate roads in a foreign country without occasional recourse to a map. No tourist would go to New York City and simply sit in his hotel room thumbing through postcards of the Statue of Liberty, the Empire State Building, Rockefeller Center, Yankee Stadium and all the rest. The tourist may have come to New York because of the postcards, and once there the postcards may even help to order and prioritize each day's activities, but only an idiot would mistake the postcards for the genuine article. As theologically developed, philosophically tested and culturally expressed in paintings and sculpture, the doctrine of the Trinity could never fit on a postcard, yet perhaps this analogy helps to clarify how the doctrine of the Trinity relates to the reality of the Triune God. Trinitarian theologians have never constructed doctrines for their own sakes, but always to serve the worshiping community that gathers in the thrice-blessed name of God.

A newly finished house built exactly to architectural specifications and employing the best labor and materials available does not for all of that automatically become a home. A humanizing spirit must breathe within the created space before lumber, nails, glass, shingles and wire become a home. Theologians do not construct doctrines in the expectation that the living God will immediately move in and take up residence. That would be sheer presumption. Theology, if the "queen of the sciences," goes forward only in fear, trembling and humility. To do less would be to spite the object of all theological inquiry, the living God. Even so, if a house needs a humanizing spirit, a doctrine needs a divinizing spirit, none other than the Spirit of God. Regardless of how "homey" any structure may be, few if any would live their entire lives cooped up within their house. God can likewise not be confined to any doctrine, not even the doctrine of the Trinity.

Undeniably, God transcends every conceptual structure humanity has ever or could ever desire. This insight, while true enough, should not lead to a "holy agnosticism" where one mark of sophistication is how much *cannot* be known about God. God is not impressed by human sophistication. John Wesley said that the Holy Spirit, and by extension the Father and Son also, was given "to assist our faith, not gratify our curiosity."[65] Understanding all mysteries, possessing all knowledge, having all faith—even to remove mountains—fails to impress God unless love is present (1 Cor 13:2). In Jesus Christ love has become fully present, love of a markedly different character than is typically observed in the fallen world. Christian love is not calculating but unconditional, motivated by service not prestige. "The more one grows in love, the more one chooses the form God himself has chosen: poverty, humiliation, insults."[66]

These three experiences—poverty, humiliation and insults—would never be respectfully attached to a respectable God by decent people. The paradox of Christmas, God's appearance in a manger, is what sets the Christian God apart from every other intuition about the divine. No right-thinking, genteel person would ever attach poverty, humiliation and insults to God. God could only attach them to himself, not for God's benefit, but so that humans might learn how to be divine.

While the twentieth century has witnessed a noteworthy revival of interest in the Trinity, led by Karl Barth, detractors have arisen. God's triunity is charged with being logically impossible and philosophically misguided. Sensing common cause with Jews and Muslims, some have wanted to dilute trinitarianism so that Christianity becomes another unmediated, "naked" monotheism. Yet others, sympathetic to feminist concerns, are terribly uncomfortable with designations such as Father, Son, Lord and King. These words, they say, hurt more than they heal, for they reflect an entrenched patriarchal view that, among other ills, has led humankind to subdue and dominate rather than nurture and care for the earth.[67]

My task has been more expositional and contemplative than apologetic, and thus I cannot offer detailed refutations of every criticism recently mounted against the Triune God. What was earlier said of Ultimate Mystery can now be said of the Trinity (since they are in fact the same): God holds his own. Critics of the Trinity are more often than not insightful and without question sincere, yet they often ignore the central claim that triune theology advances. At its bare minimum, the Trinity is "a teaching about God's life with us and our life with each other."[68] Theology, the orthodoxy of God's life with us, unavoidably leads to ethics, the orthopraxis of shared life that creates community. This necessary balance between theology and ethics is at least a partial answer to the Trinity's critics. The philosophically minded lose the ethical impulse amid their speculations, while many feminists seem concerned only about ethics, not fully appreciating that right conduct must flow out of right understanding.

The doctrine of the Trinity suffers as much from neglect by Christians as from attack by disbelievers. Since any traditional or classical form of Christianity is impossible without the Trinity, it must grieve God that the doctrine of the Trinity is thought by many Christians to be optional instead of central. Of course, God is not distressed over mere doctrinal omission, but he must be troubled that his very substance and nature are not recognized for what they are: self-communicating love, eternally generated by Father, Son and Spirit. Humankind, created because of love and meant by God to live in love with God, self and others, destroyed love through its sin, and can be restored to the Father's love only by the Son's sacrifice implanted within by the Holy Spirit. Triune love is nothing if not sacrificial, and it invites every Christian to live not for self, but for others. "There is no room for egoism in the Trinity. It has no . . . selfhood as such."[69] The modern human seizes on selfhood. Not to become "a fully functioning" individual is, according to the gospel of human achievement, not to become at all. The Christian gospel, however, points to a cross, and after it a resurrection, as totally defining of selfhood in God's eyes. To live triunely is to see the self, the world and others with the vision of God.

Christian life is visionary life. It is life that looks to Jesus, "the pioneer and perfecter of our faith, who for the sake of the joy that was set before him endured the cross, disregarding its shame, and has taken his seat at the right hand of the throne of God" (Heb 12:2). Christian life remembers and appropriates the past, endures and perseveres in the present, and works in hope and anticipation toward the future when, in John Wesley's words, "there will be a deep, an intimate, an uninterrupted union with God; a continual enjoyment of the Three-One God, and of all the creatures in him!"[70] Eternal love and perfect communion among Father, Son and Holy Spirit infuse human life with divine possibility, not only as a future hope but also as a present reality, a current communion of becoming "drowned in the overwhelming seas of the love of God,"[71] as Thomas Kelly once put it.

A world gorged on sensual pleasure cannot know that the purest pleasure of all is the knowledge of God within the soul, achieved by Christ's blood and confirmed by the Holy Spirit. Wesley's calling to a "continual enjoyment of the Three-One God" was anticipated in the seventeenth century by the Westminster Shorter Catechism. To the question "What is the chief end of man?" the catechism simply yet penetratingly answers, "Man's chief end is to glorify God, and to enjoy him forever."[72] True joy is triune joy, God's uninterrupted bliss that beckons everyone to speak the thrice-blessed name. Speaking, we praise, and praising, we live.

Father, God, thy love we praise
Which gave thy Son to die;
Jesus, full of truth and grace,
Alike we glorify;

Spirit, Comforter divine,
Praise by all to thee be given,
Till we in full chorus join,
And earth is turned to heaven.[73]

Notes

Introduction

[1]Bernard Lonergan, *The Way to Nicea*, trans. Conn O'Donovan (Philadelphia: Westminster Press, 1976), pp. 24-25.

[2]A. Okechukwu Ogbonnaya, *On Communitarian Divinity: An African Interpretation of the Trinity* (New York: Paragon, 1994), p. 16.

[3]Rob Staples, *Outward Sign and Inward Grace: The Place of Sacraments in Wesleyan Spirituality* (Kansas City, Mo.: Beacon Hill, 1991), p. 131.

[4]Ibid.

[5]H. Richard Niebuhr, *Christ and Culture* (New York: Harper Torchbooks, 1975), pp. 209-10.

[6]Ogbonnaya, *On Communitarian Divinity*, pp. 16-17.

[7]Nicholas Lash, *Believing Three Ways in One God: A Reading of the Apostles' Creed* (London: SCM Press, 1992), p. 60.

[8]A. W. Argyle, *God in the New Testament* (London: Hodder & Stoughton, 1965), p. 179.

[9]Thomas à Kempis, *The Imitation of Christ*, trans. Leo Sherley-Price (London: Penguin, 1952), p. 27 (bk. 1, chap. 1).

[10]William Cowper, "Light Shining out of Darkness," in *The New Oxford Book of Christian Verse*, ed. Donald Davie (New York: Oxford University Press, 1988), p. 199.

Chapter 1: God's Name Revealed

[1]Philip Gleeson, "Mystery," in *The New Dictionary of Theology*, ed. Joseph A. Komonchak, Mary Collins and Dermot A. Lane (Wilmington, Del.: Glazier, 1987; reprint Pasay City, Philippines: St. Paul Publications, 1991).

[2]Jaroslav Pelikan, *The Melody of Theology: A Philosophical Dictionary* (Cambridge, Mass.: Harvard University Press, 1988), pp. 168-69.

[3]Ibid., p. 168.

[4]This formula, that the Son is begotten of the Father in or by the Holy Spirit, is the thesis of Thomas G. Weinandy, *The Father's Spirit of Sonship* (Edinburgh: T & T Clark, 1995).

[5]*John Wesley's Sermons: An Anthology,* ed. Albert C. Outler and Richard P. Heitzenrater (Nashville: Abingdon, 1991), p. 535; hereafter cited as *Anthology.* Also in *Sermons,* ed. Albert C. Outler, in *The Works of John Wesley,* ed. Frank Baker and Richard P. Heitzenrater, Bicentennial ed. (Oxford: Clarendon, 1975-1983; Nashville: Abingdon, 1984-), 4:66; hereafter cited as *Works.*

[6]*Anthology,* pp. 535-36; *Works,* 4:66-67.

[7]*Anthology,* p. 438; *Works,* 3:99.

[8]Quoted in Eberhard Jüngel, *The Doctrine of the Trinity: God's Being Is in Becoming* (Grand Rapids, Mich.: Eerdmans, 1976), p. 58.

[9]Jürgen Moltmann, *The Crucified God,* trans. R. A. Wilson and John Bowden (New York: Harper & Row, 1974), p. 222.

[10]Jürgen Moltmann argues for a social approach to the Trinity in *The Trinity and the Kingdom,* trans. Margaret Kohl (San Francisco: Harper & Row, 1981). Moltmann believes that trinitarian theology must begin with the history of the Son. See pp. 61-96.

[11]*Anthology,* p. 90; *Works,* 1:150. John Wesley preached this sermon, but it was written and first preached by Charles Wesley.

[12]*Anthology,* p. 50; *Works,* 3:544.

[13]Catherine Mowry LaCugna, *God for Us: The Trinity and Christian Life* (San Francisco: HarperCollins, 1991), p. 245.

[14]*Anthology,* p. 92; *Works,* 1:154.

[15]Karl Rahner, *Theological Investigations,* trans. Kevin Smyth (New York: Crossroad, 1982), 4:330. Quoted in H. Ray Dunning, *Grace, Faith and Holiness* (Kansas City, Mo.: Beacon Hill, 1988), p. 116.

[16]Quoted in Alister E. McGrath, *Understanding the Trinity* (Grand Rapids, Mich.: Zondervan, 1988), p. 143.

[17]Quoted in W. Waite Willis Jr., *Theism, Atheism and the Doctrine of the Trinity: The Trinitarian Theologies of Karl Barth and Jürgen Moltmann in Response to Protest Atheism* (Atlanta: Scholars Press, 1987), p. 1.

[18]Catherine Mowry LaCugna, "The Practical Trinity," *The Christian Century,* July 15-22, 1992, p. 682.

[19]Jaroslav Pelikan, *The Christian Tradition,* vol. 1, *The Emergence of the Catholic Tradition (100-600)* (Chicago: University of Chicago Press, 1971), p. 1.

[20]Wolfhart Pannenberg, *The Church,* trans. Keith Crim (Philadelphia: Westminster Press, 1983), p. 74.

[21]McGrath, *Understanding the Trinity*, pp. 62-77.

[22]W. E. McCumber, *The Bible Speaks to Me About My Beliefs* (Kansas City, Mo.: Beacon Hill, 1989), p. 21.

[23]LaCugna, *God for Us*, p. 15.

[24]Quoted in Willis, *Trinity*, p. 5.

[25]Claude Welch, *In This Name: The Doctrine of the Trinity in Contemporary Theology* (New York: Charles Scribner's Sons, 1952), p. 277.

[26]Urban T. Holmes, *A History of Christian Spirituality* (San Francisco: Harper & Row, 1980), p. 2.

[27]Thomas C. Oden, *The Living God*, vol. 1 of *Systematic Theology* (San Francisco: Harper & Row, 1987), pp. 188-94.

[28]Arthur W. Wainwright, *The Trinity in the New Testament* (London: S.P.C.K., 1962), pp. 30-40; Edmund J. Fortman, *The Triune God* (Grand Rapids, Mich.: Baker Book House, 1982), pp. 4-6.

[29]Oden, *Living God*, p. 188.

[30]Wolfhart Pannenberg, *Systematic Theology*, trans. Geoffrey W. Bromiley, 2 vols. (Grand Rapids, Mich.: Eerdmans, 1991), 1:276.

[31]Ibid., 1:275.

[32]Karl Rahner, *The Trinity*, trans. Joseph Donceel (Tunbridge Wells, Kent: Burns & Oates, 1970), pp. 40-41.

[33]Ibid., p. 41.

[34]Ibid., p. 42.

[35]Dunning, *Grace, Faith and Holiness*, p. 208.

[36]The plural *us* and *our* have often been read as meaning the Three-in-One God. In truth, however, they reflect the Hebrew *Elohim*, a plural form of addressing God.

[37]Alasdair I. D. Heron, *The Holy Spirit* (Philadelphia: Westminster Press, 1983), p. 173.

[38]Wainwright, *Trinity in the New Testament*, p. 41.

[39]William G. Rusch, ed., *The Trinitarian Controversy* (Philadelphia: Fortress, 1980), p. 2.

[40]LaCugna, *God for Us*, p. 129; Owen C. Thomas, *Introduction to Theology*, rev. ed. (Wilton, Conn.: Morehouse-Barlow, 1983), pp. 60-61.

[41]LaCugna, *God for Us*, p. 129.

[42]Daniel L. Migliore, *Called to Freedom: Liberation Theology and the Future of Christian Doctrine* (Philadelphia: Westminster Press, 1980), p. 65.

[43]Dunning, *Grace, Faith and Holiness*, p. 209.

[44]Emil Brunner, *The Mediator*, trans. Olive Wyon (Philadelphia: Westminster Press, 1947), p. 276.

[45]Pelikan, *Melody*, p. 53.

[46]Emil Brunner, *The Christian Doctrine of God*, trans. Olive Wyon (Philadel-

phia: Westminster Press, 1950), p. 206.

[47]Ibid. Compare Donald G. Bloesch, *Essentials of Evangelical Theology*, 2 vols. (San Francisco: Harper & Row, 1978), 1:10.

[48]LaCugna, *God for Us*, p. 130.

[49]Ibid., pp. 21, 130.

[50]Quoted in Bloesch, *Evangelical Theology*, 1:78.

[51]Willis, *Trinity*, p. 14.

[52]Clark H. Pinnock, "From Augustine to Arminius: A Pilgrimage in Theology," in *The Grace of God, the Will of Man*, ed. Clark H. Pinnock (Grand Rapids, Mich.: Zondervan, 1989), p. 23.

[53]Moltmann, *Trinity*, p. 12.

[54]Clark Pinnock, "Systematic Theology," in Clark Pinnock et al., *The Openness of God: A Biblical Challenge to the Traditional Understanding of God* (Downers Grove, Ill.: InterVarsity Press, 1994), p. 103.

[55]Ibid.

[56]Ibid., p. 117.

[57]Thomas O. Chisholm, "Great Is Thy Faithfulness," in *Sing to the Lord*, ed. Ken Bible (Kansas City, Mo.: Lillenas, 1993), p. 44.

[58]Moltmann, *Crucified God*, p. 239.

[59]Ibid., p. 255.

[60]Brunner, *Doctrine of God*, p. 235.

[61]Quoted in Willis, *Trinity*, p. 41.

[62]Quoted in John J. O'Donnell, *The Mystery of the Triune God* (New York: Paulist, 1989), p. 21.

[63]Karl Barth, *Church Dogmatics* 2/1, *The Doctrine of God*, ed. G. W. Bromiley and T. F. Torrance (Edinburgh: T & T Clark, 1957), pp. 262-63.

[64]Karl Barth, *The Word of God and the Word of Man*, trans. Douglas Horton (Gloucester, Mass.: Peter Smith, 1978), p. 196.

[65]Quoted in Willis, *Trinity*, p. 41.

[66]Quoted in Jüngel, *Trinity*, p. 15.

[67]Quoted in ibid., p. 24.

[68]Walter Kasper, *Theology and Church*, trans. Margaret Kohl (New York: Crossroad, 1989), p. 138.

[69]*Anthology*, p. 161; *Works*, 1:383.

[70]Pelikan, *Melody*, p. 168.

[71]Avery Dulles, *Models of the Church*, expanded ed. (New York: Image, 1987), p. 17.

[72]T. F. Torrance, *Reality and Evangelical Theology* (Philadelphia: Westminster Press, 1982), p. 24. Quoted in Dunning, *Grace, Faith and Holiness*, p. 230.

[73]Rahner, *Trinity*, p. 22. Quoted in LaCugna, *God for Us*, p. 211.

[74]LaCugna, *God for Us*, p. 22.

[75]Quoted in Pelikan, *Emergence of Catholic Tradition*, p. 222.

[76]LaCugna, *God for Us*, p. 2.

[77]Søren Kierkegaard, *Philosophical Fragments*, trans. David F. Swenson (Princeton, N.J.: Princeton University Press, 1962), p. 43.

[78]*Anthology*, p. 334; *Works*, 2:185.

[79]Albert C. Outler, ed., *John Wesley* (New York: Oxford University Press, 1964), p. 494. I am indebted to K. Steve McCormick of Eastern Nazarene College for this quotation.

[80]*Anthology*, p. 282; *Works*, 2:39.

[81]See Clark Pinnock et al., *The Openness of God*, for five perspectives on how a truly biblical outlook corrects and purifies the traditional—static and cumbersome—approach to God.

[82]LaCugna, "Practical Trinity," p. 678.

[83]Weinandy, *Father's Spirit of Sonship*, p. 125.

[84]Ibid., p. 131.

[85]Ibid.

[86]Hans Urs von Balthasar, *Theo-Drama* (San Francisco: Ignatius, 1992), 3:508. Quoted in ibid.

[87]Pelikan, *Melody*, p. 42.

[88]See Oden, *Living God*, and Thomas Oden, *The Word of Life*, vol. 2 of *Systematic Theology* (San Francisco: Harper & Row, 1989).

[89]Quoted in Pelikan, *Melody*, pp. 43, 264.

[90]Quoted in Pelikan, *Emergence of Catholic Tradition*, p. 223.

[91]Ruth C. Duck, *Gender and the Name of God: The Trinitarian Baptismal Formula* (New York: Pilgrim, 1991), p. 47.

[92]Heron, *Holy Spirit*, p. viii.

[93]John C. Meagher, *The Truing of Christianity: Visions of Life and Thought for the Future* (New York: Doubleday, 1990), p. 331.

[94]Sallie McFague, *Models of God: Theology for an Ecological, Nuclear Age* (Philadelphia: Fortress, 1987), pp. 78-87.

[95]Quoted in Frank N. Magill and Ian P. McGreal, eds., *Christian Spirituality* (San Francisco: HarperSanFrancisco, 1988), p. 181.

[96]Julian of Norwich, *Showings*, trans. Edmund Colledge and James Walsh (New York: Paulist, 1978), p. 293.

[97]Quoted in Cyril C. Richardson, "The Enigma of the Trinity," in *A Companion to the Study of St. Augustine*, ed. Roy W. Battenhouse (New York: Oxford University Press, 1955), p. 248.

[98]Quoted in Migliore, *Called to Freedom*, p. 67.

[99]Quoted in Moltmann, *Trinity*, p. 58.

[100]Duck, *Gender and God*, p. 63.

[101]Quoted in Moltmann, *Crucified God*, p. 241.

Chapter 2: God's Name Rooted

[1]Leonard Hodgson, *The Doctrine of the Trinity* (London: Nisbet, 1943), p. 59.

[2]Donald G. Bloesch, *Essentials of Evangelical Theology*, 2 vols. (San Francisco: Harper & Row, 1978), 1:35-36.

[3]Nicholas Lash, *Believing Three Ways in One God: A Reading of the Apostles' Creed* (London: SCM Press, 1992), p. 95.

[4]Quoted in ibid., p. 14.

[5]Jaroslav Pelikan, *The Melody of Theology: A Philosophical Dictionary* (Cambridge, Mass.: Harvard University Press, 1988), p. 53.

[6]Ibid, pp. 53-54.

[7]Lash, *Believing Three Ways*, p. 28.

[8]Hodgson, *Trinity*, pp. 83-84.

[9]Lash, *Believing Three Ways*, p. 73.

[10]Ibid., p. 80.

[11]Ibid., p. 79.

[12]Edmund J. Fortman, *The Triune God* (Grand Rapids, Mich.: Baker Book House, 1982), p. 20.

[13]See Arthur W. Wainwright, *The Trinity in the New Testament* (London: S.P.C.K., 1962), pp. 260-65. Fortman, *Triune God*, p. 29, says, "John goes further than any other New Testament writer in awareness of the trinitarian problem."

[14]Donald G. Bloesch, *God the Almighty: Power, Wisdom, Holiness, Love* (Downers Grove, Ill.: InterVarsity Press, 1995), p. 169.

[15]Ibid.

[16]Royce Gordon Gruenler, *The Trinity in the Gospel of John* (Grand Rapids, Mich.: Baker Book House, 1986), p. 28.

[17]Ibid., p. xvi.

[18]Ibid., p. 123.

[19]Emil Brunner, *The Christian Doctrine of God*, trans. Olive Wyon (Philadelphia: Westminster Press, 1950), p. 207.

[20]W. E. McCumber, *The Bible Speaks to Me About My Beliefs* (Kansas City, Mo.: Beacon Hill, 1989), p. 39.

[21]William G. Rusch, ed., *The Trinitarian Controversy* (Philadelphia: Fortress, 1980), p. 1.

[22]H. Ray Dunning, *Grace, Faith and Holiness* (Kansas City, Mo.: Beacon Hill, 1988), p. 90.

[23]R. P. C. Hanson, *The Attractiveness of God: Essays in Christian Doctrine* (London: S.P.C.K., 1973), p. 74.

[24]J. B. Lightfoot, ed., *The Apostolic Fathers* (Grand Rapids, Mich.: Baker Book House, 1956), ninth parable, sec. 1, p. 220. Quoted in Lash, *Believing Three Ways*, p. 99.

[25]J. N. D. Kelly, *Early Christian Doctrines*, rev. ed. (San Francisco: Harper & Row, 1978), p. 92. Cf. Lightfoot, *Apostolic Fathers*, Ephesians 9, p. 65; Fortman, *Triune God*, pp. 39-40.

[26]Lightfoot, *Apostolic Fathers*, "An Ancient Homily," sec. 1, p. 44. Quoted in Jürgen Moltmann, *The Trinity and the Kingdom*, trans. Margaret Kohl (San Francisco: Harper & Row, 1981), p. 130.

[27]Hanson, *Attractiveness*, p. 75.

[28]Ibid., p. 76.

[29]Kelly, *Early Christian Doctrines*, p. 100.

[30]Hanson, *Attractiveness*, pp. 76-77.

[31]Quoted in Kelly, *Early Christian Doctrines*, p. 98.

[32]Bernhard Lohse, *A Short History of Christian Doctrine*, trans. by F. Ernest Stoeffler (Philadelphia: Fortress, 1966), pp. 43-44.

[33]Hanson, *Attractiveness*, p. 78.

[34]Geoffrey W. Bromiley, *Historical Theology: An Introduction* (Grand Rapids, Mich.: Eerdmans, 1978), p. 17.

[35]Kelly, *Early Christian Doctrines*, p. 107.

[36]Catherine Mowry LaCugna, *God for Us: The Trinity and Christian Life* (San Francisco: HarperCollins, 1991), p. 27.

[37]Ibid.

[38]Rusch, *Trinitarian Controversy*, p. 7.

[39]Jean Danielou, *A History of Early Christian Doctrine Before the Council of Nicaea*, vol. 2, *Gospel Message and Hellenistic Culture*, trans. John Austin Baker (Philadelphia: Westminster Press, 1973), p. 359.

[40]Hanson, *Attractiveness*, p. 78.

[41]Alexander Roberts and James Donaldson, eds., *The Ante-Nicene Fathers* (Grand Rapids, Mich.: Eerdmans, 1981), vol. 1, *The Apostolic Fathers: Justin Martyr-Irenaeus*, pp. 487-88, *Against Heresies* 4.20.1. Quoted in Kelly, *Early Christian Doctrines*, p. 106.

[42]Ibid., p. 463, preface to bk. 4, sec. 4.

[43]Ibid., p. 577, *Fragments of Irenaeus*, 53. Quoted in Colin E. Gunton, *The Promise of Trinitarian Theology* (Edinburgh: T & T Clark, 1991), p. 36.

[44]Kelly, *Early Christian Doctrines*, p. 106.

[45]Gunton, *Promise*, pp. 146-47.

[46]Gustaf Wingren, *Man and the Incarnation* (Edinburgh: Oliver and Boyd, 1959), p. 4.

[47]Roberts and Donaldson, *Ante-Nicene Fathers*, vol. 1, *The Apostolic Fathers: Justin Martyr-Irenaeus*, pp. 442-43, *Against Heresies* 3.16.6. Quoted in LaCugna, *God for Us*, p. 26.

[48]Mary Ann Donovan, "Irenaeus: At the Heart of Life, Glory," in *Spiritualities of the Heart*, ed. Annice Callahan (New York: Paulist, 1990), p. 13.

[49]Quoted in ibid., p. 14. See *Against Heresies* 4.20.7. A more traditional translation is "For the glory of God is a living man; and the life of man consists in beholding God."

[50]Hanson, *Attractiveness*, p. 79.

[51]Ibid., p. 78.

[52]Moltmann, *Trinity*, p. 137.

[53]Ibid.

[54]Alexander Roberts and James Donaldson, eds., *The Ante-Nicene Fathers* (Grand Rapids, Mich.: Eerdmans, 1980), vol. 3, *Latin Christianity: Its Founder, Tertullian*, p. 603, *Against Praxeas*, chap. 8; as quoted in Bernard Lonergan, *The Way to Nicea*, trans. Conn O'Donovan (Philadelphia: Westminster Press, 1976), pp. 45-46. Cf. Kelly, *Christian Doctrines*, pp. 112-13; Lohse, *Short History*, p. 45.

[55]Lash, *Believing Three Ways*, p. 30.

[56]Ibid.

[57]Kelly, *Early Christian Doctrines*, p. 122.

[58]Moltmann, *Trinity*, p. 137.

[59]Pelikan, *Melody*, p. 182.

[60]Maurice Wiles, *The Christian Fathers* (London: SCM Press, 1977), p. 33.

[61]Justo L. Gonzalez, *The Story of Christianity*, vol. 1, *The Early Church to the Dawn of the Reformation* (San Francisco: HarperSanFrancisco, 1984), p. 78.

[62]Lonergan, *Way to Nicea*, p. 65.

[63]Quoted in Fortman, *Triune God*, p. 55.

[64]Alexander Roberts and James Donaldson, eds., *The Ante-Nicene Fathers* (Grand Rapids, Mich.: Eerdmans, 1982), vol. 4, *Fathers of the Third Century*, pp. 247-48; *On First Principles* 1.2.6. Quoted in Rusch, *Trinitarian Controversy*, p. 14.

[65]Ibid., p. 247; 1.2.4. Quoted in Fortman, *Triune God*, p. 55.

[66]Ibid.

[67]I am summarizing the presentation in Hanson, *Attractiveness*, pp. 80-81.

[68]Ibid., p. 80.

[69]Quoted in Kelly, *Early Christian Doctrines*, p. 129.

[70]Lonergan, *Way to Nicea*, p. 61.

[71]Hanson, *Attractiveness*, p. 83.

[72]Lonergan, *Way to Nicea*, p. 60.

[73]Ibid., p. 62.

[74]Ibid.

[75]Friedrich Schleiermacher, *The Christian Faith*, ed. H. R. Macintosh and J. S. Stewart (Edinburgh: T & T Clark, 1928), p. 747. Cf. Lohse, *Short History*, p. 46.

[76]Lohse, *Short History*, p. 46.

[77]Wolfhart Pannenberg, *Systematic Theology*, trans. Geoffrey Bromiley, 2 vols. (Grand Rapids, Mich.: Eerdmans, 1991), 1:271. Cf. Kelly, *Early Christian Doctrines*, p. 132; Rusch, *Trinitarian Controversy*, p. 15.

[78]Lonergan, *Way to Nicea*, p. 63.

[79]Rusch, *Trinitarian Controversy*, p. 15.

[80]Hanson, *Attractiveness*, p. 81.

[81]Pannenberg, *Systematic Theology*, 1:275.

[82]Robert C. Gregg and Dennis E. Groh, *Early Arianism: A View of Salvation* (Philadelphia: Fortress, 1981), p. 109.

[83]LaCugna, *God for Us*, pp. 34-35.

[84]Lonergan, *Way to Nicea*, p. 49.

[85]Maurice Wiles, *The Making of Christian Doctrine* (Cambridge: Cambridge University Press, 1975), p. 33.

[86]Quoted in Kelly, *Early Christian Doctrines*, p. 227.

[87]Arthur C. McGill, *Suffering: A Test of Theological Method* (Philadelphia: Westminster Press, 1982), p. 72.

[88]Kelly, *Early Christian Doctrines*, pp. 228-29.

[89]Pelikan, *Melody*, p. 117.

[90]Kelly, *Early Christian Doctrines*, p. 230.

[91]Quoted in Daniel L. Migliore, *Called to Freedom: Liberation Theology and the Future of Christian Doctrine* (Philadelphia: Westminster Press, 1980), p. 71.

[92]G. A. Studdert Kennedy, *The Hardest Part* (London: n.p., 1918), p. 42. Quoted in Moltmann, *Trinity*, p. 35.

[93]McGill, *Suffering*, p. 73.

[94]Moltmann, *Trinity*, pp. 133-34.

[95]Wiles, *Making of Christian Doctrine*, p. 33.

[96]Quoted in Kelly, *Early Christian Doctrines*, pp. 243-44.

[97]Pannenberg, *Systematic Theology*, 1:275.

[98]Ibid., p. 279.

[99]Ibid., p. 322.

[100]Ibid.

[101]Kelly, *Early Christian Doctrines*, p. 233.

[102]Quoted in ibid., p. 258.

[103]Quoted in Lohse, *Short History*, pp. 59-60.

[104]Timothy Ware, *The Orthodox Church*, 2nd ed. (New York: Penguin, 1993), p. 208.

[105]See ibid., pp. 231-38, for a description of being "a partaker of the divine nature."

[106]C. S. Lewis, *Mere Christianity* (New York: Macmillan, 1954), p. 160.

[107]Ibid., p. 158.

[108]LaCugna, *God for Us*, p. 284.

[109]Ware, *Orthodox Church*, p. 231.

[110]Quoted in J. S. Whale, *Christian Doctrine* (Cambridge: Cambridge University Press, 1952), p. 110.

[111]Quoted in Kelly, *Early Christian Doctrines*, p. 238.

[112]Lohse, *Short History*, p. 56.

[113]Robert W. Jenson, *The Triune Identity: God According to the Gospel* (Philadelphia: Fortress, 1982), p. 89.

[114]Pelikan, *Melody*, p. 35.

[115]G. L. Prestige, *God in Patristic Thought* (London: S.P.C.K., 1952), p. xiv.

[116]LaCugna, *God for Us*, p. 61.

[117]Laurence Cantwell, *The Theology of the Trinity* (Notre Dame, Ind.: Fides, 1969), p. 36.

[118]Quoted in Pelikan, *Emergence of Catholic Tradition*, p. 223.

[119]Pannenberg, *Systematic Theology*, 1:323.

[120]Fortman, *Triune God*, p. 79.

[121]Quoted in Jenson, *Triune Identity*, p. 90.

[122]Quoted in Wiles, *Making of Christian Doctrine*, p. 139.

[123]Cyril C. Richardson, "The Enigma of the Trinity," in *A Companion to the Study of St. Augustine*, ed. Roy W. Battenhouse (New York: Oxford University Press, 1955), p. 238.

[124]Moltmann, *Trinity*, p. 189. Cf. Pelikan, *Emergence of Catholic Tradition*, p. 223.

[125]Jenson, *Triune Identity*, p. 105.

[126]Ibid., p. 104.

[127]Kelly, *Early Christian Doctrines*, p. 265.

[128]Philip Schaff and Henry Wace, eds., *The Nicene and Post-Nicene Fathers* (Grand Rapids, Mich.: Eerdmans, 1983), vol. 8, *St. Basil: Letters and Select Works*, p. 137, letter 38, secs. 2-3. Quoted in Thomas Hopko, "Apophatic Theology and the Naming of God in Eastern Orthodox Tradition," in *Speaking the Christian God: The Holy Trinity and the Challenge of Feminism*, ed. Alvin F. Kimel Jr. (Grand Rapids, Mich.: Eerdmans, 1992), p. 148.

[129]Ibid.

[130]Fortman, *Triune God*, p. 80.

[131]Jenson, *Triune Identity*, p. 106.

[132]Ibid.

[133]Philip Schaff and Henry Wace, eds., *The Nicene and Post-Nicene Fathers* (Grand Rapids, Mich.: Eerdmans, 1983), vol. 7, *S. Cyril of Jerusalem & S. Gregory Nazianzen*, p. 375, "Oration on Holy Baptism," sec. 41. Quoted in Hopko, "Apophatic Theology," p. 149.

[134]Ibid., p. 356. "Oration on Holy Lights," sec. 12. Quoted in Hopko, "Apophatic Theology," p. 149.

[135]Richardson, "Enigma of the Trinity," p. 245.

[136]Ibid., p. 251.

[137]Adolf von Harnack said that "Augustine only gets beyond Modalism by the mere assertion that he does not wish to be a Modalist, and by the aid of ingenious distinctions between different ideas." Quoted in Fortman, *Triune God*, p. 143.

[138]Quoted in Cantwell, *Trinity*, p. 54.

[139]Augustine, *The Trinity*, trans. Edmund Hill (Brooklyn, N.Y.: New City, 1991), p. 242; 8.1.2. Quoted in Kelly, *Early Christian Doctrines*, p. 272.

[140]Diagram is from W. J. Audsley and G. Audsley, *Handbook of Christian Symbolism* (London: Day and Son, 1865), p. 50, pl. 3; reproduced in Oden, *Living God*, p. 220.

[141]Augustine, *Trinity*, p. 214; 6.2.12. Quoted in LaCugna, *God for Us*, p. 86. Cf. Richardson, "Enigma of the Trinity," p. 246; Fortman, *Triune God*, p. 141.

[142]Richardson, "Enigma of the Trinity," p. 247.

[143]Ibid., p. 248.

[144]Quoted in Migliore, *Called to Freedom*, p. 67.

[145]Karl Barth, *Credo*, trans. J. Strathearn McNab (London: Hodder & Stoughton, 1936), p. 136. Quoted in D. M. Baillie, *God Was in Christ* (New York: Charles Scribner's Sons, 1948), p. 141.

[146]Quoted in Claude Welch, *In This Name: The Doctrine of the Trinity in Contemporary Theology* (New York: Charles Scribner's Sons, 1952), p. 186.

[147]Richardson, "Enigma of the Trinity," p. 245.

[148]Raimundo Panikkar, *The Trinity and the Religious Experience of Man* (Maryknoll, N.Y.: Orbis, 1973), p. 68.

[149]Dunning, *Grace, Faith and Holiness*, p. 224.

[150]Fortman, *Triune God*, p. 149.

[151]Richardson, "Enigma of the Trinity," p. 253.

[152]Gunton, *Promise*, p. 51.

[153]Ibid., p. 106.

[154]Welch, *In This Name*, p. 180. For a discussion of triads in the history of religion, see Geoffrey Parrinder, "Triads," in *Encyclopedia of Religion*, ed. Mircea Eliade (New York: Macmillan, 1987).

[155]LaCugna, *God for Us*, p. 93.

[156]Barth discusses this in *Church Dogmatics* 1/1, ed. G. W. Bromiley and T. F. Torrance (Edinburgh: T & T Clark, 1957), pp. 333-47. See also Welch, *In This Name*, p. 180; Eberhard Jüngel, *The Doctrine of the Trinity: God's Being Is in Becoming* (Grand Rapids, Mich.: Eerdmans, 1976), p. 13; W. Waite Willis Jr., *Theism, Atheism and the Doctrine of the Trinity: The Trinitarian Theologies of Karl Barth and Jürgen Moltmann in Response to Protest Atheism* (Atlanta: Scholars Press, 1987), p. 40.

[157]Michel René Barnes, "Augustine in Contemporary Trinitarian Theology,"

Theological Studies 56 (June 1995): 237.

[158]Stephen McKenna, introduction to *Saint Augustine: The Trinity* (Washington, D.C.: Catholic University of America Press, 1963). Quoted in Gunton, *Promise*, p. 32.

[159]Christopher B. Kaiser, *The Doctrine of God: An Historical Survey* (London: Marshall, Morgan and Scott, 1982), p. 81. Quoted in Gunton, *Promise*, p. 95.

[160]Gunton, *Promise*, p. 43.

[161]Karl Rahner, *The Trinity*, trans. Joseph Donceel (Tunbridge Wells, Kent: Burns & Oates, 1970), p. 58.

[162]Moltmann, *Trinity*, p. 19.

[163]Bloesch, *God the Almighty*, p. 187.

[164]Ibid., p. 203

[165]Moltmann, *Trinity*, p. 129.

[166]Migliore, *Called to Freedom*, p. 67.

Chapter 3: God's Name Bestowed

[1]Jaroslav Pelikan, *The Melody of Theology: A Philosophical Dictionary* (Cambridge, Mass.: Harvard University Press, 1988), p. 138.

[2]Ibid.

[3]Quoted in Claude Welch, *In This Name: The Doctrine of the Trinity in Contemporary Theology* (New York: Charles Scribner's Sons, 1952), p. 186.

[4]Cyril C. Richardson, "The Enigma of the Trinity," in *A Companion to the Study of St. Augustine*, ed. Roy W. Battenhouse (New York: Oxford University Press, 1955), p. 253.

[5]Albert C. Outler and Richard P. Heitzenrater, eds., *John Wesley's Sermons: An Anthology* (Nashville: Abingdon, 1991), p. 334. Hereafter cited as *Anthology*. Also in Frank Baker and Richard P. Heitzenrater, eds., *The Works of John Wesley*, Bicentennial ed. (Oxford: Clarendon, 1975-83; Nashville: Abingdon, 1984-), vols. 1-4: *Sermons I-IV*, ed. Albert C. Outler, 2:185. Hereafter cited as *Works*.

[6]Pelikan, *Melody*, p. 138.

[7]Quoted in David L. Miller, *Three Faces of God: Traces of the Trinity in Literature and Life* (Philadelphia: Fortress, 1986), p. 13.

[8]Jacques Ellul, as quoted in Annie Dillard, *Pilgrim at Tinker Creek* (New York: Harper's Magazine, 1974), p. 33.

[9]Quoted in Paul Merritt Bassett, "The Holiness Movement and the Protestant Principle," *Wesleyan Theological Journal* 18 (Spring 1983): 10.

[10]Immanuel Kant, *Religion Within the Limits of Reason Alone*, trans. Theodore M. Greene and Hoyt H. Hudson (New York: Harper Torchbooks, 1960), p. 133.

[11]Quoted in Langdon Gilkey, "Ordering the Soul: Augustine's Manifold

Legacy," *The Christian Century*, April 27, 1988, p. 429.

¹²*The Confessions of Saint Augustine*, trans. John K. Ryan (New York: Doubleday, 1960), p. 43.

¹³*Anthology*, p. 437; *Works*, 3:97.

¹⁴Mildred Bangs Wynkoop, *Foundations of Wesleyan-Arminian Theology* (Kansas City, Mo.: Beacon Hill, 1967), pp. 35-37.

¹⁵See Wesley's tract "Predestination Calmly Considered" in *John Wesley*, ed. Albert C. Outler (New York: Oxford University Press, 1964), pp. 425-72; also found in *The Works of John Wesley*, 14 vols. (London: Wesleyan Methodist Book Room, 1872; reprint Kansas City, Mo.: Beacon Hill, 1979), 10:204-59 (page references are to reprint edition).

¹⁶Quoted in J. Bruce Long, "Love," in *The Encyclopedia of Religion*, ed. Mircea Eliade (New York: Macmillan, 1987).

¹⁷Karl Barth, *The Doctrine of the Word of God (Prolegomena to Church Dogmatics 1/1)*, trans. G. T. Thomson (Edinburgh: T & T Clark, 1936), p. 157. Quoted in D. M. Baillie, *God Was in Christ* (New York: Charles Scribner's Sons, 1948), p. 136.

¹⁸Karl Barth, *The Knowledge of God and the Service of God According to the Teaching of the Reformation*, trans. J. L. M. Haire and Ian Henderson (London: Hodder & Stoughton, 1938), p. 31. Quoted in Baillie, *God Was in Christ*, p. 136.

¹⁹Martin Luther, "A Mighty Fortress Is Our God," in Ken Bible, ed., *Sing to the Lord* (Kansas City, Mo.: Lillenas, 1993), p. 30.

²⁰Catherine Mowry LaCugna, *God for Us: The Trinity and Christian Life* (San Francisco: HarperCollins, 1991), p. 410.

²¹Ibid., pp. 288-92.

²²Quoted in Welch, *In This Name*, p. 96.

²³This was suggested by nineteenth-century American pastor and theologian Horace Bushnell.

²⁴R. J. Stanislaw, "Crosby (Van Alstyne), Fanny Jane (1820-1915)," in *Dictionary of Christianity in America*, ed. Daniel G. Reid (Downers Grove, Ill.: InterVarsity Press, 1990).

²⁵Fanny J. Crosby, "Blessed Assurance," in Bible, ed., *Sing to the Lord*, no. 442.

²⁶Quoted in Eberhard Jüngel, *The Doctrine of the Trinity: God's Being Is in Becoming* (Grand Rapids, Mich.: Eerdmans, 1976), p. 40.

²⁷Thomas O. Chisholm, "O to Be Like Thee," in Bible, ed., *Sing to the Lord*, no. 490.

²⁸Barth, *Knowledge of God*, p. 31. Quoted in Baillie, *God Was in Christ*, p. 136.

²⁹Baillie, *God Was in Christ*, p. 143.

³⁰Henry Lederer of the School of Medicine, University of Cincinnati. Quoted in Richard S. Taylor, *Exploring Christian Holiness*, vol. 3, *The Theological*

Formulation (Kansas City, Mo.: Beacon Hill, 1985), p. 105.

[31]John J. O'Donnell, *The Mystery of the Triune God* (New York: Paulist, 1989), p. 107.

[32]Ibid.

[33]John Zizioulas, "The Ontology of Personhood," paper prepared for the British Council of Churches' Study Commission on Trinitarian Doctrine Today (1985), p. 9. Quoted in Colin E. Gunton, *The Promise of Trinitarian Theology* (Edinburgh: T & T Clark, 1991), p. 97.

[34]Quoted in Walter H. Principe, "Boethius," in *Encyclopedia of Early Christianity*, ed. Everett Ferguson (New York: Garland, 1990).

[35]Augustine, *The Trinity*, trans. Edmund Hill (Brooklyn, N.Y.: New City, 1991), pp. 228-29, bk. 7, sec. 11. Quoted in Thomas G. Weinandy, *The Father's Spirit of Sonship* (Edinburgh: T & T Clark, 1995), p. 111.

[36]Barth, *Church Dogmatics* 1/1, *The Doctrine of the Word of God*, p. 355.

[37]Karl Rahner, *The Trinity*, trans. Joseph Donceel (Tunbridge Wells, Kent: Burns & Oates, 1970), p. 109. Cf. Weinandy, *Father's Spirit of Sonship*, p. 118.

[38]Clark Pinnock, "Systematic Theology," in Clark Pinnock et al., *The Openness of God: A Biblical Challenge to the Traditional Understanding of God* (Downers Grove, Ill.: InterVarsity Press, 1994), p. 108.

[39]Weinandy, *Father's Spirit of Sonship*, pp. 119-20.

[40]Robert W. Jenson, *The Triune Identity: God According to the Gospel* (Philadelphia: Fortress, 1982), p. 105.

[41]Daniel L. Migliore, *Called to Freedom: Liberation Theology and the Future of Christian Doctrine* (Philadelphia: Westminster Press, 1980), p. 73.

[42]Gunton, *Promise*, p. 164.

[43]Joseph A. Bracken, *What Are They Saying About the Trinity?* (New York: Paulist, 1979), p. 15.

[44]LaCugna, *God for Us*, p. ix.

[45]Carl E. Braaten, "The Triune God: The Source and Model of Christian Unity and Mission," *Missiology: An International Review* 18 (October 1990): 415.

[46]Bernard of Clairvaux, *Song of Songs*, sermon 71. Quoted in Vincent Brümmer, *The Model of Love* (Cambridge: Cambridge University Press, 1993), p. 71.

[47]*Works*, 2:380.

[48]Gustaf Aulén, *The Faith of the Christian Church*, trans. Eric H. Wahlstrom (Philadelphia: Muhlenberg, 1960), p. 332. Quoted in Rob Staples, *Outward Sign and Inward Grace: The Place of Sacraments in Wesleyan Spirituality* (Kansas City, Mo.: Beacon Hill, 1991), p. 102.

[49]Pelikan, *Melody*, p. 107.

[50]*Anthology*, p. 282; *Works*, 2:39.

[51]Wesley, *Works* (1872 ed.), 10:392. I am indebted to Geoffrey Wainwright for

this quotation. See *Geoffrey Wainwright on Wesley and Calvin* (Melbourne: Uniting Church Press, 1987), p. 17.

[52]*Anthology,* p. 50; *Works,* 3:544.

[53]Quoted in *Anthology,* p. 491; *Works,* 3:208.

[54]*Anthology,* p. 491; *Works,* 3:208.

[55]Augustine, *Confessions,* p. 43.

[56]Ibid.

[57]Edmund J. Fortman, *The Triune God* (Grand Rapids, Mich.: Baker Book House, 1982), p. 149.

[58]Ibid., p. 148.

[59]Paul Tillich, *The Shaking of the Foundations* (London: SCM Press, 1949), p. 161.

[60]Charles Wesley, "Celebrate Immanuel's Name," in Bible, ed., *Sing to the Lord,* no. 162.

[61]See the parable of the dog kennel and the palace in Thomas C. Oden, ed., *The Parables of Kierkegaard* (Princeton, N.J.: Princeton University Press, 1989).

[62]*The United Methodist Hymnal* (Nashville: United Methodist Publishing House, 1989), p. 79.

Chapter 4: God's Name Restored

[1]Thomas A. Langford, *Practical Divinity: Theology in the Wesleyan Tradition* (Nashville: Abingdon, 1983), p. 180.

[2]Robert James Waller, *The Bridges of Madison County* (London: Mandarin Paperbacks, 1993), p. viii.

[3]Paul Tillich, *Systematic Theology,* 3 vols. in 1 (Chicago: University of Chicago Press, 1967), 1:122-23.

[4]Johannes Tauler, *Sermons,* trans. Maria Shrady (New York: Paulist, 1985), p. 103.

[5]Rob Staples, *Outward Sign and Inward Grace: The Place of Sacraments in Wesleyan Spirituality* (Kansas City, Mo.: Beacon Hill, 1991), p. 183.

[6]Quoted in J. N. D. Kelly, *Early Christian Doctrines,* rev. ed. (San Francisco: Harper & Row, 1978), p. 98.

[7]Bernhard Lohse, *A Short History of Christian Doctrine,* trans. F. Ernest Stoeffler (Philadelphia: Fortress, 1966), pp. 43-44.

[8]Edmund J. Fortman, *The Triune God* (Grand Rapids, Mich.: Baker Book House, 1982), p. 79.

[9]Quoted in Robert W. Jenson, *The Triune Identity: God According to the Gospel* (Philadelphia: Fortress, 1982), p. 90.

[10]Emil Brunner, *The Christian Doctrine of God,* trans. Olive Wyon (Philadelphia: Westminster Press, 1950), p. 205.

[11]Paul Tillich, *Dynamics of Faith* (New York: Harper Torchbooks, 1958), p. 42.

[12]Douglas John Hall, *God and Human Suffering: An Exercise in the Theology of the Cross* (Minneapolis: Augsburg, 1986), p. 112.

[13]Langford, *Practical Divinity*, p. 20.

[14]Hans Urs von Balthasar, *The Von Balthasar Reader*, ed. Medard Kehl and Werner Loser (New York: Crossroad, 1982), p. 113.

[15]Daniel L. Migliore, *Called to Freedom: Liberation Theology and the Future of Christian Doctrine* (Philadelphia: Westminster Press, 1980), p. 75.

[16]Jürgen Moltmann, *The Crucified God*, trans. R. A. Wilson and John Bowden (New York: Harper & Row, 1974), p. 240.

[17]Quoted in Martin E. Marty, "Theologian: Genus and Species," *The Christian Century*, April 27, 1988, p. 439.

[18]Kelly, *Early Christian Doctrines*, p. 120.

[19]Moltmann, *Crucified God*, p. 246.

[20]Ibid., p. 241.

[21]Quoted in ibid.

[22]John J. O'Donnell, *The Mystery of the Triune God* (New York: Paulist, 1989), p. 62.

[23]Albert C. Outler and Richard P. Heitzenrater, eds., *John Wesley's Sermons: An Anthology* (Nashville: Abingdon, 1991), p. 126. Hereafter cited as *Anthology*. Also in Frank Baker and Richard P. Heitzenrater, eds., *The Works of John Wesley*, Bicentennial ed. (Oxford: Clarendon Press, 1975-83; Nashville: Abingdon, 1984-), vols. 1-4: *Sermons I-IV*, ed. Albert C. Outler, 1:223. Hereafter cited as *Works*.

[24]Ibid., p. 479; *Works*, 2:427.

[25]Daniel Day Williams, *The Spirit and the Forms of Love* (New York: Harper & Row, 1968), p. 166.

[26]Jürgen Moltmann, *The Trinity and the Kingdom*, trans. Margaret Kohl (San Francisco: Harper & Row, 1981), p. 4.

[27]Kelly, *Christian Doctrines*, p. 298; cited in Geoffrey Wainwright, *Doxology: The Praise of God in Worship, Doctrine and Life* (New York: Oxford University Press, 1980), pp. 208, 515 (n. 481).

[28]Wainwright, *Doxology*, pp. 66, 208.

[29]*The Methodist Hymn-Book* (London: Methodist Publishing House, 1933), no. 191. Quoted in Wainwright, *Doxology*, pp. 208-9.

[30]*The New Oxford Book of Christian Verse*, ed. Donald Davie (New York: Oxford University Press, 1988), p. 146.

[31]Dietrich Bonhoeffer, *Letters and Papers from Prison. The Enlarged Edition* (London: SCM Press, 1971), p. 360. Quoted in Moltmann, *Crucified God*, p. 47.

[32]Patriarch Philareth of Moscow. Quoted in Moltmann, *Trinity*, p. 83.

[33]*Works,* 2:385.

[34]John of the Cross, *Selected Writings,* ed. Kieran Kavanaugh (New York: Paulist, 1987), p. 303.

[35]Thomas Benson Pollock, as quoted in Paul K. Jewett, *God, Creation and Revelation: A Neo-evangelical Theology* (Grand Rapids, Mich.: Eerdmans, 1991), p. 306.

[36]Wilhelm Pauck, ed., *Melanchthon and Bucer* (Philadelphia: Westminster Press, 1969), pp. 21-22.

[37]Søren Kierkegaard, "The Unchangeableness of God," trans. David F. Swenson, in *For Self-Examination* and *Judge for Yourselves!* trans. Walter Lowrie (Princeton, N.J.: Princeton University Press, 1944), p. 240.

[38]Ibid.

[39]Bonaventure, quoted in Alasdair I. D. Heron, *The Holy Spirit* (Philadelphia: Westminster Press, 1983), p. 87.

[40]Meister Eckhart, as quoted in W. R. Inge, *Christian Mysticism* (London: Methuen, 1948), p. 151.

[41]*Anthology,* p. 170; *Works,* 1:396.

[42]Ibid., p. 86; *Works,* 1:143.

[43]Walter Kasper, *Theology and Church,* trans. Margaret Kohl (New York: Crossroad, 1989), p. 153.

[44]*Anthology,* p. 92; *Works,* 1:154.

[45]John Powell, *The Mystery of the Church* (Milwaukee: Bruce, 1967), p. 8. Quoted in Avery Dulles, *Models of the Church,* expanded ed. (New York: Image, 1987), p. 26.

[46]Kasper, *Theology and Church,* p. 152.

[47]See chapter 3, "Spirit of God—Spirit of Christ," in Heron, *Holy Spirit.*

[48]*Anthology,* p. 536; *Works,* 4:67.

[49]Søren Kierkegaard, *Concluding Unscientific Postscript,* trans. David F. Swenson (Princeton, N.J.: Princeton University Press, 1941), p. 206.

[50]*Anthology,* p. 449; *Works,* 2:482.

[51]Ibid., p. 340; *Works,* 2:194.

[52]Thomas O. Chisholm, "O to Be Like Thee," in Ken Bible, ed., *Sing to the Lord* (Kansas City, Mo.: Lillenas, 1993), no. 490.

[53]*Anthology,* p. 486; *Works,* 3:200.

[54]Ibid., p. 105; *Works,* 1:171.

[55]Ibid., p. 334; *Works,* 2:185.

[56]C. S. Lewis, *Mere Christianity* (New York: Macmillan, 1954), p. 159.

[57]John R. Tyson, ed., *Charles Wesley: A Reader* (New York: Oxford University Press, 1989), pp. 225-26; cf. Davie, *New Oxford Book of Christian Verse,* pp. 157-58.

[58]Lewis, *Mere Christianity,* p. 160.

[59]Louis Bouyer, *A History of Christian Spirituality*, vol. 1, *The Spirituality of the New Testament and the Fathers*, trans. Mary P. Ryan (New York: Seabury, 1963), p. 490.

[60]Augustine, *The Trinity*, trans. Edmund Hill (Brooklyn, N.Y.: New City, 1991), p. 214; 6.2.12. Quoted in Catherine Mowry LaCugna, *God for Us: The Trinity and Christian Life* (San Francisco: HarperCollins, 1991), p. 86. Cf. Cyril C. Richardson, "The Enigma of the Trinity," in *A Companion to the Study of St. Augustine*, ed. Roy W. Battenhouse (New York: Oxford University Press, 1955), p. 246; Fortman, *Triune God*, p. 141.

[61]Leonardo Boff, *Trinity and Society*, trans. Paul Burns (Maryknoll, N.Y.: Orbis, 1988), p. 5.

[62]Quoted in Inge, *Mysticism*, p. 151.

[63]Quoted in Louis Dupre and James A. Wiseman, eds., *Light from Light: An Anthology of Christian Mysticism* (New York: Paulist, 1988), p. 383.

[64]Carl J. Peter, "Sanctification," in *The New Dictionary of Theology*, ed. Joseph A. Komonchak, Mary Collins and Dermot A. Lane (Wilmington, Del.: Glazier, 1987; reprint Pasay City, Philippines: St. Paul Publications, 1991).

[65]*Part III: The Christian Testament Since the Bible* (London: Firethorn, 1985), p. 317.

[66]Symeon the New Theologian, *The Discourses*, trans. C. J. de Catanzaro (New York: Paulist, 1980), p. 28.

[67]*Anthology*, pp. 186-87; *Works*, 1:435.

[68]J. Edwin Orr, "Cleanse Me," in Bible, ed., *Sing to the Lord*, p. 516.

[69]Peter Erb, introduction to Johann Arndt, *True Christianity*, trans. Peter Erb (New York: Paulist, 1979), p. 6.

[70]Geoffrey Wainwright, "Christian Spirituality," in *Encyclopedia of Religion*, ed. Mircea Eliade (New York: Macmillan, 1987).

[71]Columba Hart, introduction to Hadewijch, *The Complete Works* (New York: Paulist, 1980), p. 38.

[72]Albert C. Outler, ed., *John Wesley* (New York: Oxford University Press, 1964), p. 179.

[73]*Anthology*, p. 169; *Works*, 1:395.

[74]*Anthology*, p. 170; *Works*, 1:396.

[75]Heron, *Holy Spirit*, p. 173.

[76]Claus Westermann, *The Praise of God in the Psalms* (Richmond, Va.: John Knox Press, 1965), pp. 159-61. Quoted in LaCugna, *God for Us*, p. 336.

[77]Francis of Assisi, "All Creatures of Our God and King," in Bible, ed., *Sing to the Lord*, p. 77.

[78]Catherine of Siena, *The Dialogue*, trans. Suzanne Noffke (New York: Paulist, 1980), p. 364.

[79]*Works*, vol. 7, *A Collection of Hymns for the Use of the People Called Methodists*,

ed. Franz Hildebrandt and Oliver A. Beckerlegge (Oxford: Oxford University Press, 1983; reprint Nashville: Abingdon), p. 335.
[80]Jenson, *Triune Identity*, p. 47.
[81]Lewis, *Mere Christianity*, p. 127.
[82]*Works*, 7:324.
[83]LaCugna, *God for Us*, p. 345.
[84]Quoted in Anders Nygren, *Agape and Eros*, trans. Philip S. Watson (Chicago: University of Chicago Press, 1982), p. 518.
[85]Bernard of Clairvaux, *Selected Works*, trans. G. R. Evans (New York: Paulist, 1987), p. 195.
[86]Ibid.
[87]*Anthology*, p. 105; *Works*, 1:171.
[88]Catherine of Siena, *Dialogue*, p. 365.
[89]William W. How, "For All the Saints," in Bible, ed., *Sing to the Lord*, no. 685.

Chapter 5: God's Name Extended

[1]Adrienne von Speyr, quoted in Jürgen Moltmann, *The Church in the Power of the Spirit*, trans. Margaret Kohl (New York: Harper & Row, 1977), p. 60.
[2]Catherine Mowry LaCugna, *God for Us: The Trinity and Christian Life* (San Francisco: HarperCollins, 1991), p. 377.
[3]Anthony Kelly, *The Trinity of Love: A Theology of the Christian God* (Wilmington, Del.: Glazier, 1989), p. 182.
[4]Quoted in David L. Miller, *Three Faces of God: Traces of the Trinity in Literature and Life* (Philadelphia: Fortress, 1986), p. 26.
[5]LaCugna, *God for Us*, p. 100.
[6]Laurence Cantwell, *The Theology of the Trinity* (Notre Dame, Ind.: Fides, 1969), p. 91.
[7]LaCugna, *God for Us*, p. 100.
[8]Leonardo Boff, *Trinity and Society*, trans. Paul Burns (Maryknoll, N.Y.: Orbis, 1988), p. 175.
[9]Quoted in ibid., p. 222.
[10]Quoted in ibid., p. 220.
[11]Ibid., p. 221.
[12]Ibid., p. 133.
[13]Albert C. Outler and Richard P. Heitzenrater, eds., *John Wesley's Sermons: An Anthology* (Nashville: Abingdon, 1991), p. 435. Hereafter cited as *Anthology*. Also in Frank Baker and Richard P. Heitzenrater, eds., *The Works of John Wesley*, Bicentennial ed. (Oxford: Clarendon, 1975-83; Nashville: Abingdon, 1984-), vols. 1-4: *Sermons I-IV*, ed. Albert C. Outler, 3:94-95. Hereafter cited as *Works*.
[14]Quoted in George M. Newlands, *Theology of the Love of God* (Atlanta: John

Knox Press, 1980), p. 210.

[15]Hadewijch, *The Complete Works* (New York: Paulist, 1980), p. 117.

[16]Albert C. Outler, *John Wesley's Sermons: An Introduction* (Nashville: Abingdon Press, 1991), p. 67. Reprinted from *Works*, vol. 1.

[17]Paul Ramsey, *Basic Christian Ethics* (Chicago: University of Chicago Press, 1980), p. 243.

[18]Reinhold Niebuhr, *An Interpretation of Christian Ethics* (London: SCM Press, 1936), p. 131.

[19]John M. Nielson, president of Asia-Pacific Nazarene Theological Seminary, Metro Manila, Philippines, provided this insight.

[20]Hadewijch, *Works*, pp. 99-100.

[21]Edward LeRoy Long Jr., *A Survey of Recent Christian Ethics* (New York: Oxford University Press, 1982), p. 55.

[22]LaCugna, *God for Us*, pp. 400-401.

[23]Quoted in Alister E. McGrath, *Understanding the Trinity* (Grand Rapids, Mich.: Zondervan, 1988), p. 110.

[24]Quoted in Boff, *Trinity*, p. 19; compare Jürgen Moltmann, *The Crucified God*, trans. R. A. Wilson and John Bowden (New York: Harper & Row, 1974), p. 238; and Jürgen Moltmann, *The Trinity and the Kingdom*, trans. Margaret Kohl (San Francisco: Harper & Row, 1981), p. 6.

[25]Quoted in John J. O'Donnell, *The Mystery of the Triune God* (New York: Paulist Press, 1989), p. 108.

[26]Colin E. Gunton, *The Promise of Trinitarian Theology* (Edinburgh: T & T Clark, 1991), pp. 4, 28.

[27]Jürgen Moltmann, *God in Creation: A New Theology of Creation and the Spirit of God*, trans. Margaret Kohl (San Francisco: Harper & Row, 1985), pp. 258-59.

[28]LaCugna, *God for Us*, p. 228.

[29]Catherine Mowry LaCugna, "Trinity," in *Encyclopedia of Religion*, ed. Mircea Eliade (New York: Macmillan, 1987).

[30]F. W. Green, "The Later Development of the Doctrine of the Trinity," in *Essays on the Trinity and the Incarnation*, ed. A. E. J. Rawlinson (London: Longmans, Green, 1933), p. 294.

[31]LaCugna, "Trinity."

[32]James M. Gustafson, *Ethics from a Theocentric Position*, vol. 1, *Theology and Ethics* (Chicago: University of Chicago Press, 1983), p. 95.

[33]LaCugna, "Trinity."

[34]*Works*, 7:545.

[35]LaCugna, "Trinity."

[36]Geoffrey Wainwright, *Doxology: The Praise of God in Worship, Doctrine and Life* (New York: Oxford University Press, 1980), p. 23.

[37]O'Donnell, *Mystery of the Triune God*, p. 108.

[38]Paul L. Lehmann, *Ethics in a Christian Context* (New York: Harper & Row, 1963), p. 49.

[39]Ibid., p. 111.

[40]Quoted in J. N. D. Kelly, *Early Christian Doctrines*, rev. ed. (San Francisco: Harper & Row, 1978), p. 264.

[41]Green, "Later Development," p. 292.

[42]Cantwell, *Trinity*, p. 90; cf. Peter Drilling, *Trinity and Ministry* (Minneapolis: Fortress, 1991), p. 34.

[43]LaCugna, *God for Us*, p. 272.

[44]Quoted in Eberhard Jüngel, *The Doctrine of the Trinity: God's Being Is in Becoming* (Grand Rapids, Mich.: Eerdmans, 1976), p. 33.

[45]Drilling, *Trinity*, pp. 34-35; cf. LaCugna, *God for Us*, p. 272.

[46]Drilling, *Trinity*, p. 35.

[47]Quoted in Mercy Amba Oduyoye, "The Doctrine of the Trinity—Is It Relevant for Contemporary Christian Theology?" in *Naming God*, ed. Robert P. Scharlemann (New York: Paragon, 1985), pp. 151-52.

[48]Wainwright, *Doxology*, p. 210.

[49]Donald Davie, ed., *The New Oxford Book of Christian Verse* (New York: Oxford University Press, 1988), p. 158.

[50]Sidney Callahan, *In Good Conscience: Reason and Emotion in Moral Decision Making* (San Francisco: HarperCollins, 1991), p. 214.

[51]Ibid., p. 17.

[52]Sean Fagan, "Conscience," in *The New Dictionary of Theology*, ed. Joseph A. Komonchak, Mary Collins and Dermot A. Lane (Wilmington, Del.: Glazier, 1987; reprint Pasay City, Philippines: St. Paul Publications, 1991).

[53]C. E. Nelson, "Conscience," in *Harper's Encyclopedia of Religious Education*, ed. Iris V. Cully and Kendig Brubaker Cully (San Francisco: Harper & Row, 1990).

[54]John Deschner, *Wesley's Christology: An Interpretation* (Grand Rapids, Mich.: Zondervan, 1988), p. 97.

[55]*Anthology*, p. 491; *Works*, 3:207.

[56]Karl Barth, *Ethics*, trans. Geoffrey W. Bromiley (New York: Seabury, 1981), p. 477.

[57]Dietrich Bonhoeffer, *Ethics* (New York: Macmillan, 1955), p. 55. Quoted in Edward LeRoy Long Jr., *A Survey of Christian Ethics* (New York: Oxford University Press, 1967), p. 154.

[58]Quoted in Lehmann, *Ethics*, p. 366.

[59]Eric Mount, *Conscience and Responsibility* (Richmond: John Knox Press, 1969), p. 172-73. Quoted in Long, *Survey of Recent Christian Ethics*, p. 116.

[60]William R. Cannon, *The Theology of John Wesley* (New York: Abingdon-

Cokesbury, 1946), p. 218.

[61]Callahan, *Conscience*, p. 14.

[62]Fagan, "Conscience."

[63]*Works*, 7:454-55.

[64]Quoted in Pelikan, *The Melody of Theology: A Philosophical Dictionary* (Cambridge, Mass.: Harvard University Press, 1988), p. 7.

[65]*Anthology*, p. 444; *Works*, 2:474.

[66]O'Donnell, *Mystery of the Triune God*, p. 73.

[67]Geoffrey Wainwright, *Geoffrey Wainwright on Wesley and Calvin* (Melbourne: Uniting Church Press, 1987) pp. 67-68, n. 67. Wainwright claims that the biggest threats to the doctrine of the Trinity today are from those who desire to align Christianity with other religions, especially "monotheistic" ones, as well as from "philosophical apologists" who are closer to a deistic outlook. Scientists, secularists and radical feminists are also opposed to the classic Christian view of God for various reasons. See Wainwright's article "The Doctrine of the Trinity: Where the Church Stands or Falls," *Interpretation* 45 (April 1991): 117-32.

[68]LaCugna, *God for Us*, p. 1.

[69]Raimundo Panikkar, *The Trinity and the Religious Experience of Man* (Maryknoll, N.Y.: Orbis, 1973), p. 61.

[70]*Anthology*, p. 500; *Works*, 2:510.

[71]Thomas R. Kelly, *A Testament of Devotion* (New York: Harper & Row, 1941), p. 77.

[72]Philip Schaff, *The Creeds of Christendom*, 3 vols. (Grand Rapids, Mich.: Baker Book House, 1966), 3:676.

[73]*Works*, 7:347.

Select Bibliography

Augustine. *The Trinity*. Translated and introduced by Edmund Hill. Brooklyn, N.Y.: New City, 1991.

Barth, Karl. *Church Dogmatics*. Vol. 1, *The Doctrine of the Word of God* (pt. 1). Translated by G. W. Bromiley. Edinburgh: T & T Clark, 1975.

Bloesch, Donald G. *The Battle for the Trinity*. Ann Arbor, Mich.: Servant, 1985.

Boff, Leonardo. *Trinity and Society*. Translated by Paul Burns. Maryknoll, N.Y.: Orbis, 1988.

Bracken, Joseph A. *What Are They Saying About the Trinity?* New York: Paulist, 1979.

Cantwell, Laurence. *The Theology of the Trinity*. Notre Dame, Ind.: Fides, 1969.

Corless, Roger, and Paul F. Knitter, eds. *Buddhist Emptiness and Christian Trinity: Essays and Explorations*. New York: Paulist, 1990.

Drilling, Peter. *Trinity and Ministry*. Minneapolis: Fortress, 1991.

Duck, Ruth C. *Gender and the Name of God: The Trinitarian Baptismal Formula*. New York: Pilgrim, 1991.

Erickson, Millard J. *God in Three Persons: A Contemporary Interpretation of the Trinity*. Grand Rapids, Mich.: Baker, 1995.

Fortman, Edmund J. *The Triune God: A Historical Study of the Doctrine of the Trinity*. Grand Rapids, Mich.: Baker, 1982.

Gruenler, Royce Gordon. *The Trinity in the Gospel of John: A Thematic Commentary on the Fourth Gospel*. Grand Rapids, Mich.: Baker, 1986.

Gunton, Colin E. *The Promise of Trinitarian Theology*. Edinburgh: T & T Clark, 1991.

Hodgson, Leonard. *The Doctrine of the Trinity*. London: Nisbet, 1943.

Jenson, Robert W. *The Triune Identity: God According to the Gospel*. Philadelphia·

Fortress, 1982.

Jüngel, Eberhard. *The Doctrine of the Trinity: God's Being Is in Becoming*. Grand Rapids, Mich.: Eerdmans, 1976.

Kelly, Anthony. *The Trinity of Love: A Theology of the Christian God*. Wilmington, Del.: Glazier, 1989.

Kelly, J. N. D. *Early Christian Doctrines*. Revised ed. San Francisco: Harper & Row, 1978.

Kimel, Alvin F., Jr., ed. *Speaking the Christian God: The Holy Trinity and the Challenge of Feminism*. Grand Rapids, Mich.: Eerdmans, 1992.

LaCugna, Catherine Mowry. *God for Us: The Trinity and Christian Life*. San Francisco: HarperSanFrancisco, 1993.

Lash, Nicholas. *Believing Three Ways in One God: A Reading of the Apostles' Creed*. London: SCM Press, 1992.

Lee, June Young. *The Trinity in Asian Perspective*. Nashville: Abingdon, 1996.

Lohse, Bernard. *A Short History of Christian Doctrine*. Translated by F. Ernest Stoeffler. Philadelphia: Fortress, 1966.

Lonergan, Bernard. *The Way to Nicea: The Dialectical Development of Trinitarian Theology*. Translated by Conn O'Donovan. Philadelphia: Westminster Press, 1976.

Lowry, Charles W. *The Trinity and Christian Devotion*. New York: Harper & Brothers, 1946.

McGrath, Alister E. *Understanding the Trinity*. Grand Rapids, Mich.: Zondervan, 1988.

Miller, David L. *Three Faces of God: Traces of the Trinity in Literature and Life*. Philadelphia: Fortress, 1986.

Moltmann, Jürgen. *The Crucified God*. Translated by R. A. Wilson and John Bowden. San Francisco: Harper & Row, 1974.

––––––. *History and the Triune God: Contributions to Trinitarian Theology*. Translated by John Bowden. New York: Crossroad, 1992.

––––––. *The Trinity and the Kingdom*. Translated by Margaret Kohl. San Francisco: Harper & Row, 1981.

O'Donnell, John J. *The Mystery of the Triune God*. New York: Paulist, 1989.

Ogbonnaya, A. Okechukwu. *On Communitarian Divinity: An African Interpretation of the Trinity*. New York: Paragon, 1994.

Panikkar, Raimundo. *The Trinity and the Religious Experience of Man*. Maryknoll, N.Y.: Orbis, 1973.

Peters, Ted. *God as Trinity: Relationality and Temporality in Divine Life*. Louisville, Ky.: Westminster/John Knox, 1993.

Rahner, Karl. *The Trinity*. Translated by Joseph Donceel. Tunbridge Wells, Kent, U.K.: Burns & Oates, 1970.

Richardson, Cyril C. *The Doctrine of the Trinity*. New York: Abingdon, 1958.

Rusch, William G., ed. and trans. *The Trinitarian Controversy.* Philadelphia: Fortress, 1980.

Segundo, Juan Luis. *Our Idea of God.* Maryknoll, N.Y.: Orbis, 1974.

Studer, Basil. *Trinity and Incarnation: The Faith of the Early Church.* Edited by Andrew Louth. Translated by Matthias Westerhoff. Edinburgh: T & T Clark, 1993.

Thompson, John. *Modern Trinitarian Perspectives.* New York: Oxford University Press, 1994.

Toon, Peter. *Our Triune God: A Biblical Portrayal of the Trinity.* Wheaton, Ill.: Victor, 1996.

Toon, Peter, and James D. Spiceland, eds. *One God in Trinity: An Analysis of the Primary Dogma of Christianity.* Westchester, Ill.: Cornerstone Books, 1980.

Torrance, T. F. *The Trinitarian Faith.* Edinburgh: T & T Clark, 1988.

Wainwright, Arthur W. *The Trinity in the New Testament.* London: S.P.C.K., 1962.

Wainwright, Geoffrey. *Doxology: The Praise of God in Worship, Doctrine and Life.* New York: Oxford University Press, 1980.

Weinandy, Thomas G. *The Father's Spirit of Sonship: Reconceiving the Trinity.* Edinburgh: T & T Clark, 1995.

Welch, Claude. *In This Name: The Doctrine of the Trinity in Contemporary Theology.* New York: Charles Scribner's Sons, 1952.

Willis, W. Waite, Jr. *Theism, Atheism and the Doctrine of the Trinity: The Trinitarian Theologies of Karl Barth and Jürgen Moltmann in Response to Protest Atheism.* Atlanta: Scholars Press, 1987.

Zizioulas, John D. *Being as Communion: Studies in Personhood and the Church.* Crestwood, N.Y.: St. Vladimir's Seminary Press, 1985.